Designer's Notebook

Designer's
Notebook

Second Edition

IAN NICOLSON C. Eng. F.R.I.N.A.

W · W · NORTON & COMPANY
New York   London

Copyright © 1987, 1970 by Ian Nicolson
First American Edition, 1988.

Printed in the United States of America.

Library of Congress Cataloging-in-Publication Data

Nicolson, Ian, 1928–
    Designer's notebook.

    1. Yachts and yachting—Furniture, equipment, etc.
I. Title.
VM331.N5   1987   623.8′223   88-5126

ISBN 0-393-03325-2

W. W. Norton & Company, Inc., 500 Fifth Avenue, New York, N. Y. 10110
W. W. Norton & Company Ltd., 37 Great Russell Street, London WC1B 3NU

1 2 3 4 5 6 7 8 9 0

To my son, David,
in thanks for crewing on our boats

Contents

Ideas . . . Ideas . . . Ideas

Introduction to the Second Edition

Bright ideas cure problems. Sometimes the use of a brain wave occurs generations after the first flash of ingenuity sparks the concept. My father invented 'flight refuelling' in 1927, but it only truly came into its own during the Falklands War, in 1982, and he died in 1947.

Boats generate problems faster than anything except perhaps cars and aeroplanes. However, people who go afloat are ingenious, and some of the ways they overcome difficulties are shown in this book . . . and in other comparable books I have written.

We are all in debt to the owners, builders, designers, draughtsmen, foremen, charge hands, riggers, sail-makers, mast-makers – the list is endless – who have dreamed up the gadgets and tricks shown here. It is not fair to name anyone because so often a gadget appears in two widely separated places at the same time.

I'm sure there was a startled look from some stone-age man as he rounded the bend of the river Euphrates in his log canoe, a million years ago, and saw to his intense irritation that some other fellow had also thought up the idea of borrowing his wife's wolf-skin, and setting it as a sail.

Not all ideas work well. When we all had solid wood masts, and it was getting difficult to find long straight trees, someone came up with the 'tubular join'. They got the conception from studying fishing rods which were made up from pieces of wood held together by short sections of piping. The idea of making up a long thin elegant mast from two quite short trees and a few feet of bronze tubing seemed brilliant. It worked for a few years, but the trouble was that water seeped in and caused hidden rot inside the tube. This sort of mast tended to break at extraordinary times, when there was hardly any wind and just enough swell to cause the yacht to pitch and make the mast whip.

The saddest tale of failed ingenuity comes from the cruising world. A family wanted to go off for a week's holiday, and could not take their goldfish with them. So they set the goldfish bowl under the telephone bell, which was one of the old-fashioned sort, on the wall, with an external clapper. This clapper vibrates against the bell when the phone rings. They tied a packet of fish-food to the bell clapper, and cut a small hole in the bottom of the packet. Then every time the phone rang, the clapper shook some fish food into the bowl below. Now all they had to do was to phone home each day from wherever they were, and the goldfish would automatically be fed.

What they had not bargained for was that a friend phoned them the first day they were away. As the phone was not answered, he tried again an hour later, and again after another hour, and again . . . and again . . . and again.

And so the goldfish became bloated with food that first day, but died of starvation before the end of the week.

So it does pay to develop gadgets, and not expect total success right away. The drawings in this book are for the most part not dimensioned because the size of anything made will depend on the size of the boat it is to fit. What never changes is the need for excellent materials and fastenings. The cost of good glassfibre or stainless steel or varnish is little more than the shoddiest type; and the cost of materials is only a small percentage of the total cost.

My thanks are due to the owners, editor and staff of *Yachts and Yachting*, where many of these drawings first appeared.

Ian Nicolson
Cove, Loch Long
1986

Hull Construction

Like the rest of this book, this chapter is absolutely not an exhaustive treatise on its subject. It is a collection of jottings picked up over the years. A skilful designer will be able to adopt techniques thought up for one material into boat-building in another. Because of course there never were so many yacht building styles and fashions and basic materials. What with carbon fibres, epoxides and polyesters, low carbon steels and shatter-proof plywoods combined with and in competition with traditional commodities, the choice has never been bigger; the opportunities for ingenuity and development are also greater than ever.

The ideas sketched here are simple ones, so that even an amateur builder beginning his first boat will probably be able to use most of them. However designers may get into trouble trying to persuade certain boat-yards to use some of these suggestions because yards have their own traditions and techniques. Plenty of yards make a mess of a job which is too far removed from their normal working practice. They have that built-in resistance to change which is the hall-mark of some fine craftsmen. This is understandable because to do a job well takes time and practice. Once the skill has been acquired it is natural to be reluctant to go off at a tangent, and so the skilful designer takes trouble to ensure his plans suit the building yard.

When using any of these ideas it is normally best to design in plenty of strength first. Next the structure or detail can be examined with a view to reducing weight and complexity. Simplification is a great thing, much to be admired and pursued, but within clear limits. No boat is simpler than the traditional inshore fishing boat. But look at their dreadful lodging and hanging knees, great massive pieces of timber only 20% effective because each arm of every knee has only two bolts. What is worse, the outer bolt is far from the end of the arm, often not properly tightened, sometimes without a washer under the nut, sometimes hammered into a hole drilled too big, or forced into an undersize hole so that the knee is split.

Many of the suggestions here will save time and money but in every case only the best materials and fastenings should be used. These cost very little more than lower quality commodities; in the long run there is always a saving.

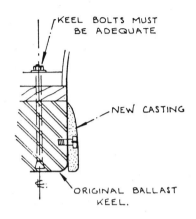

Adding weight

When a yacht will not stand up to the wind she is no fun to own. She is uncomfortable due to the large angle of heel, and may be unsafe. If the keel is iron it may be taken off and replaced by a lead one. Adding internal ballast is seldom enough. Re-rigging is sometimes the answer, when a heavy wood spar can be changed for a light alloy one.

Sometimes the addition of side pieces to the keel is worthwhile. This is often economical but needs careful fairing if it is not to look botched-up. The strength of the keel bolts and floors must be above suspicion.

New side pieces may be attached by multiple bolts threaded into the original keel. The additions must sweep in at each end and taper at the top to give the ballast keel bulb-shape. It is important to design the addition carefully and work to a drawing properly prepared to ensure a professional appearance and improved performance.

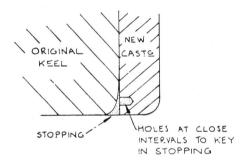

Stopping in awkward corners

Sketched here is a difficult stopping-up job. A new addition has been fitted to the side of a ballast keel (a specialised job not to be lightly undertaken, incidentally). Where the old keel has been rounded-off along the edge there is a tapered gap which must be filled properly.

It is not easy to get any stopping material to stay in such an aperture.

The trick is to drill a series of holes along the inner face of the new casting before fitting it. These holes need to be as big as possible without taking away a lot of useful weight. They also need to be fairly close, to be effective. A suggested set of dimensions might be ⅝ inch holes about ¾ inch deep spaced 2 or 3 inches apart.

This keying-in technique may be used in wood or metal at all sorts of different localities. Care must be taken to work the stopping firmly into the holes so that the keying is really effective.

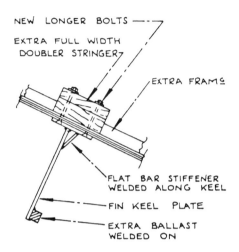

NEW LONGER BOLTS

EXTRA FULL WIDTH
DOUBLER STRINGER

EXTRA FRAME

FLAT BAR STIFFENER
WELDED ALONG KEEL

FIN KEEL PLATE

EXTRA BALLAST
WELDED ON

More ballast on a twin-keeler

Some small twin bilge keel cruisers are underballasted
for sea work. This applies in particular to early versions,
whilst later models often have more weight hung below.
Adding weight is not easy since it must be done with due
respect to the rest of the structure. Many of these little
cruisers would carry an extra 20% of ballast without any
trouble. One easy way to add weight is to weld a steel bar
on to the bottom of each bilge keel. The ends of the bar
must be faired, either by cutting at an angle or by fitting
wood ends.

The plate keel may be stiffened at the top flange with a
length of flat bar the same thickness as the plate and
about three inches wide, almost the full length of the
plate. A wood fairing piece should fill each end of the
triangular gap.

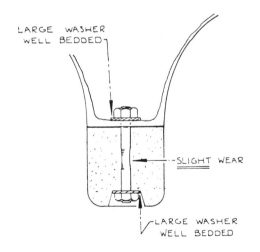

LARGE WASHER
WELL BEDDED

SLIGHT WEAR

LARGE WASHER
WELL BEDDED

Low cost keel bolts

This idea is only for those who truly know what they are
doing and it must be used with caution. When building a
sailing yacht the ballast keel bolts can be a costly item.
One wants good material, such as aluminium bronze for
a lead keel. A cheap way to obtain this material is to use
old propeller shafts. But it is important to select only
those shafts which have a small amount of wear and
locate the worn part so that it is well clear of the threaded
part.

In the sketch the worn part cannot cause leaks. Only
about 5% wear is acceptable and by far the best plan is to
cut the shaft into lengths so that worn sections are not
used at all.

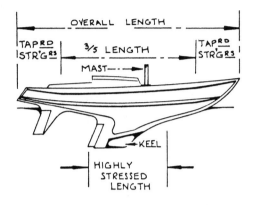

OVERALL LENGTH

TAPᴿᴰ STRᴵGᴿˢ | ³/₅ LENGTH | TAPᴿᴰ STRᴵGᴿˢ

MAST

KEEL

HIGHLY STRESSED LENGTH

Strength with lightness

It is usual when putting the stringers into a yacht to taper the ends. Some Lloyd's rules allow a 25% reduction, but only over the first and final fifth of the boat. In theory the very end of a stringer could be reduced to a point, since at the extreme end there is no bending stress. In practice there must be at least enough material to join the ends to the stem and transom.

Lloyd's rules are drawn up with a view to covering a wide variety of craft and they err, quite rightly, on the side of excess strength. When building for racing, especially if the yacht is not expected to last long, the width and depth of the stringers can be less than Lloyd's allow – especially aft. Clear of the mast and ballast keel the stresses diminish towards the yacht's ends.

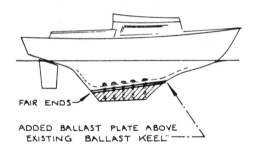

FAIR ENDS

ADDED BALLAST PLATE ABOVE EXISTING BALLAST KEEL

Better ballasting

Many modern small cruisers are under-ballasted. This failing stems largely from economics, but that does not help the man who wants his boat to stand up to a gale. What is required is extra weight low down.

On a 'traditional' shape of yacht like the one in the sketch one of the best ways to improve the ballasting is to insert a steel plate above the iron casting. The easiest way to do the job is to remove the ballast keel and to make a plywood template of the top to obtain the exact shape and the position of the bolt holes. This can be given to a steel stockist who has a profile cutter for cutting out. As a guide, a square foot of steel plate ⅛ inch thick weighs about 5 lbs. Ensure that the extra piece of ballast is thoroughly epoxy painted to reduce corrosion.

CABIN SOLE

WOOD SOLE BEARER
LINED UP CAREFULLY

STEEL FLOOR WITH
PREDRILLED HOLES
FOR BEARER

When the floors carry the sole

It is quite hard to make up a set of metal floors with their top edges exactly in line once installed in a ship. There are so many factors from a foreman's bad eyesight to an apprentice's ham-fistedness which can cause small discrepancies. This means that it is not always easy to use the floors as sole bearers directly. If the floors are of steel plate they can have a wood packing piece instead of putting a flange across the top. The wood packing acts as a flange and its height can be adjusted to suit the sole.

Among the advantages of this scheme are: a small error in lining up the sole bearer pieces is easily corrected and electric wires and small pipes can be run through between the underside of the sole and the top of the steel plates.

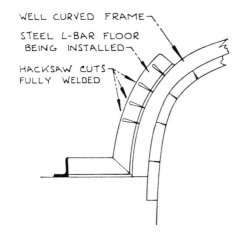

WELL CURVED FRAME

STEEL L-BAR FLOOR
BEING INSTALLED

HACKSAW CUTS
FULLY WELDED

Shaped floors without heat

Where the bilge of a yacht is curvaceous the builder may have difficulty in making metal floors to fit. They must fit precisely if they are to be effective. There are various alternatives which can be used. The shape can be reproduced on cardboard or ply templates and the floors made by a blacksmith; wood packing pieces may be used in conjunction with straight floor arms; plate floors might be burned or laboriously hand cut to shape.

Perhaps one of the easiest solutions is to make a row of hacksaw cuts almost across the arms of the floors. The floor is then bent exactly to shape. A little epoxy glue may be used to hold the curve though this is generally not needed. Once the glue has set the floor is taken out and each cut is welded up, prior to galvanising.

The attraction of this scheme is that most of the work can be done by someone with little skill.

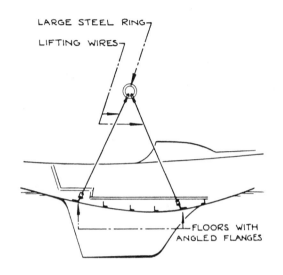

LARGE STEEL RING

LIFTING WIRES

FLOORS WITH ANGLED FLANGES

Lifting plates

If external webbing slings are used, fitted round the belly of a boat, to lift her into or out of the water, there is a good chance that grit on the slings will scratch the hull surface. Proper lifting wires designed to fit accurately onto lifting plates are much better.

One simple way to fit lifting plates is to angle two of the vertical floor flanges. On most boats it does not matter whether the floor flanges are upright or tilted. The hole for the lifting wire shackles should be amply large. The ring at the top of the wires should have a big internal diameter so that even a dockside crane hook can be accommodated.

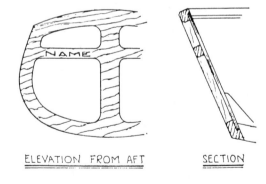

NAME

ELEVATION FROM AFT   SECTION

A stern of character

There is no denying that a big transom can look unsightly. Large flat areas relieved only by name and port are not particularly pleasing to the eye. There is a good case for fitting the transom framing made of fine varnished hardwood on the aft side. Naturally the framing – or cumblades as it is sometimes called – must be beautifully made.

One advantage of the external framing is that the name and port can be carved in. In this connection it is important to remember to do the carving before setting up the transom, especially if the rake is as shown in the sketch, otherwise the carver will have a difficult job. For the carving enthusiast, external framing presents an area of hardwood just asking for traditional adornment.

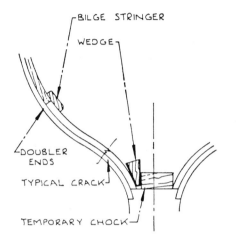

BILGE STRINGER

WEDGE

DOUBLER ENDS

TYPICAL CRACK

TEMPORARY CHOCK

Bent frame repairs

It is common for bent timbers to crack at the reverse turn above the garboard. When doing a doubling repair, a good shipwright takes trouble to make the new work blend as much as possible with the existing structure.

A good place to start the new doubler is under the bilge stringer, so that the end is concealed. The bottom end is best taken right to the top of the keel. It is advisable to use a chock and wedge to secure the heel of the doubler while it is being fastened in place. Also, clamps should be used to hold the doubler tight to the adjacent frame prior to fastening.

Any doubler should extend for at least the width of two and a half planks beyond the crack and a lap of four planks is by no means too much. Fastenings should be staggered in the doubler and also in each plank to reduce the risk of splitting. There should be two or three fastenings through the doubler into each plank.

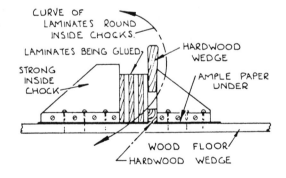

CURVE OF LAMINATES ROUND INSIDE CHOCKS.

LAMINATES BEING GLUED

STRONG INSIDE CHOCK

HARDWOOD WEDGE

AMPLE PAPER UNDER

WOOD FLOOR

HARDWOOD WEDGE

Laminating techniques

The laminating of timber is easy and gives such satisfactory results that it deserves to be more widely used. Laminating should be done on a firm base such as floor or bench. The shape of the laminate is first marked on the floor and a series of chocks screwed accurately in position on the inside of the curve. A number of layers of newspaper or a piece of waxed paper or polythene should be placed between the laminate and the base to prevent them sticking together. While the glue is setting the laminates must be held together rigidly. Screws or through bolts can be used or a very satisfactory method is to fasten chocks to the outside of the curve and drive in hardwood wedges as shown in the sketch. If you are lucky enough to have an adequate supply of cramps, chocks and wedges will not be required but make sure that the cramps are staggered and not all tightened up along the top or the bottom edge of the assembly being glued.

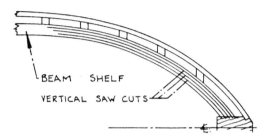

BEAM SHELF

VERTICAL SAW CUTS

Easier fitting

Large size wood scantlings such as beam shelves can be awkward to fit. It is not only their massive weight which needs special handling, they are also difficult to bend into place.

To get a beam shelf to conform to a tight bow bend may call for every man in the yard, struggling and heaving. Instead of wasting all this time one or more vertical cuts in the shelf will make it easy to coax in. A good gap-filling epoxy glue is run into the slits before fitting, so that the shelf is virtually a laminated member once it has been bolted or clenched at every frame and the glue has set.

Notice how the aft ends of the cuts are staggered to avoid a sudden bend in the timber. Also a fairly fine saw should be used to avoid a rough cut. In most yards the circular saw will be used, carefully following a pencilled line. If a band saw is used then a guide must be set up to ensure straight cuts.

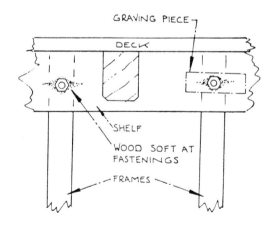

GRAVING PIECE

DECK

SHELF

WOOD SOFT AT FASTENINGS

FRAMES

A common defect

Many wood yachts suffer from softening of the wood where bolts pass through the beam shelf. This occurs where there is a deck leak, just a tiny weep as a rule, and where the ventilation and paint are less than perfect. It is a big job to renew the shelf and not necessary provided that the trouble is caught in time.

There are various cures, but the most common is the fitting of a graving piece. This is an inlaid piece of wood, which must match the timber of the shelf if this is varnished. Otherwise it should be a hardwood which is fairly stable. The graving piece must be fitted very carefully and glued in place after the whole area has dried out. Nothing that is saturated with salt will ever dry properly, so once the bad wood has been cut away wash the area with hot water to dissolve the salt. Fix the graving piece using plenty of epoxy glue but wait until the whole area is dry.

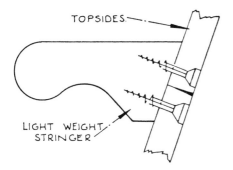

Moulded stringer for wood boats

Where a wood boat is longitudinally framed, there is always a difficulty in deciding the best shape of the stringers. If they are made of any rectangular section, then water will lodge on top in long puddles. Some designers have got over this by sloping the stringers down towards the stern, but this looks rather unskilled when it is 'in the solid'. An attractive stringer section is drawn here. It has plenty of timber at the outer edge to take two rows of screws. The middle is machined away for lightness and there is a bulb on the inner face for strength. Shelves, bunks and other furniture items can easily be fitted to the top surface. Painting is easy and the appearance good.

Possibly the biggest snag is that the outside bevel changes, both along the length of the ship and around the girth of the hull. However, on many motor boats, especially hard shine craft, this change of bevel is not so great and much, if not all, of the outside bevel can be machined to the correct angle quickly.

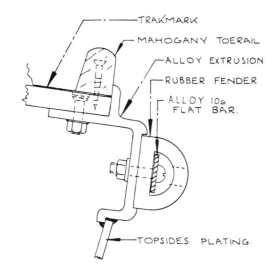

Alloy edge extrusion

Because there is a sudden change in the shape of the shell the gunwale is a likely place for leaks and a point where high local stresses are common. When building in aluminium alloy it is an excellent idea to use one of the special extrusions available. This particular extrusion is sensible because it gives an ample landing for the deck, with a rebate which ensures sufficient width of bedding. There should be a slight amount of flexibility at the angle, with no join close by. At least two inches below the edge, the topsides come in, being held by two lines of full welding. The lips which hold the rubber fender add stiffness to the extrusion, though their main function is to prevent the rubber from being forced up or down when alongside a quay.

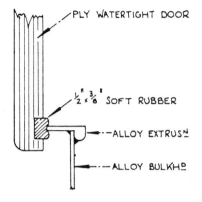

PLY WATERTIGHT DOOR

½" × ³⁄₈" SOFT RUBBER

--ALLOY EXTRUS.ᴺ

--ALLOY BULKH.ᴰ

Lightweight watertight door

On an aluminium yacht the appearance can be improved by having the doors in watertight bulkheads of wood.

Each door is made from a piece of thick ply, with a rebate machined all round to take the rubber seal. The sharp edge of the bulkhead boundary extrusion bites into the rubber, to form the seal. The rebate can be made slightly on the narrow side, so that even without glue the rubber will tend to stay safely in place. Ply has little tendency to distort and even if it does to a small degree, this arrangement should remain watertight.

It is worth remembering that one of the prime advantages of an aluminium yacht, or a steel one for that matter, is that the bulkheads are welded easily to the shell so that they are fully watertight and this makes watertight doors of special interest.

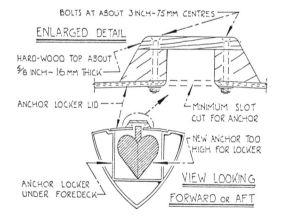

BOLTS AT ABOUT 3 INCH~75 MM CENTRES

ENLARGED DETAIL

HARD-WOOD TOP ABOUT ⁵⁄₈ INCH~16 MM THICK

ANCHOR LOCKER LID

MINIMUM SLOT CUT FOR ANCHOR

NEW ANCHOR TOO HIGH FOR LOCKER

ANCHOR LOCKER UNDER FOREDECK

VIEW LOOKING FORWARD or AFT

Enlarging an anchor locker

Many yachts have anchor lockers under the foredeck. So as not to take too much space out of the fore cabin, designers tend to make these lockers just the right size for the anchor, with no space to spare. If the anchor is lost and a larger one has to replace it, or if the anchor is too small for the kind of cruising the owner enjoys, there is a serious problem.

Often enough, the larger anchor is only a couple of inches deeper than the original one, so if a little box can be built in the locker lid this will be enough to make it possible to close the lid. There is no need to make a new lid, and this sketch shows just how simple and cheap the alteration can be. The new anchor is put into the locker and, with the lid open, the height the anchor protrudes is measured. Provided it is no more than a few inches, the lid is marked and cut away, then the boxing is built over the hole.

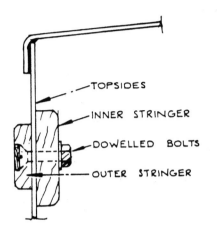

TOPSIDES

INNER STRINGER

DOWELLED BOLTS

OUTER STRINGER

Topside stiffening

It is often a problem to know how to stiffen a glassfibre yacht. A flimsy hull can sometimes be made more rigid by fitting carefully designed rubbing strakes a little below the deck. There must be internal wood stringers opposite the outside strakes and these can be made quite large. Both the inner and outer stringers should be well bedded because the outer surface of the hull is unlikely to be perfectly free from slight undulations, while the inner surface will certainly not be completely smooth.

Though bolts through both stringers are shown in the sketch, it is possible to use screws. Ideally the screws should go through the smaller scantling into the larger, but where the inner and outer strakes are about the same size it makes sense to put the screws from inside outwards, so as to avoid dowelling.

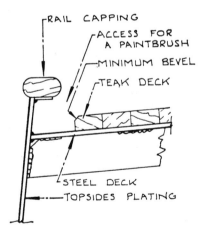

RAIL CAPPING

ACCESS FOR A PAINTBRUSH

MINIMUM BEVEL

TEAK DECK

STEEL DECK

TOPSIDES PLATING

Sheathing a metal deck

Although this sketch is drawn for a teak sheathing on a steel deck the detail and principles apply to other comparable structures. The outboard deck plank is not laid right out against the toerail as it would be hard to make the vertical join watertight. Instead a gap is left and the outer plank is bevelled. This bevel is kept small, otherwise anyone treading on it might feel a tendency to be tipped outwards.

As the rail capping extends inwards, there is no chance that anyone will accidentally jam a foot in the scupper. However enough space is left for cleaning and painting the scupper. It has to be admitted that this arrangement is not as smart as a fully covered deck but it is appreciably cheaper. It also makes it easy to add extra deck fittings. For instance a sheet lead or stanchion base can be welded to the exposed metal deck.

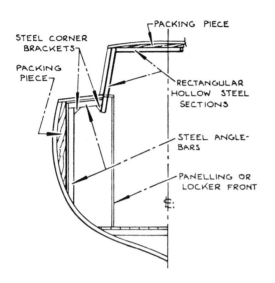

STEEL CORNER
BRACKETS

PACKING
PIECE

PACKING PIECE

RECTANGULAR
HOLLOW STEEL
SECTIONS

STEEL ANGLE-
BARS

PANELLING OR
LOCKER FRONT

Steel for strength

Steel is a useful material for stiffening up a yacht's structure because it is cheap and easily available. If it is galvanised then painted after degreasing, before installation, it will last a long time.

This sketch shows steel being used to make a cabin top stronger – perhaps for deep-sea cruising.

Where the steel will show it is best in the form of square or rectangular-sectioned pipe, called Rectangular Hollow Section, because it looks neat. Where the stiffening is out of sight the cheaper and universally stocked common angle-bar is used. As facilities for bending steel scantlings are not always available it is often necessary to use shaped filler pieces of wood.

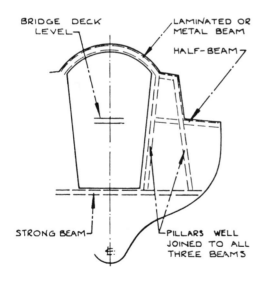

BRIDGE DECK
LEVEL

LAMINATED OR
METAL BEAM

HALF-BEAM

STRONG BEAM

PILLARS WELL
JOINED TO ALL
THREE BEAMS

Cabin access

There have been rumours circulating concerning the structural rigidity of glassfibre yachts. What is certain is that a glassfibre yacht is likely to be hard driven because it does not usually leak, so after going hard to windward for a few hours there may be no splosh and swish of bilge water to encourage caution. Because the material itself is expensive, builders take trouble to use the minimum amount in construction.

What increases the problem is the demand for easy access through the yacht. No longer will owners put up with slightly awkward cabin doorways. It is important, therefore, to provide adequate extra stiffening to bulkheads with large doorways. This sketch shows how a bulkhead can be stiffened where a large walk way has been cut out. All the stiffeners must be joined thoroughly at the intersections.

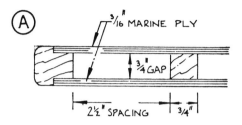

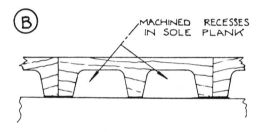

Super sole

These days the owner who wants to win races cuts his crew's hair to save weight. Many of us have reached a stage where the weight-saving battle is at a high pitch. For this reason it is worth seeing what is left which can safely be pared down.

The limit has long been reached with the structural components of the typical out-and-out racing machine, but the sole may warrant attention, especially as it often soaks up water and so grows heavier with the passing months.

Two alternative forms of construction are sketched here. Method A is attractive where large panels of flooring are required. It must be glued carefully and fastened with a few barbed ring nails or maybe screws – not many because of their weight. Method B is especially interesting because there are instances when existing floorboards can be treated in this fashion, by routing out the major part of the under side.

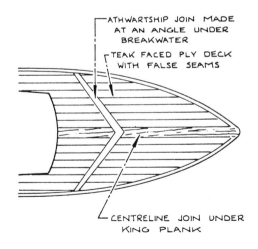

Smart decks

Now that laid teak decks are seldom seen, except on large yachts, it is difficult to know how to produce a good looking deck. There is one attractive substitute for a teak deck – plywood with a teak face veneer. On the surface black or white lines are painted by the manufacturer, giving the appearance of a planked teak deck. Unfortunately the manufacturing process is such that the lines on one ply board will not always line up exactly with those on another.

In this sketch one way of surmounting this difficulty is shown – the joins in the ply panels being covered by either the breakwater or the king plank. There will be some waste, as it is important to slope the breakwater back about 35 degrees, so that at each end of the board the corner must be cut to conform with this angle.

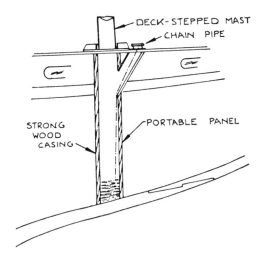

DECK-STEPPED MAST
CHAIN PIPE
STRONG WOOD CASING
PORTABLE PANEL

A chain locker in the right place

Most owners like to keep the weight of their anchor chain away from the extreme bow so as to improve the performance of their yacht, but appreciate that if the chain is too far aft it is awkward to stow and run out. Quite a few opt for a chain stowage level with the mast, possibly in conjunction with an anchor winch at waist level on the mast.

All this is sound, well-established practice. An unusual idea is to use the mast supporting structure as the chain locker. The structure might be of 1¼ inch thick teak or mahogany for a 35 footer, carefully bolted and glued together in the form of a vertical trunking. It must be securely fastened at top and bottom, as well as down the sides, where fillet pieces may be needed.

Some sort of access to the inside is highly desirable. This might be in the form of a removable panel, which extends part of the depth of the casing. It is also important to make provision for securing the inboard end of the chain, to prevent it all running out if it is let go out of control.

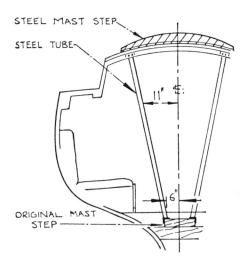

STEEL MAST STEP
STEEL TUBE
11" ℄
6"
ORIGINAL MAST STEP

Putting the mast on deck

One of the reasons for changing a keel-stepped mast to a deck-stepped one is to get better space in the cabin. It is pleasant to be able to change a 5 inch wide mast for a 1½ inch diameter steel pillar.

The advantage can be improved still further, as this sketch shows. Instead of putting a single pillar under the mast, a pair of struts may be used so that there is a central walk-way through the boat. Naturally the mast stresses still have to be absorbed correctly.

By angling a pair of pillars, their feet can be fastened on to the old mast step or a new scantling in the same location. The tops are bolted to a new beam which supports an athwartship mast step. Provided there is about 22 inches of space at shoulder level and about 12 inches at sole level, access will be comfortable.

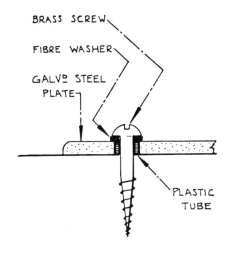

BRASS SCREW
FIBRE WASHER
GALV⁰ STEEL
PLATE
PLASTIC
TUBE

Common problem

One of the most usual boat-building problems today is the interaction of metals. In theory all that has to be done is to fasten every fitting with screws and bolts of the same material as the fitting. But it never works out that way.

Some galvanised bolts last no time – especially if they are not 'hot-dipped' – though galvanised fittings are usually satisfactory. Stainless bolts are hard to find except in small sizes. Bronze is fine but costly for fittings, brass is OK for screws on deck fittings but no good for the fittings themselves. And so it goes on.

A good compromise is to use simple inexpensive galvanised fittings with brass screws and bolts. The fastenings are easily available and not expensive by comparison with other materials. By using fibre washers under the heads of the fastenings and light plastic tubing bushes in the holes the different metals are kept apart. Three good coats of varnish over all keeps the seawater away.

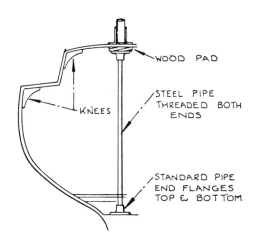

WOOD PAD
STEEL PIPE
THREADED BOTH
ENDS
KNEES
STANDARD PIPE
END FLANGES
TOP & BOTTOM

Mast pillar for pocket cruisers

To support a deck-stepped mast on a very small cruiser, just take a length of 1 inch bore steel water pipe, thread both ends and screw on pipe flanges. The flanges can be screwed up to adjust for height, taking care that there are at least five complete circles of thread in each flange piece.

If the boat is a little bigger, it might make sense to go for a 1½ inch bore pipe. This should normally support a mast carrying up to say 220 sq ft of canvas.

It will not take into account racking or diagonal stresses, which must be met by knees or strength bulkheads. Also it may need a pad at the bottom to spread the load over a wide area of the hull, to avoid leaks at the garboard.

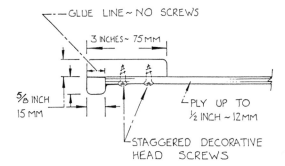

GLUE LINE ~ NO SCREWS

3 INCHES ~ 75MM

⅝ INCH
15 MM

PLY UP TO
½ INCH ~ 12MM

STAGGERED DECORATIVE
HEAD SCREWS

Doorway in bulkhead

The section through the ply bulkhead edge shown here suits very thin ply, down to 4 mm, and also the common bulkhead thickness of 12 mm (½ inch nominal). As both wood pieces are the same thickness, and the smaller piece is square section, the circular saw and planer need the minimum setting – and this saves time, which is money. This type of bulkhead edging is quick and easy to make; it involves no rebating, and it needs no precision work. The staggered screws should be set at precisely the same intervals all the way down to give a neat appearance, and of course all the screw slots must be in line.

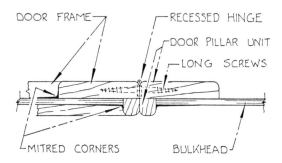

DOOR FRAME

RECESSED HINGE

DOOR PILLAR UNIT

LONG SCREWS

MITRED CORNERS

BULKHEAD

Matching door frame and posts

Amateur and professional boat-builders find it useful to be able to use one section of machined wood for more than one purpose. A good example is shown here, as the bulkhead edging which forms the door post is the same as the framework round the ply door. The larger pieces of wood are the same thickness as the smaller ones, and the latter are square section, so the work in the timber mill is kept to a minimum. The door hinges are recessed and have really long screws for strength, but for a cabin door there should always be three or four hinges.

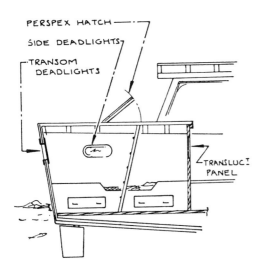

PERSPEX HATCH

SIDE DEADLIGHTS

TRANSOM DEADLIGHTS

TRANSLUCT PANEL

Lighting small cabins

If a small cabin is not to be miserable, it must be well lit. Cleverly contrived cabins under the aft decks of 35 ft motor-cruisers and those short fo'c's'les on 30 footers can be delightful, tolerable or hellish, according to the amount of daylight.

Where possible the best technique is to have ports all round. In this sketch there are deadlights in the transom, which break up the big flat area of the stern. The side deadlights will have to be arranged to fit in with the framing system but it is usually cheaper to fit one large one rather than a pair of small ones each side.

Both the Perspex hatch and the translucent panel will be large in area and relatively inexpensive. To prevent anyone looking into the cabin the Perspex should be rubbed on the under side with emery paper.

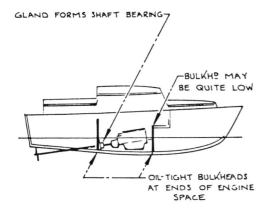

GLAND FORMS SHAFT BEARING

BULKHD MAY BE QUITE LOW

OIL-TIGHT BULKHEADS AT ENDS OF ENGINE SPACE

Oil in the bilges

Under the engines of most motor-cruisers there is always at least a little oil – sometimes a sizeable puddle.

It is a great boon if there is some impassable barrier at each end of the engine compartment to stop the oil coating the whole bilge. A well-made deep floor is effective till the boat rolls heavily. Best of all is a watertight bulkhead, which need not extend more than half-way up the topsides. Where each propeller shaft passes through this bulkhead there must be a gland, to stop bilge water and oil getting through, even though the bilge water should never be allowed this high because the shafts will whirl it up and all over the place. These glands serve as shaft bearings, limiting whip, but they are not as effective as proper bearings. Special arrangements must be made for pumping the separate bilge compartments.

Rudders, Tillers and Steering Gear

My sailing days started in Poole harbour. On the moorings near my boat was a motor-cruiser which had been built by a shipyard, as opposed to a yacht-yard. Those shipbuilders appeared to have been thoroughly mixed up in their attempts to scale down from their normal products. In short, that powerboat was a shocker. One day she was cruising down the Wareham river, which is narrow and twisty, when a well-laden tripper boat came in sight heading up-river. The two craft met at a bend in the river. When the helmsman of the cruiser tried to turn the bend, he found the rudder would not answer, and there was nearly a serious accident. The fisherman at the tiller of the tripper boat, amid the gale of oaths, somehow steered clear of impending doom by ramming the bank, which was well padded with reeds.

The explanation was simple. In the cruiser the steering wires from the wheel passed over various sheaves leading to the quadrant. One of these sheaves was in a casing secured to the floorboards of the aft cabin. The very first time the helm was put hard over quickly the floorboards lifted . . . !

When designing and making steering equipment it is certainly worth thinking about the consequences of failure at sea. It can be worse to lose steering ability than to lose a mast. In addition, for many people much of the pleasure of going afloat lies in the delicious feel of the helm. This means that the whole steering linkage must be carefully thought out and well engineered.

As a general principle rudder bearings probably cannot be too big. They ought to be of self-lubricating material, and this needs machining with due allowance for expansion when wet. The material manufacturers will advise on what expansion to expect with soakage, but, if in doubt, work on the principle that a little slack is better than a seized rudder.

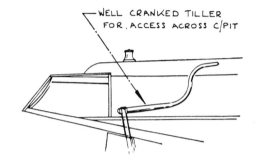

WELL CRANKED TILLER
FOR ACCESS ACROSS C/PIT

Sensible tiller shape

A popular argument in favour of wheel steering on small sailing yachts is based on the fact that a tiller takes up too much space in the cockpit. Actually it is not the tiller which occupies so much area, but the *sweep* of the tiller. In this sketch is shown a subtle way of minimising this sweeping disadvantage.

By maintaining the main length of the tiller down at sole level, the crew can very easily step over it. When going across the cockpit during tacking it is not difficult to avoid the tiller because during that part of the operation the boat is about upright. Naturally this type of tiller needs to be made carefully if it is to be adequately strong. Here is a case for laminating or carefully formed tubing. The tiller and its end fitting must be strong enough to withstand misplaced crew weight.

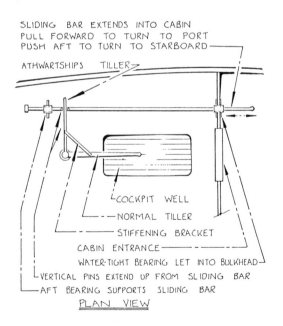

SLIDING BAR EXTENDS INTO CABIN
PULL FORWARD TO TURN TO PORT
PUSH AFT TO TURN TO STARBOARD

ATHWARTSHIPS TILLER

COCKPIT WELL
NORMAL TILLER
STIFFENING BRACKET
CABIN ENTRANCE
WATER-TIGHT BEARING LET INTO BULKHEAD
VERTICAL PINS EXTEND UP FROM SLIDING BAR
AFT BEARING SUPPORTS SLIDING BAR
PLAN VIEW

Steering from inside the cabin

Automatic steering devices are not cheap, and some of them do not work in rough weather. Those which work through a wind vane do not like very light conditions either. This gadget works in all weathers, costs very little, suits a great range of craft, and allows the crew to sail from the comfort of the cabin.

A practised helmsman can steer and cook or navigate at the same time. There must be a compass near the inside steering position, and the helmsman should look out every so often to avoid bashing into rocks and ships.

The fore and aft sliding bar may be of wood or metal, and it needs end stops to prevent it being pushed too far either way.

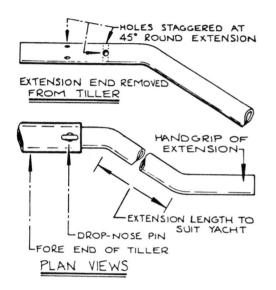

HOLES STAGGERED AT
45° ROUND EXTENSION

EXTENSION END REMOVED
FROM TILLER

HANDGRIP OF
EXTENSION

EXTENSION LENGTH TO
SUIT YACHT

DROP-NOSE PIN

FORE END OF TILLER

PLAN VIEWS

Keel boat tiller extension

Many cruisers would be improved by the addition of a tiller extension. However, the dinghy type with a universal joint and a delicate stick to the helmsman's hand is not always suitable. The extension sketched here consists of a length of stainless tube which fits into the end of a tubular tiller. The extension is cranked to carry it to windward, allowing the helmsman to sit well outboard.

So that the extension can be rotated and fixed in a number of positions to vary the height of the handle, a number of holes are drilled in the aft end of the extension. The extension is secured by a drop-nose pin.

The extension can be used from the leeward side, or turned so that the handle is raised, if the helmsman wants to stand to look over the cabin top when coming to moorings.

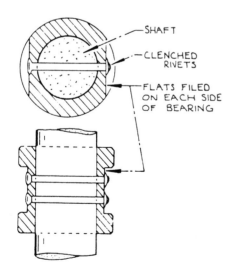

SHAFT

CLENCHED
RIVETS

FLATS FILED
ON EACH SIDE
OF BEARING

Rudder bearing

On a counter-sterned yacht the rudder can present something of a problem. If no bearings are fitted, then the stock and tube will wear. Repairs will be expensive, especially if the tube is glassed in. To get round this problem on a new boat, one designer has proposed a simple Tufnol bearing clenched through the stock. Repairs will be easy, since the rivet heads are soon filed off, the clenches knocked out and an identical new bearing slipped in place and riveted up.

With those two flats filed on the bearing it would be possible to use bolts instead of clenches. This idea is easy to imitate, even where facilities are limited. The bearing should have ample length above and below the fastenings.

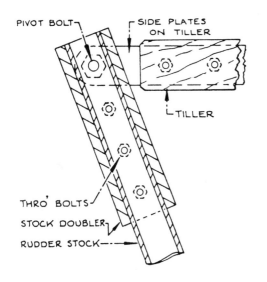

Rudder head

This design is suitable for small keelboats and cruisers up to about 20 ft on the waterline. Above that size the stresses call for either a more sophisticated design, or massive components.

The rudder stock, which is probably tubular for lightness and minimum cost, is doubled at the top. The doubling tube must be a good fit and ideally should be epoxy glued to the stock. A minimum of three bolts fasten the doubler to the stock, while a larger bolt takes the tiller plates. These in turn must have four fastenings through the tiller.

A great attraction of this design is that it can be fabricated without special tools. There is no keyway to cut so an amateur can make it quickly in his own workshop. The bottom end of the doubler pipe can rest on a suitably angled plate to carry the weight of the rudder.

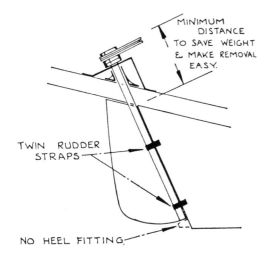

A broken principle

As every apprentice boat-builder knows after his first two years, rudders should be hung with heel fittings. This bottom end support not only takes the weight of the rudder but it protects it when grounding or slipping and acts as the main bearing which works well even after a lot of wear has taken place.

There are disadvantages to this heel fitting which get less publicity. It makes the removal of the rudder most awkward. It can be costly to make and fit. Often it is heavy, and it is likely to be subject to corrosion.

Sketched here is a diagram showing a rudder designed for easy removal. The stock is short so that the rudder does not have to be lowered down into a hole in the ground to get it free. Two identical broad bands hold the stock to the fin, the bottom one being well down near the heel of the rudder.

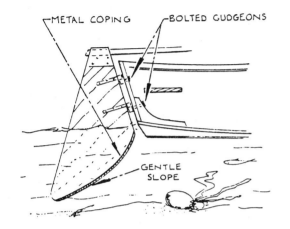

Safe rudder

There has been so much written and said about ideal rudder shapes but most of it applies only to racing boats operating in deep clear water. For small knockabout boats, whether power or sail, which go into deep water only occasionally, the ideal shape might be modified to give reliability. If a lifting rudder is fitted, then there are more moving parts, more things to go wrong, more expense. Also a very large proportion of lifting rudders soon become slightly floppy, so that the helmsman does not have perfect control. A rudder which is designed to cope with grounding by riding over the mud is not difficult to make. It is only suitable for boats up to about 20 ft and it must be thick, strongly assembled and properly protected with a metal leading edge. The pintles and gudgeons must be through bolted and very strongly made.

One final point – make sure that the transom is really well attached to the hull!

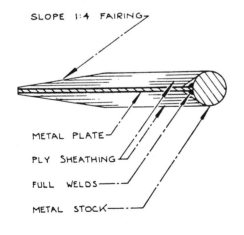

Rudder construction

Of the many ways of making a rudder, this one can be recommended on the score of strength, cheapness and simplicity. It is not as long-lasting as all-bronze, nor as elegant as an all-teak one, but it would suit a wide variety of power and sailing vessels.

The stock is of steel with a rudder plate welded down the aft side with a full penetration weld. This assembly is drilled then galvanised. The next job is to coat the metal-work very thoroughly with epoxy paint after degreasing. Finally the fairing of ply is clenched through the previously drilled holes in the plate and the aft edge is faired away.

The ply prevents the galvanising from getting scratched, especially if the wood extends just beyond the metal all round.

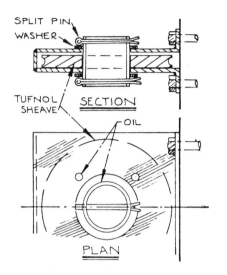

Ideal steering sheaves

The smoothness of many wheel steering arrangements is ruined because the wire linking the wheel to the quadrant has to contort itself at every sheave. There is no such thing as an oversize sheave for this type of job.

Naturally very big sheaves can be heavy but by using a material like Tufnol and by drilling it with a fair number of lightening holes the weight is kept down. For the axle a large-bore bronze or stainless steel tube serves well, provided it has regular lubrication. Though many of the plastics used for sheaves are self-lubricating, a drop of oil once a month is advisable. A small axle might at first sight seem lighter but it would wear locally so that the axle hole in the sheave would soon be too large and the sheave would run roughly. Another important feature is the rigidity of the sheave casing and its fastenings and base.

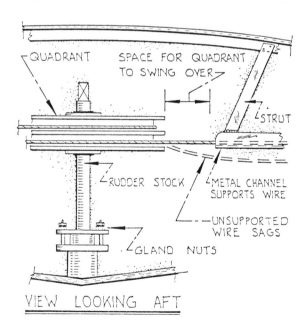

Steering wire safety feature

One persistent fault in all steering systems which use wire or chain led to a quadrant is that the lead is angled wrongly. As the wire loosens with use it sags, as shown on the right of the picture. It then comes onto the quadrant from below. In time the wire gets slacker still and fails to stay on the quadrant.

What is needed is an open-topped channel on each side to feed the wire or chain at the right level onto the quadrant. These channels should be made of metal, securely fixed in place, with well belled-out ends so that there is no wear and the channels can cope with such problems as the wire swinging about slightly as the boat plunges in a seaway. The insides of the channels should be greased monthly, or more often if the vessel is continuously at sea.

Cabin Tops and Cockpits

Design for Force 10' is not a bad motto. Less severe weather conditions are safer and more comfortable, so any yacht which can deal with the upper range of the Beaufort scale will be satisfactory in moderate weather. Also there is nothing like visible signs of strength and security to give peace of mind, which is the basis of all good cruises.

For racing weight-saving and the reduction of windage, as well as the best siting of winches, are among the considerations which dominate designers' thinking. This means the considerations are very different from cruising.

In the cockpit it is not enough to avoid sharp edges and protruding peninsulas of structure. The cruising crew will spend most of the time at sea in this area, and they will probably be at least slightly cramped. So every part of the structure should be angled to give the most comfort.

It is no bad thing, after designing a cockpit, to heel the drawing twenty or thirty degrees, and see how the crew are going to be affected. Can they reach the opposite seats with their feet, or will they tend to slide off the windward side all the time? Will locker lids and doors stay tight? How much water will trickle into the cabin through the companionway hatch and doors?

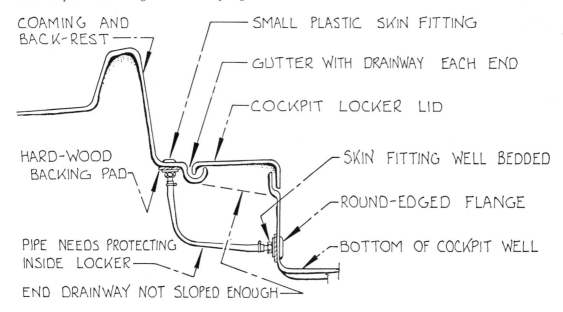

COAMING AND BACK-REST

SMALL PLASTIC SKIN FITTING

GUTTER WITH DRAINWAY EACH END

COCKPIT LOCKER LID

HARD-WOOD BACKING PAD

SKIN FITTING WELL BEDDED

ROUND-EDGED FLANGE

BOTTOM OF COCKPIT WELL

PIPE NEEDS PROTECTING INSIDE LOCKER

END DRAINWAY NOT SLOPED ENOUGH

Cockpit seat locker drain

The sketch shows a typical cockpit locker. When the boat heels a lot water lies between the seat backrest and the seat base. There may be sloped drains at each end of each locker lid but, unless these are steeply angled, in bad weather water will trickle into the lockers.

Drain pipes at each end of each lid will take away the accumulating puddles, but they should be at least ½ inch, and better still ¾ inch, internal diameter to prevent blockage by rubbish. If the pipes are plastic they must be bent round gentle curves or they will kink and become even more easily blocked by debris besides being inefficient as drains.

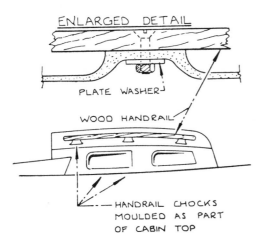

ENLARGED DETAIL

PLATE WASHER

WOOD HANDRAIL

HANDRAIL CHOCKS
MOULDED AS PART
OF CABIN TOP

Cabin top handrails

It really is very important that grabrails are not only particularly substantial, but firmly fitted as well. On a glassfibre cabin top, the chocks which lift the rail clear can be moulded into the deck. This gives the moulder an easy chance to thicken up the skin in way of the fastenings. It also means that the nut and washer plate will be recessed on the underside, and not reach out to scalp everyone who passes below. Notice how the biggest possible plate washer is used. This system can be used where the cabin top is rounded forward, since the wood rail can be bent. In fact the wood can be bent both down and inboard forward to give an attractive appearance.

Incidentally, the bolt diameter must not exceed one fifth the width of the wood or too much strength will be lost.

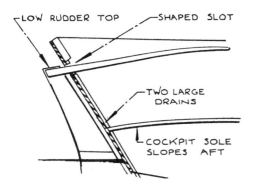

LOW RUDDER TOP   SHAPED SLOT

TWO LARGE
DRAINS

COCKPIT SOLE
SLOPES AFT

Modern trend

One way to squeeze every inch of accommodation into a yacht is to run the cockpit back to the transom. This idea can be applied to power or sailing yachts and it has various advantages.

The tiller is brought through a port in the transom provided the cockpit is self-draining, and this gives a short, light tiller and lowers the rudder head. Draining the cockpit is easy; all that is needed is a pair of long slots at sole level with neoprene flaps on the outside.

Naturally the cockpit must slope aft, and it would be worth rounding the slope down at the aft end, where no one will normally tread. The cockpit sole should always be at least 8 inches above sea level, almost regardless of the size of the boat. On yachts over 24 ft waterline the aim will be to achieve a minimum of 10 inches when at rest in calm water.

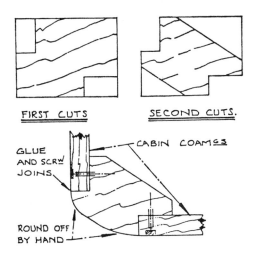

FIRST CUTS   SECOND CUTS.

GLUE AND SCREW JOINS

CABIN COAMG

ROUND OFF BY HAND

Machined corner posts

When making up a cabin top or wheelhouse the sides should always be joined by rebated corner posts. This is by far the best way to combine strength with good appearance and watertightness.

In the sketch the two rebates for the side and front coamings are exactly the same even though the post is not square. Then the inner bevel (to reduce the weight and improve appearance of the post) is chamfered off at the same angle as the outer cut. This last is a time-saver prior to the fairing off which will be undertaken after the coamings are screwed and glued though some of the rough may be taken off before assembly. Even an amateur who has a portable electric drill and saw attachment is well advised to have a saw-mill do the corner post machining.

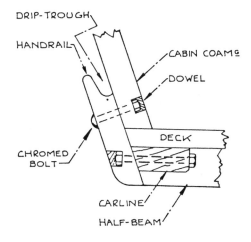

DRIP-TROUGH

HANDRAIL

CABIN COAMG

DOWEL

DECK

CHROMED BOLT

CARLINE

HALF-BEAM

Cabin top coamings

It is surprisingly difficult to get coamings to stay watertight, especially when there are highly stressed fittings like the main sheet horse mounted on them. This layout has the advantage that the components are pulled tightly together by rows of bolts which are more effective than screws and can be tightened after a few years, even though this means removing the dowels. Another real asset of this type of carline and coaming is that water has to negotiate at least two lines of join before it can get into the cabin. Naturally all the faying surfaces will be well bedded with a non-hardening compound like Secomastic. Also this layout provides that drips from ports are caught in the handrail where they can be mopped up every so often, instead of landing on the berths below. Notice how the handrail is as thick as the coaming.

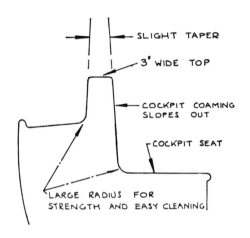

SLIGHT TAPER

3' WIDE TOP

COCKPIT COAMING SLOPES OUT

COCKPIT SEAT

LARGE RADIUS FOR STRENGTH AND EASY CLEANING

Glassfibre cockpit coamings

It is both a convenience and a comfort to have a variety of seats for helmsman and crew in any yacht. On long trips they can change round. Coming to moorings they can sit high for a good view, and in bad weather, low for shelter.

For these reasons it makes sense to have cockpit coamings which are at least 3 inches wide at the top and are reasonably comfortable for sitting on. This arrangement also ensures that the coamings gain stiffness from their width. By tapering them slightly they are easier to get off a mould, and provide a slight outward rake to the cockpit seat back which makes for increased comfort. Naturally the side decks must not be made too narrow and on a small boat it may be best to keep the coaming wide only in way of the forward end of the tiller. A tiller extension will be needed if the helmsman is to sit on the coaming top.

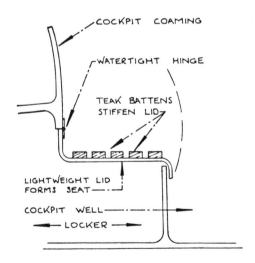

COCKPIT COAMING

WATERTIGHT HINGE

TEAK BATTENS STIFFEN LID

LIGHTWEIGHT LID FORMS SEAT

COCKPIT WELL

LOCKER

Glassfibre cockpit

As a material glassfibre is heavy and rather expensive. It is therefore usual to use it as thinly as possible. For a cockpit locker lid a thickness of 1/16 inch would be ample for keeping the water out on a coastal cruiser but would be too thin to carry the weight of a man sitting on the seat lid.

One answer to this situation is to make the locker lids quite light and then stiffen them with teak battens, giving the advantages of a slatted seat. The teak looks smart as well as making sure that the crew are not forced to sit in a puddle.

In this sketch the lid is moulded up the cockpit side so that spray collecting on the lee seat does not drip into the locker via the hinge line.

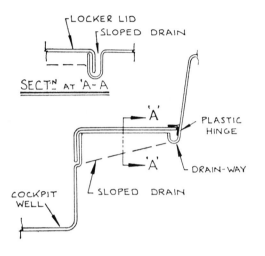

SECTᴺ ᴀᴛ 'A-A

Watertight cockpit lockers

These are hard to achieve because even if the sides are good and keep out the drips, the outer edge is always a vulnerable one. On a glassfibre yacht it is fairly easy to use the deep trough technique. This allows water to get into the cracks round the lid where it can run away.

These ways must slope very sharply as otherwise they will not drain when the boat is heeled heavily. They should be wide so that they are easy to clean and can cope when a solid wave comes aboard. It may be thought that the seat tops could be fully portable to make it easy to get sail bags into the lockers. However loose lids are never safe and tend to get blown overboard in just those gale conditions when they are most wanted. What is needed to get those bulky packages into the lockers is a clip to hold the locker lid fully open.

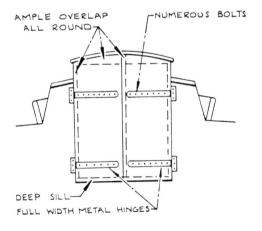

Offshore cabin doors

The tendency for an increasing number of yachts to make long voyages offshore underlines the need for special deep-sea scantlings. A yacht going offshore for long periods is bound to meet very bad weather and should be suitably equipped.

One of the weaknesses of every yacht is the cabin doors and surrounding structure. A heavy sea from aft will break in a flimsy pair of doors with horrifying efficiency and then flood the yacht. To avoid this trouble the doors should be made of at least 1 inch thick plywood, or high grade hardwood. This thickness should not be decreased on a small yacht since the weight of sea breaking on a 2 ft wide companionway does not decrease with the yacht's size.

To stiffen the doors a pair of full width metal hinges is recommended.

Hatches and Ventilation

Hatches tend to be the only source of ventilation on many small craft. This is a pity because without good and constant ventilation glassfibre yachts tend to suffer from condensation and sometimes the smell of the g.r.p. Wooden yachts without ventilation will rot, and steel ones corrode faster than they should.

Hatches are important because they are the front and back door of a boat, a source of structural weakness, leaks and general trouble. It pays to make them with skill, then fit them with cunning.

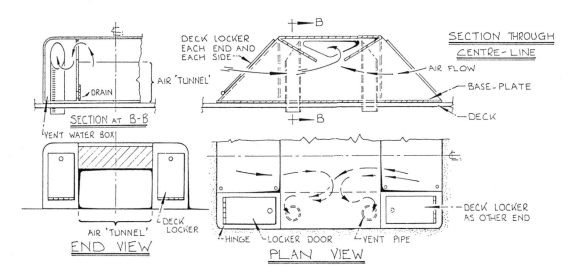

Deck lockers and vents

This combined fitting can be made of glassfibre, wood or metal. It suits all sorts of craft from massive power yachts down to small coast-hoppers. It has all sorts of special advantages, such as steeply sloped ends which do not catch sheets, and a ventilating system which works regardless of whether the wind is blowing from aft or forwards. This suits boats kept in marinas. The sloped roof of the 'tunnel' makes the wind speed up, and under certain conditions the venting will be from inside the boat outwards.

The lockers will not be watertight unless they have rubber seals around the doors, so they need drain holes at the corners. The drains in the vent boxes must have neoprene flaps on the outside, to let water out but prevent it getting in when seas sweep solid over the deck.

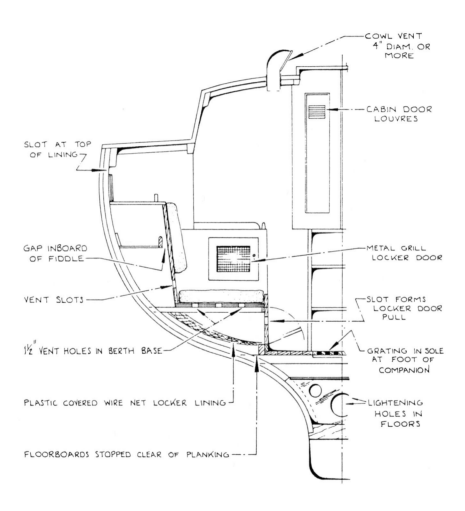

COWL VENT
4" DIAM. OR
MORE

CABIN DOOR
LOUVRES

SLOT AT TOP
OF LINING

GAP INBOARD
OF FIDDLE

VENT SLOTS

METAL GRILL
LOCKER DOOR

SLOT FORMS
LOCKER DOOR
PULL

1½" VENT HOLES IN BERTH BASE

GRATING IN SOLE
AT FOOT OF
COMPANION

PLASTIC COVERED WIRE NET LOCKER LINING

LIGHTENING
HOLES IN
FLOORS

FLOORBOARDS STOPPED CLEAR OF PLANKING

Circulation and ventilation

Whatever construction material is used for a boat it is essential to have adequate ventilation. This is fairly easy to achieve on a limited scale, but to do a thorough job calls for persistence. First there must be at least two good ventilators, one to let the air in, the second to suck it away. In practice even on a boat 24 ft overall it pays to fit four vents or more.

Any inlet or outlet of less than 4 inch diameter is likely to be relatively ineffective unless there is a strong wind blowing. Even in half a gale, a 2 inch diameter ventilator which leads the breeze through a complex water-box will not let in much fresh air.

Once inside, the air should be encouraged to trickle in and out of every locker and corner, collecting errant moisture as it goes. A locker, like the hull of the boat, must have both an inlet and an outlet for the draught. A slot less than 6×2 inches is too small to let air pass through easily. Likewise it is essential that areas such as the bilges, behind the lining and under the mattresses have an adequate circulation of air. Fitting out is a good time to improve the air circulation, since any cuts in glassfibre or wood or metal will need protecting with paint or re-glassing and this is the best opportunity. As a basic rule, it is impossible to have too many slots, holes and gratings for ventilation. It is worth remembering too, that the addition of these air vents is lightening the craft.

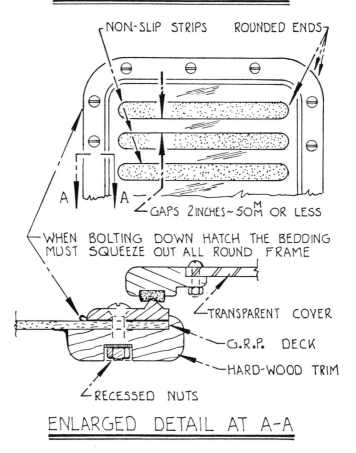

PLAN VIEW OF HATCH

NON-SLIP STRIPS   ROUNDED ENDS

GAPS 2 INCHES ~ 50 MM OR LESS

WHEN BOLTING DOWN HATCH THE BEDDING MUST SQUEEZE OUT ALL ROUND FRAME

TRANSPARENT COVER

G.R.P. DECK

HARD-WOOD TRIM

RECESSED NUTS

ENLARGED DETAIL AT A-A

Fitting a modern hatch

Virtually all boats have bought-in rather than boat-yard made hatches nowadays. These hatches, which usually have aluminium frames, need very careful bolting down, with ample bedding material all round, otherwise there will be leaks under the frame.

The bolts should have nuts recessed into wood trim, or be otherwise protected, to prevent them catching sails and the clothing of anyone scrambling through the hatchway. As the top is normally of Perspex or a similar slippery material, non-skid strips set close together are needed for safety.

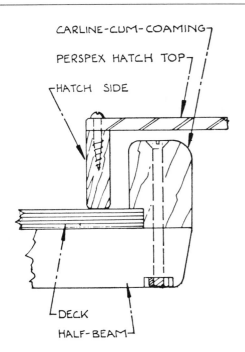

CARLINE-CUM-COAMING
PERSPEX HATCH TOP
HATCH SIDE
DECK
HALF-BEAM

Lightweight forehatch

Saving weight is best achieved by leaving things out rather than planing off pounds of shavings to thin down the scantlings until they are perhaps dangerously light.

Typical of the way weight can be saved is this idea for combining the forehatch inner coaming and the carline. The carline is put on top of the beam and must be bolted since screws, even with glue, cannot be relied upon to hold. Hardwood must be used for the carline-cum-coaming. Rounding its top edges makes it much more comfortable for anyone climbing through the forehatch, besides giving a better appearance.

The rebate for the deck is to be strongly recommended as it makes a much tighter join than a simple butt. If the half-beam is held temporarily, the deck laid and finally the carline-cum-coaming bolted down with ample bedding in the rebate, a very tight join is achieved.

This type of latch with no rubber seal is only suitable for inshore craft.

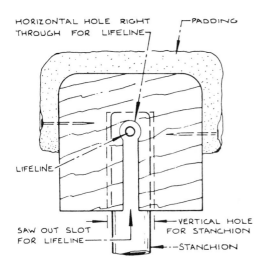

HORIZONTAL HOLE RIGHT THROUGH FOR LIFELINE
PADDING
LIFELINE
SAW OUT SLOT FOR LIFELINE
VERTICAL HOLE FOR STANCHION
STANCHION

Winter cover protection

Even a glassfibre boat should be protected with an overall cover if it is laid up in the open for the winter. On some yachts it is difficult to remove the stanchions. In many cases it is advisable to leave them in place in order to provide crawling headroom over the side decks and to provide extra support for the cover. If the tops of the stanchions are unprotected they will chafe through the cover.

To prevent chafe, a padded wood chock may be fitted to the top of each stanchion. It should be a cube of about 4 inches with a vertical hole giving about ⅛ inch clearance for the stanchion. A horizontal hole is drilled at the level of the lifeline and a slot sawn out. Finally the top of the chock is rounded and padded.

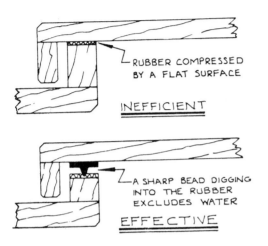

RUBBER COMPRESSED BY A FLAT SURFACE

INEFFICIENT

A SHARP BEAD DIGGING INTO THE RUBBER EXCLUDES WATER

EFFECTIVE

Hatch seals

It is always best to put a rubber seal round a hatch, to keep water out. Various types of high coaming, inner and outer coamings, even triple coamings are all very helpful. But in the final event, what is needed is some continuous well-bedded seal all round.

However there are degrees of excellence in the matter of seals. It is important to have a sharp edge, often called a bead, digging firmly into the rubber. This technique is tough on the rubber, which will need regular renewal, probably every other year or so. But that is a small price to pay for an absolutely watertight hatch.

To keep the bead forced well into the rubber, four or six strong clasps are needed.

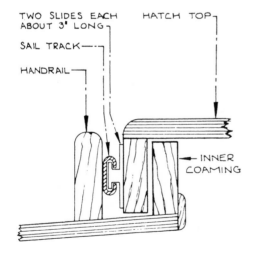

TWO SLIDES EACH ABOUT 3' LONG

SAIL TRACK

HANDRAIL

HATCH TOP

INNER COAMING

An easy hatch

Some amateur shipwrights tend to shy from making a sliding hatch because they feel that a small error in the assembly will result in a hatch that jams.

In practice many chandlers, though they stock no brass bar, have short lengths of sail track. It is not unusual to find short lengths of track in boat yards, offcuts left after a new mast or boom has been made.

This design has many advantages which will appeal to the relatively inept. For instance the inner coamings can be slightly off the vertical, without causing trouble. Just disguise the fact by rounding the top edges well. The depth of the hatch sides can vary and be planed to the correct depth after trial. It is usual to use ply for the hatch top as solid timber tends to dry out and leak at the seams.

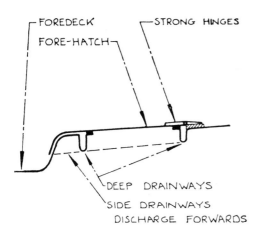

FOREDECK
FORE-HATCH
STRONG HINGES
DEEP DRAINWAYS
SIDE DRAINWAYS
DISCHARGE FORWARDS

Glassfibre forehatch

A forehatch moulded from fibreglass to blend in with the fore end of the cabin top can look smart and present the minimum windage. It will also be light in weight if carefully engineered.

The hatch beds down on a rubber strip set on the all-round horizontal ridge inboard of the drainway. This means that water has first to seek a way between the hatch and the cabin top, then fill the drainway and finally get past the seal before it is able to find its way below.

An essential feature of this arrangement is the strength of the hinges. They have to be able to withstand the pressure caused by closing the hatch on the rubber seal. The rigidity of the hatch and cabin top is greatly increased by using large-radius curves.

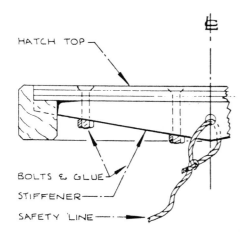

HATCH TOP
BOLTS & GLUE
STIFFENER
SAFETY LINE

Hatch without hinges

On the hulls of cats and tris it is usual to fit simple access hatches. Even on the smallest craft these hatches are necessary to make it possible to bail out bilge-water, stow gear and so on. It is quite usual to make the hatch tops very simple, without hinges, often for the good reason that small hinges are flimsy.

A hatch of this sort needs a very good safety line. Otherwise when it is taken off or blows off, it can go overboard quickly and easily. It is no good tying a safety line to a screw-eye, it pulls out too easily. A good idea is to fix a strong stiffener across the hatch, so that it can stand being walked upon. The stiffener should be drilled for the Terylene safety line. The inboard end must be made fast to a frame or similar strong-point inside.

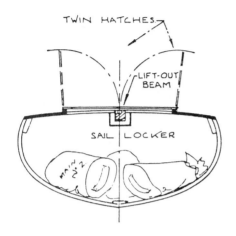

Improved aft hatch

There is nothing so useful as that locker in the counter, but often there is nothing so awkward to get into. A hinged hatch usually has to be fairly small if it is not to hang outboard when open and there is seldom room for a really large sliding hatch, big enough to swallow a full sail-bag.

A good way round the problem is to make the hatch in two halves with hinges outboard. The central beam is portable so that for removing large objects it can be lifted out. The beam may have a central gutter to take any drips that seep between the hatches which will be piped out through the transom.

With this central beam the hatch tops can be quite light, say ⅜ inch ply, and be safe to climb about on.

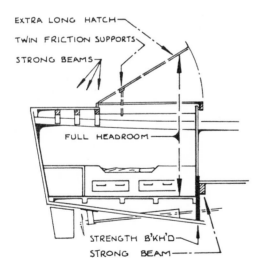

Adequate headroom

Naval architects spend hours struggling to achieve full headroom whilst retaining an attractive appearance.

This technique applies in particular to aft cabins. In the sketch a scheme giving ample headroom is shown. True, the headroom extends only over the forward two or three feet of the cabin, but this is adequate for dressing. A long hatch cuts into the structural strength of a boat which explains the need for stout beams, a pair of half bulkheads linked by a deep floor and a strong sole bearer just forward of the bulkhead.

The hatch cover should extend well forward when shut, so that it covers the opening when the hatch is open and so excludes the rain.

Hatch side curtains will also improve weather protection.

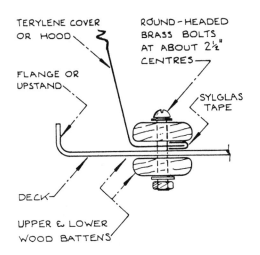

TERYLENE COVER OR HOOD

FLANGE OR UPSTAND

ROUND-HEADED BRASS BOLTS AT ABOUT 2½" CENTRES

SYLGLAS TAPE

DECK

UPPER & LOWER WOOD BATTENS

Keeping out spray

On a glassfibre or metal boat it is not always easy to fit a cover over a forehatch.

One technique which can be used is to sandwich the bottom seam of the cover between hardwood battens. The battens are drawn together by bolts or screws. In practice screws have to be rather carefully driven and the batten taking the thread must be thick so bolts are probably best. Notice how the Sylglas tape is folded over the Terylene and is clear of the bolts; it tends to snarl up if a drill is put through it. Another detail to note is the flange. If none exists, one should be fitted to hold back drips which get under the cover.

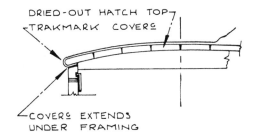

DRIED-OUT HATCH TOP
TRAKMARK COVERS

COVERS EXTENDS UNDER FRAMING

Hatch repair

The traditional type of hatch with a planked top has one recurring disadvantage – it will dry out and leak. There are various means of checking this from using well-seasoned teak to paying the seams with a rubber compound which expands and contracts with the wood.

However, on an old boat it is sometimes impossible to cure the leaking top without some form of sheathing. An easy approach is to lay Trakmark or Treadmaster over the whole of the hatch. The edges of the former are best wrapped right round and fastened under the fore and aft runners. The fore and aft ends may be secured by the end beams so that no edge of the material is left out to curl, shrink or otherwise spoil the appearance. Treadmaster is stopped just short of the edges. Some owners use ordinary canvas for this type of covering but it does not wear well and even when well painted seems to collect and hold water, then rot. Though canvas is cheap, it is not all that much cheaper than Trakmark, which does not need painting.

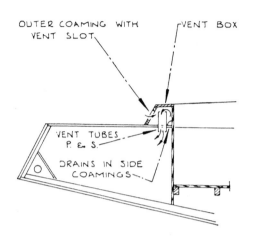

OUTER COAMING WITH
VENT SLOT

VENT BOX

VENT TUBES
P. & S.

DRAINS IN SIDE
COAMINGS

Aft ventilation

It is not easy to fit ventilators aft of the cockpit without cluttering up the aft deck.

By using the aft coaming of the cockpit as one upright of a ventilator box, the whole problem can be solved rather conveniently. The cockpit side coamings are often carried aft a short distance anyway so all that is needed is an extra aft coaming and a top.

There should be *two* tubes through the deck to provide both an inlet and an outlet since it is constant circulation of air that is required. Ideally the tubes should be of over 4 inch diameter, otherwise the air is slow to trickle through them except when there is a Force 6 wind.

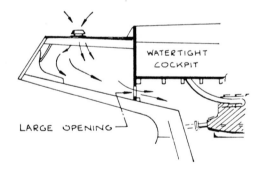

WATERTIGHT
COCKPIT

LARGE OPENING

Aft end vent

To induce air-flow through the end of the counter it is essential to have an inlet and an outlet. As most mass-produced cruisers only have a single aft vent, air only seeps slowly in and out of the counter locker. With a substantial aperture in the bottom of the bulkhead the draught will flow effortlessly and when the engine is started it will draw air from aft. Incidentally this may raise engine efficiency a trifle because the usual enclosing casing sometimes restricts breathing.

It is usual to drill a row of 1 inch diameter holes when 'opening up' an over-compartmented boat, but a much better plan is to make holes about 4 inches or more in diameter. This size lets a proper flow take place, whereas any smaller size needs too much change of pressure on one side (i.e. the equivalent of a strong breeze) to induce a draught.

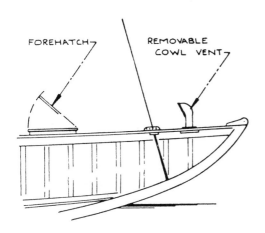

FOREHATCH

REMOVABLE
COWL VENT

Fore end vent

Most yachts spend more than 80% of their lives on moorings or in marinas. They can therefore have vents right forward which are too vulnerable at sea and have to be taken off before getting under way. Boats which are under 25 feet long, or have low freeboard, or are built of wood should have this type of vent.

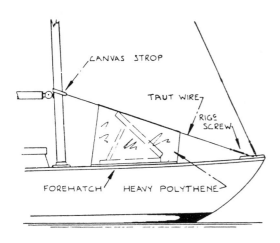

CANVAS STROP

TAUT WIRE

RIGG
SCREW

FOREHATCH   HEAVY POLYTHENE

Getting the best from a forehatch

On a small yacht headroom forward is sometimes obtained by opening the forehatch. However, this is not so good in the rain.

By fitting a heavy polythene sheet over the forehatch, as shown, the rain will be excluded and there will be good permanent ventilation all the time the boat is occupied and on moorings. In fact with a little care this scheme can even be used at sea in moderate weather.

The cover can be made of 1500 gauge polythene which is available from builders' merchants. It is very tough and should be rolled, not folded, when stowed. It will let in plenty of light, and can be obtained with netting worked into the polythene, which provides strength and gives some privacy, if the toilet is located below the forehatch.

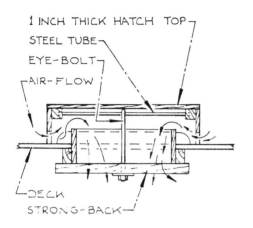

1 INCH THICK HATCH TOP
STEEL TUBE
EYE-BOLT
AIR-FLOW
DECK
STRONG-BACK

Anti-pilferage

Yachts deteriorate more through internal dampness than they do through over-use. Most owners appreciate this and would like to leave hatches open all day, every day. Nowadays there are two reasons why they cannot do this: the risk of pilferage and the fact that there is no watchman available in the typical yacht yard to go round all the yachts each night to close the hatches. This oversize hatch cover is held down by a strong-back beam and a vertical eyebolt. The sides of the cover are cut away to allow ventilation holes to a height of half an inch less than the hatch coaming. Also the sides are set well outside the coamings, so that the air-flow has an easy path and wide slots to go through.

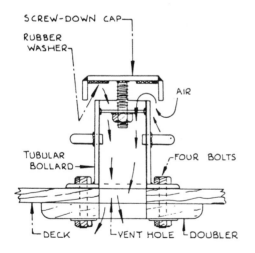

SCREW-DOWN CAP
RUBBER WASHER
AIR
TUBULAR BOLLARD
FOUR BOLTS
DECK
VENT HOLE
DOUBLER

Fore peak ventilation

In any craft, be she an offshore racer, family cruiser, chrome trimmed gin palace or scruffy tub, there is almost invariably a clutter on the foredeck. Seldom is there room for a ventilator of adequate size right forward where it is needed most. One way of overcoming the problem and saving valuable deck space into the bargain is to fit a combined mooring bollard and ventilator. The fitting illustrated here can be made from a length of 3 inch diameter pipe welded to a ¼ inch thick base plate about 8 inches square; the horns are of ¾ inch diameter rod. The cap is fabricated from a length of larger diameter pipe blanked off at the top. The ½ inch diameter bolt welded to the cap runs through a hole in a length of 1 inch by ¼ inch bar with a nut welded on.

Vent through bulkhead with coat-hook

This simple vent is made up of a framework which surrounds a hole in the bulkhead, with a standard plastic or metal vent grill secured to it. In practice the grill plate might be secured between the frame and the bulkhead.

The coat-hook is a simple spike made of timber which may match or contrast with the bulkhead. It can be made truly massive, strong enough to carry a large sail bag. This is most convenient, because it is not easy to buy strong coat-hooks.

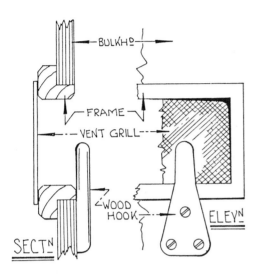

Escape hatch

Yachts which race offshore have to have means whereby the main hatch can be secured and opened from inside and from the cockpit. On boats built with hatch locks on the outside which are inaccessible from inboard, it can be difficult to work out a viable scheme to conform with the rules.

A simple way round the problem is to cut a circle in the top weather-board, and bolt on a Henderson hatch. Anyone inside the cabin who wants to escape simply takes off the hatch cover, which is put on with its top inside the cabin, reaches through and twists the lock knob.

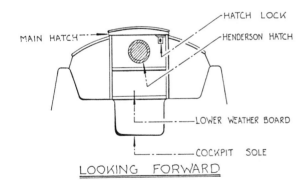

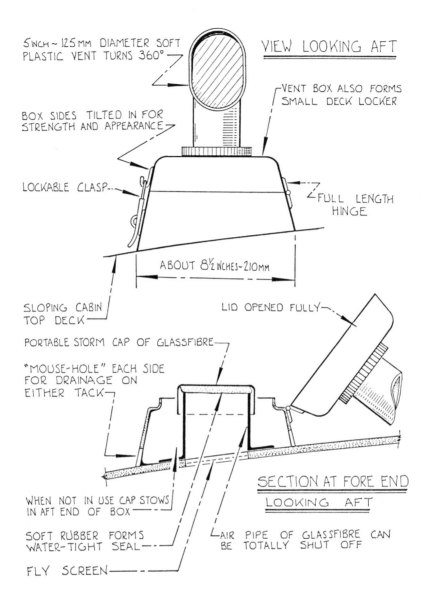

5 INCH ~ 125 mm DIAMETER SOFT PLASTIC VENT TURNS 360°

VIEW LOOKING AFT

VENT BOX ALSO FORMS SMALL DECK LOCKER

BOX SIDES TILTED IN FOR STRENGTH AND APPEARANCE

LOCKABLE CLASP

FULL LENGTH HINGE

ABOUT 8½ INCHES ~ 210 mm

SLOPING CABIN TOP DECK

LID OPENED FULLY

PORTABLE STORM CAP OF GLASSFIBRE

"MOUSE-HOLE" EACH SIDE FOR DRAINAGE ON EITHER TACK

SECTION AT FORE END
LOOKING AFT

WHEN NOT IN USE CAP STOWS IN AFT END OF BOX

AIR PIPE OF GLASSFIBRE CAN BE TOTALLY SHUT OFF

SOFT RUBBER FORMS WATER-TIGHT SEAL

FLY SCREEN

Camper and Nicholson vent box design

In very severe weather this vent is quickly shut down by putting the storm cap over the internal pipe top. The vent box is strongly made and forms a deck locker for items such as halyard winch handles. Ropes slithering over the deck will not catch on the sloped ends of the box, but unless there is a bent tubular guard over the cowl they will catch on that. A metal guard of this type can double as a grab rail.

To hold the box shut there is a lockable 'over-dead-centre' type hasp so that sneak-thieves cannot make off with the winch handles.

There are drain holes on both sides of the box, because when the boat heels water would accumulate in the box and eventually run into the cabin if there were holes along one side only.

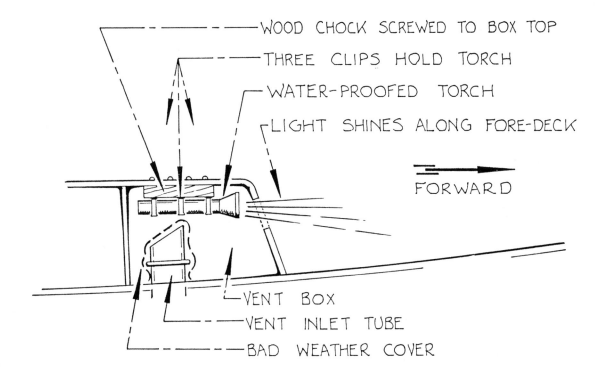

WOOD CHOCK SCREWED TO BOX TOP

THREE CLIPS HOLD TORCH

WATER-PROOFED TORCH

LIGHT SHINES ALONG FORE-DECK

FORWARD

VENT BOX

VENT INLET TUBE

BAD WEATHER COVER

Dual purpose vent box

Though the vent box shown here is built into the forward end of the cabin top, the ideas incorporated can be worked into other types of vent box, such as the common 'Dorade' vent located on top of the coach-roof.

The air inlet slot is located at the correct height to suit the flashlight which is secured to the top of the vent box.

Some owners may prefer to fix a waterproof light fitting here, wired to the ship's batteries.

With the onset of very bad weather the inlet tube is blanked off with a pvc cover held by shock-cord below the sealing rim which is fixed permanently round the up-standing tube.

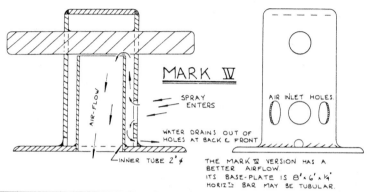

MARK IV

AIR-FLOW

SPRAY
ENTERS

WATER DRAINS OUT OF
HOLES AT BACK & FRONT

INNER TUBE 2" ⌀

AIR INLET HOLES.

THE MARK IV VERSION HAS A
BETTER AIRFLOW.
ITS BASE-PLATE IS 8" x 6' x ¼"
HORIZL BAR MAY BE TUBULAR.

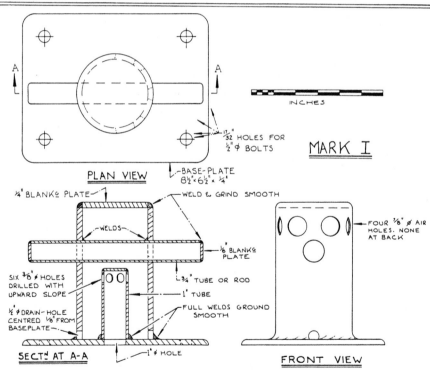

A ← ← A

17/32" HOLES FOR
½" ⌀ BOLTS

INCHES

MARK I

PLAN VIEW

BASE-PLATE
8½" x 6½" x ¼"

¼" BLANKG PLATE

WELD & GRIND SMOOTH

WELDS

⅛" BLANKG
PLATE

SIX ⅜" HOLES
DRILLED WITH
UPWARD SLOPE

¾" TUBE OR ROD

1" TUBE

½" ⌀ DRAIN-HOLE
CENTRED ⅛" FROM
BASEPLATE

FULL WELDS GROUND
SMOOTH

SECTN AT A-A

1" ⌀ HOLE

FOUR ⅛" ⌀ AIR
HOLES. NONE
AT BACK

FRONT VIEW

Bollard-Vent

My first design of the Bollard-Vent was produced when I was apprenticed. The plan was made on an improvised drawing-board under the low oak beams of the seventeenth-century cottage in Poole, where I lived then. The prototype bollard needed no alteration and a batch was made from then on every few years.

It is satisfying to see the Bollard-Vent on the foredecks of offshore racers and cruisers all round the coast. Because it is easy and reliable to moor onto it is appreciated by people who use their boats a lot and go offshore, where ventilation in bad weather is such a problem. But I have to admit that not very many yachts had these fittings, probably because they were not advertised.

Years after the first batch were made, out of the blue I had a letter from Bernard Hayman. He was building a new, rather unusual boat called *Barbican*. She is crammed with interesting ideas so I was pleased when he said he wanted to fit a Bollard-Vent. He later published a series of articles about *Barbican* and this wide-spread publicity made the vent well known. People from all over the world, especially Australia, wrote for plans.

I showed the plan of the original model, the Mark I, to my partner, Alfred Mylne. He suggested modifications, and that day I drew up Mark II. Over the next few days we made more changes so that Mark IV was born. It is simpler and therefore cheaper to make.

Sadly I have to give a warning against cheap imitations. Recently I have seen scruffy undersized under-nourished Bollard-Vents. They would not hold a dinghy in a draught, let alone a wildly plunging cruiser on an exposed lee shore. Just as bad, if not worse, these copies do not have the essential inner pipe to form a baffle, so water will get through them in moderate weather. In bad weather they will funnel tons of water into the yacht, especially as she plunges to windward.

Even on the original version if water is constantly deep over the foredeck, a plug is needed to put in the bottom of the inner tube. When this plug is removed there may be a small accumulation of water, so have a bucket ready to catch it. However the plug should only be necessary on rare occasions in the worst weather.

This fitting can be used on boats between about 22 and 52 ft long, power or sail. Though normally fitted on the foredeck, at least one boat has a pair on the *aft* deck. On any type of yacht of 30 ft or more a pair of these Bollard-Vents forward makes sense for cruising, but racing boats will not want the extra weight. The diameter of the outer tube makes it easy to surge a rope round and the proportions seem to be about right for easy quick making fast.

It can be made from mild steel galvanised, or stainless steel, or bronze unplated or chromed. The welding must be perfect, indeed this is probably the place most likely to fail, apart from the yacht's deck. All welds need grinding off fully to a nice smooth round. One friend of mine wanted to cast a Bollard-Vent and this looked rather complex. However it is quite easily done by making the inner tube and its flange the first casting and the remainder a second casting. The two castings need not be joined.

Cabin Furniture

Now that we live in the age when the last bastion of individuality, a cruising yacht, is a mass-produced item, it behoves us to avoid total monotonous conformity. Works of art attract soaring prices because they are different, attractive, lovely to look at and live with.

The same should apply to a yacht's cabin. It should be cosy yet practical. It must be free from sharp edges which can injure anyone in rough weather, well supplied with hand-grips and foot-holds, yet uncluttered. At present the majority of production-line yachts are pleasant and sensible. But there are signs that the stylist, the salesman and the advertising agents are trying to exert their dreary influence. Soon we will have yacht interiors made to look good in the coloured advertisements, but hellishly uncomfortable in a Force 7 head wind, twenty miles offshore.

In these pages are ideas which have been used by amateurs and professionals to embellish and enhance the interiors of successful yachts. They are all particularly easy to make or use, and many of them can be applied to stock boats. Virtually all these sketches can be modified to suit yachts from 20 feet to 120 feet. For instance some of the chart table ideas can be applied to the owner's or captain's desk, to the owner's wife's dressing table, to the children's cabin in the fo'c's'le where they keep their toys, and so on. In the same way some chart table suggestions can be used in the galley, and vice versa.

This chapter is of special interest to the man who buys a stock hull and finishes it off himself. If he buys the best material and takes great care he can end up with a boat which is both more attractive and more valuable than the stock yacht off an assembly line, based on the same hull. And of course finishing off a hull is both cheaper and more satisfying than buying a completed craft.

When using any of these ideas it is worth looking over a well-built boat and making a few notes for guidance. It is interesting that the best builders never leave any plywood edge showing, never use putty, often manage to conceal all the fastenings, bleach and blend their woods and so on. They avoid monotony by using wood to trim Formica, by painting the lining and bulkheads, but varnishing or more usually polishing the furniture, and by subtle contrasts.

In general it pays to stick to two colours, one dominant, the other to bring out the highlights. It is best to use one wood, or maybe two at the most. However this rule may be broken in order to achieve a matching effect. For instance one might use a mahogany faced ply and edge it with solid utile, of the same colour, simply because it may be impossible to buy solid mahogany to match the facing on the ply.

In a racing yacht the aim will be to save weight. This is more successfully done by omitting inessentials than by cutting down scantlings. A fiddle which cannot stand the lurch of a heavy man as he falls in bad weather will fail at the one time when it is most wanted. It is usually more satisfactory to put in thick battens with gaps between as a berth bottom, rather than a thin continuous battening. This, of course, is simply applied engineering, which has to be remembered when making furniture just as much as when making chainplates or engine bearers.

On a cruising boat, especially one meant for deep-sea work, it is a good idea to do a few sample calculations before cutting furniture scantlings. It will at once become clear that as most metals tend to weigh some ten times their equivalent volume of wood, weight-saving in furniture is hard to achieve successfully, and sometimes not worth much trouble.

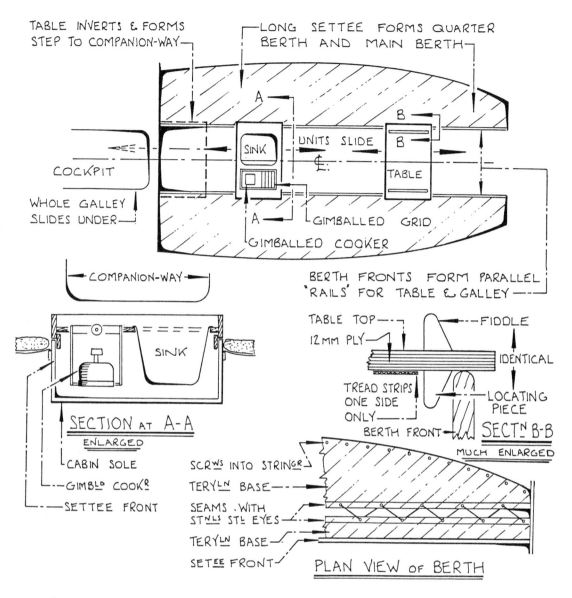

TABLE INVERTS & FORMS STEP TO COMPANION-WAY

LONG SETTEE FORMS QUARTER BERTH AND MAIN BERTH

A

B

SINK

UNITS SLIDE

B

TABLE

COCKPIT

WHOLE GALLEY SLIDES UNDER

A

GIMBALLED GRID

GIMBALLED COOKER

COMPANION-WAY

BERTH FRONTS FORM PARALLEL 'RAILS' FOR TABLE & GALLEY

SINK

TABLE TOP

12mm PLY

FIDDLE

IDENTICAL

TREAD STRIPS ONE SIDE ONLY

LOCATING PIECE

BERTH FRONT

SECTⁿ B-B

MUCH ENLARGED

SECTION AT A-A

ENLARGED

CABIN SOLE

GIMBLᴰ COOKᴿ

SETTEE FRONT

SCRᵂˢ INTO STRINGᴿ

TERYLⁿ BASE

SEAMS WITH STⁿᴸˢ STᴸ EYES

TERYLⁿ BASE

SETEE FRONT

PLAN VIEW OF BERTH

Furniture for a small cruiser

The top drawing is a plan view of the cabin of a small cruiser/racer which does not have an inboard engine. The galley consists of a box which slides between the settees. When not in use, the galley box lives under the cockpit, and at meal times it is simply slid forward. It can go as far forward as suits the other activities on board. The cooker is a single burner which is gimballed and has a grid incorporated on the gimballing so that a hot pan can be set down safely at sea, adjacent to the cooker. The cooker box is shown in section bottom left.

The galley worktop is also movable to any location fore and aft between the long settees which form two berths on each side of the boat. Normally the table forms the single step down from the cockpit to the cabin, and its top surface has non-slip tread strips on it. Turn the table upside down, and it has a good working surface for cooking.

The bottom right detail shows how the berths are made of Terylene with provision for tightening the bases when they stretch after a few months' use. A great advantage of all the ideas shown here is that they are easy to make and fit.

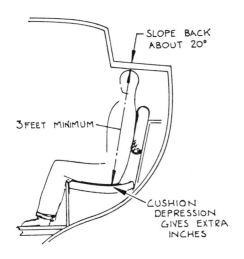

SLOPE BACK ABOUT 20°

3 FEET MINIMUM

CUSHION DEPRESSION GIVES EXTRA INCHES

Subtle sitting headroom

Amateur and professional designers alike fret and fume over the inconvenience of the human frame. It is an awkward shape and much of the time there is too much of it. People need 3 ft at least, between the top of their hair to the base of their bottom, when sitting. This distance is hard to find on small yachts, especially the light displacement type. There are two tricks to gain the extra inch or so.

By raking the seat well outboard, the vertical height is reduced below 3 ft. In addition the head is set back so that the athwartships space helps the shortage of vertical distance.

Another inch, and sometimes more, is found by fitting soft cushions, possibly with webbing or canvas bases beneath. This must not be overdone otherwise the berths become untenable in bad weather. Also too much sag can be uncomfortable but it should be possible to find at least 1 inch depression on a 4 inch cushion.

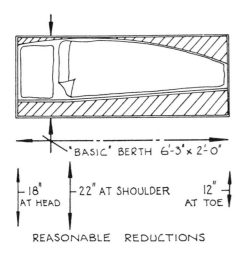

"BASIC" BERTH 6'-3" x 2'-0"

18" AT HEAD   22" AT SHOULDER   12" AT TOE

REASONABLE REDUCTIONS

Sleeping space

Not so long ago designers used to make inches in cruisers by cutting the length of one or two berths below 6 ft. This was a dubious practice, based on the theory that out of a crew of four, it was unlikely that everyone would be over 6 ft. The reckoning was that most crews included a wife or girl-friend. Statistically it seemed safe enough to provide the saloon berths about 6 ft 2 in long and the forward berths say 5 ft 11 in.

But due to a surfeit of vitamins, or some such cause, the population is getting taller. Now designers have to provide berths 6 ft 3 in at least, if they are to survive a searching Boat Show with thousands of visitors all too ready to measure berth lengths precisely.

However quite a bit of *athwartships* space can be saved. Indeed a narrowed berth has virtues at sea. The occupant rolls about less and his sleeping bag stays more cosily wrapped around him.

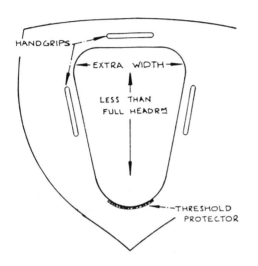

HANDGRIPS

EXTRA WIDTH

LESS THAN
FULL HEADRM

THRESHOLD
PROTECTOR

Access through a strength bulkhead

Whether a boat is built of glassfibre, metal or wood, the bulkheads are likely to be main strength members. They will give massive resistance to athwartships distortion provided they are well tied to the shell all round.

Naturally the designer will go to a lot of trouble to ensure that the opening through the bulkhead does not take away too much material. This will often result in a doorway which is less than six feet high even on a yacht of quite a respectable size. To compensate, the top of the doorway must be made extra wide, so that anyone going through can stoop sideways across the boat.

In practice the lower the entrance, the wider it should be at the top. It is a happy coincidence that yachts are so shaped that this can be achieved and still leave a good width of bulkhead all round. The handrails are important, especially if the threshold is above sole level. Fit them on both faces of the bulkhead and bolt them back to back.

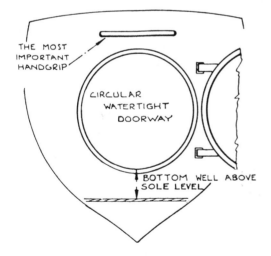

THE MOST
IMPORTANT
HANDGRIP

CIRCULAR
WATERTIGHT
DOORWAY

BOTTOM WELL ABOVE
SOLE LEVEL

The strongest type of doorway

Submarines are built on strictly practical principles. There is a very minimum of comfort but a great deal of intelligent engineering worked into these fascinating boats. The bulkheads, which seem to occur every few feet throughout the accommodation, have only small circular holes cut in them as doorways.

Anyone building a yacht should take the hint. If the boat is to be light yet strong the bulkheads should be in the form of a circular doorway. It is surprising how small a circle can be adequate. Three feet diameter is not too small though this would presumably be into a fo'c's'le or some relatively little used compartment.

If the bulkhead is to be watertight a circular door makes double sense. It is easier to get a good seal round the edge and there is less likelihood of distortion. The handgrip above the doorway is particularly important, but there should be others at the sides.

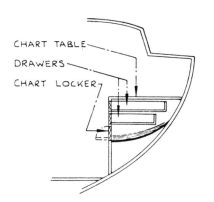

CHART TABLE

DRAWERS

CHART LOCKER

Extra chart stowage

One trouble about boats is that they are boat-shaped. They are pointed and skinny where it would be much more convenient if they were boxy. This is the main cause of trouble when arranging stowage in yachts. The skilled designer makes the best of the irregular shape he is using.

Beneath the chart table there is space for a drawer or maybe two. But below that the hull curves in, and the next drawer down is likely to be too small. It will be too narrow to hold a full width chart and so small that if it is pulled out only a short distance it will drop onto the cabin sole.

By making the space into the locker with a fold-down front, the charts can slide in easily. A piece of ⅛ inch ply curves upwards and towards the hull so that the charts slide up the back. Every chart has its name on the edge, so the correct one can be selected without pulling any others out of the locker.

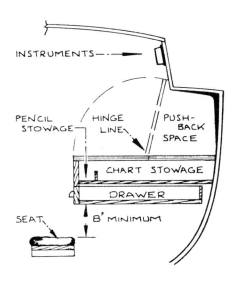

INSTRUMENTS

PENCIL STOWAGE

HINGE LINE

PUSH-BACK SPACE

CHART STOWAGE

DRAWER

SEAT

8' MINIMUM

Chart tables

If a drawer is fitted beneath the chart table for stowing the charts, the navigator has to hop off his stool and pull the drawer open half way across the cabin, to get the charts out. It is more convenient to lift the top of the table to get at the charts and perhaps have a lower drawer for seldom used charts, or for those which will be used on the next leg of the voyage.

The lift-up section should not extend right to the back of the table, then any charts and other gear on top can be pushed back to give access. It is usual to mount the navigation instruments above the chart table and under the side-deck. If they are on the cabin coaming they are likely to be in a better light and be more visible from the rest of the cabin.

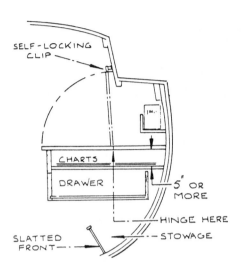

SELF-LOCKING CLIP

CHARTS

DRAWER

5" OR MORE

HINGE HERE

STOWAGE

SLATTED FRONT

Chart top table

It is common practice to make the chart table like a flat-topped desk, with lifting lid. Under the lid is a shallow box to hold the charts. To get a chart out the navigator must hold up the lid and rummage below with his spare hand, while holding on in a seaway with his ears or teeth.

A better arrangement is to have a three-quarter size lid, with a snap action clip to hold it open. This allows the navigator to push all the paraphernalia on top of the table outboard, before lifting the lid. He will have both hands free for sorting out the charts he needs and holding on. To make it possible to reach the back of the chart stowage the depth of this space should be about 5 inches. The lid must be well fitted.

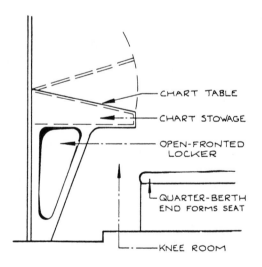

CHART TABLE

CHART STOWAGE

OPEN-FRONTED LOCKER

QUARTER-BERTH END FORMS SEAT

KNEE ROOM

Athwartships chart table

This layout is the arrangement which over the years is proving the most popular. The navigator sits on the forward end of the quarter berth and this is appropriate since the pilot usually has this bunk. He sits facing forward, which many people swear is the only way to be when working under rugged conditions. The board is sloped and fastened to a partial bulkhead. One attraction of this is that the table can be made remote from the boat and fitted at any stage during construction. It is fixed only on the forward side so that no exact fitting to a shaped surface is called for.

A space which might be wasted is made into a locker and in this location it is handy for oilies and seaboots.

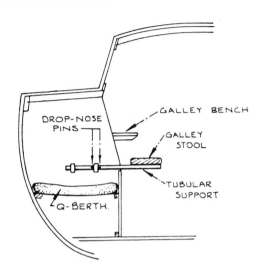

Galley seat

A seat for the cook is a pleasant ideal but often hard to achieve. A design that stows quickly and easily yet withstands the rough and tumble at sea is shown here.

On a piece of pipe (say 2 inch diameter light alloy with an ⅛ inch wall) a suitably padded seat is fitted. The tube slides in a pair of pipe holders, and is kept in place and prevented from rotating by some device like two drop-nose pins, or a couple of barrel bolts. When not in use the seat slides out board, the seat rotating by twisting the pipe, so that the whole contrivance is out of the gangway, and outboard of the edge of the bulkhead.

There are all sorts of variations on this theme. The pipe might be tiltable to deal with different angles of heel. A pair of light pipes might be used to stiffen the structure. It could be either all wood or steel. A safety strap might be incorporated to keep the cook 'in situ'.

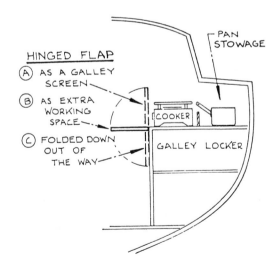

Extra working surface

The galleys of most modern yachts have two failings: they are too obtrusive and they lack working space for the cook. At one stroke the arrangement illustrated overcomes these two defects and is applicable to the majority of yachts.

A board, which can be covered with a laminated plastic on both faces and the edges, is hinged on to the inboard edge of the galley bench in way of the stove. When the galley is not in use the flap folds up and hides the stove. When the cook is working the flap is lowered to the horizontal position to extend the bench top area. If the cook wants to reach over to get at the pan stowage, then it will be necessary, on some yachts, to be able to lower the flap so that the outboard stowage at the back of the galley is within arms' reach. A barrel bolt (or better still one each side) holds the board in the correct place.

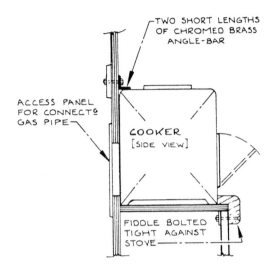

TWO SHORT LENGTHS
OF CHROMED BRASS
ANGLE-BAR

ACCESS PANEL
FOR CONNECT?
GAS PIPE

COOKER
[SIDE VIEW]

FIDDLE BOLTED
TIGHT AGAINST
STOVE

A well-fixed cooker

Most cookers are provided with small lugs for screwing down to the galley bench. But these lugs are sometimes difficult to reach. If there is a bulkhead or casing side right up against the cooker it can be impossible to get the screws in.

The bench may be of fairly thin ply, which will not provide good holding for the screws. Backing blocks under the ply are the remedy here, but there are places where these are awkward to fit. Sketched here is a simple way of holding a cooker firmly.

A hardwood fiddle is bolted along the front. Its horizontal flange is planed to exactly the right size so that it presses firmly on the front, clearing the oven door. Fiddles may also be needed down one or both sides of the cooker.

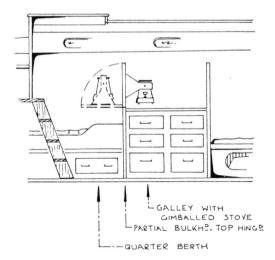

GALLEY WITH
GIMBALLED STOVE
PARTIAL BULKH?. TOP HINGE

QUARTER BERTH

More galley space

If there is one part of any yacht that is always too small, it is the galley. However cooking only takes up about one tenth of the day, so a big galley is hard to justify. In practice both quarter berths are not used during the day very much and not often just before meals. This sketch shows how the galley can be enlarged by having the gimballed stove fixed, not to the bench, but to the aft partial bulkhead. Provided no one is in the quarter berth the bulkhead is folded aft, leaving the full length of the galley bench clear.

It is possible to double this idea, putting a second stove on the forward partial bulkhead and folding that over the settee end. Or the bulkhead could be folded down to form extra working surface, without a stove on it.

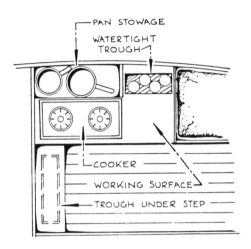

Mini-sinks

On many yachts the sink is used for about twenty minutes each day, for washing up. For much of the rest of the time it acts as a safe storage for milk cartons, gin bottles and any other similar containers in constant use. It is also a very handy storage place for dirty crockery when there is not enough of this to warrant a washing-up session. All this adds up to the conclusion that a long, narrow, trough-like sink would be very useful in many boats where there is not room for a full size sink. Even if the trough is too small for washing dishes and cannot be located in a place suitable for washing up (due perhaps to a shortage of working space) it could still be in use for 24 hours each sailing day. It can be made from nylon coated mild steel, stainless steel or even teak which cuts down breakages.

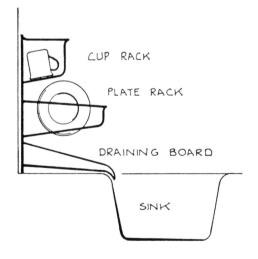

Custom-made plate rack

Most galleys are packed full of equipment, what with the stove, draining board, and lockers. There is all too little space, so that any scheme which makes for more room, especially more 'put-down' space, is welcome.

If the plates and cups are stowed in a compact rack, over a draining board, they can be put away without drying. They drip straight into the sink via the draining board. A rack which holds the individual items also prevents that maddening clink-rattle, which disturbs so many would-be sleepers.

Making up a wire or strip metal rack to fit the available space exactly is not difficult. However, it is not easy to paint it in such a way that it looks smart and yet lasts without rusting. A plastic coating is the modern way to cope with this problem, or the racks can be made of stainless steel.

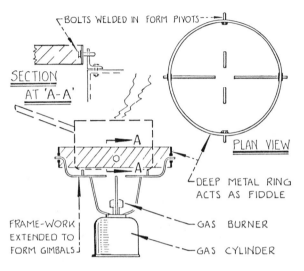

SECTION
AT 'A-A'

BOLTS WELDED IN FORM PIVOTS

PLAN VIEW

DEEP METAL RING
ACTS AS FIDDLE

FRAME-WORK
EXTENDED TO
FORM GIMBALS

GAS BURNER

GAS CYLINDER

Fully gimballed single burner stove

This set of gimbals is easy to make, and can therefore be much cheaper than a standard set sold in a chandler's. The cooker complete with its gas cylinder forms the ballast of the gimbals. One set of pivots is formed by extending the pan support structure of the stove up and outwards, with final short lengths bent horizontal and passed through holes each side of the deep metal plate ring.

This ring acts partly as a fiddle right round the pan, partly as the second unit of the gimbals. The detail top left shows how the ring is gimballed, and makes it clear that the pivots do not have to be made to a high standard of accuracy; this helps fabrication and fitting on board.

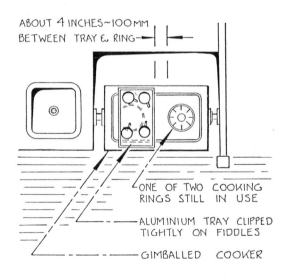

ABOUT 4 INCHES ~ 100 MM
BETWEEN TRAY & RING

ONE OF TWO COOKING
RINGS STILL IN USE

ALUMINIUM TRAY CLIPPED
TIGHTLY ON FIDDLES

GIMBALLED COOKER

Gadget for offshore cooking

On many yachts cooking outside estuaries is reduced to heating soups and tinned stews and suchlike. For this a single burner is adequate. This means that the rest of the stove top can be used as a gimballed working top.

To make this change all that is needed is a light fireproof tray which clips firmly onto the top of the swinging cooker. This is shown here in plan view, with four mugs resting on the tray.

It is important that the tray and its contents are not too heavy, otherwise the centre of gravity of the gimballed cooker will be too high and the swinging stove will throw its burden onto the cabin floor.

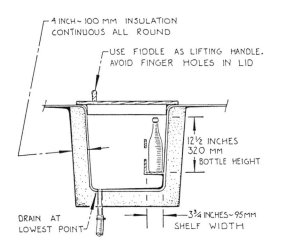

4 INCH ~ 100 MM INSULATION
CONTINUOUS ALL ROUND

USE FIDDLE AS LIFTING HANDLE.
AVOID FINGER HOLES IN LID

12½ INCHES
320 MM
BOTTLE HEIGHT

DRAIN AT
LOWEST POINT

3¾ INCHES ~ 95 MM
SHELF WIDTH

Ice box or fridge

When making up an ice box or a built-in-fridge, the outside insulation should not be less than 4 inches, and an extra insulation effect is obtained by sinking the box into the galley bench. In this way the still air in surrounding lockers helps to keep the food cold.

The bottom of the box should slope slightly, otherwise melting ice will build up an annoying puddle. Ideally there should be port and starboard drains, so that the melted water runs away on either tack.

Stowage is always a problem, and bottles in particular are best chocked off from the food. The shelf shown here has a low fiddle plus a high bar, so that it is easy to clean the shelf but the bottles will stay put even when the boat heels a lot.

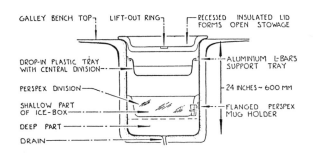

GALLEY BENCH TOP   LIFT-OUT RING   RECESSED INSULATED LID
FORMS OPEN STOWAGE

DROP-IN PLASTIC TRAY
WITH CENTRAL DIVISION

PERSPEX DIVISION

SHALLOW PART
OF ICE-BOX

DEEP PART

DRAIN

ALUMINIUM L-BARS
SUPPORT TRAY

24 INCHES ~ 600 MM

FLANGED PERSPEX
MUG HOLDER

Ice box features

If an ice box lid stands up above the surrounding work surface it gets in the way. If it is flush it may be awkward to lift out. This one is sunk, and so it forms a safe 'put-down' space where pans cannot slide away from where they have been dumped down.

The top tray holds those items wanted most often and the lowest part of the ice box (or freezer compartment) those not needed for a long time. Items of 'left-overs' can be stored in the mugs, which are held securely in the special holder (bottom right).

The 24 inch (600 mm) depth of the box is about as much as is convenient, otherwise anything right at the bottom tends to be hard to reach, especially at sea.

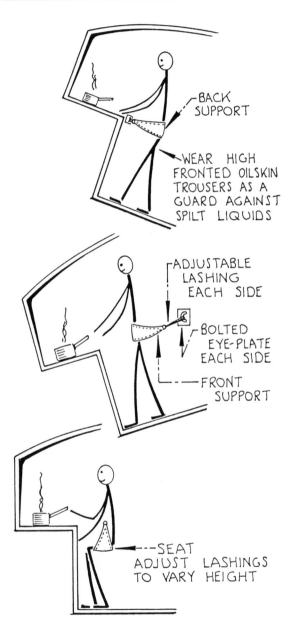

BACK
SUPPORT

WEAR HIGH
FRONTED OILSKIN
TROUSERS AS A
GUARD AGAINST
SPILT LIQUIDS

ADJUSTABLE
LASHING
EACH SIDE

BOLTED
EYE-PLATE
EACH SIDE

FRONT
SUPPORT

SEAT
ADJUST LASHINGS
TO VARY HEIGHT

Improved galley strap

Everyone knows about the standard galley strap which prevents the cook from being hurled across the cabin when working at the stove. Shown here is an improved version which has three sets of eyeplates bolted each side of the galley.

One set is for the port tack, one set is for the starboard tack, and one set turns the strap into a comfy seat for use in calmer weather. When sitting, the cook must have good lodging points for his feet, and it may pay to fit wood toerails in just the right locations on the galley sole.

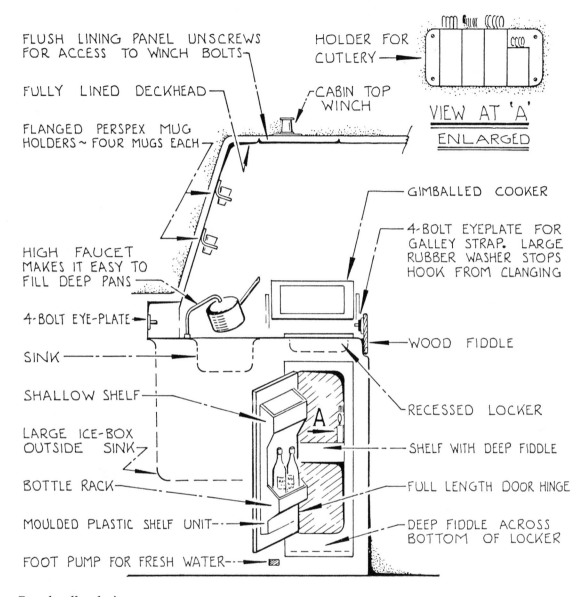

FLUSH LINING PANEL UNSCREWS FOR ACCESS TO WINCH BOLTS

HOLDER FOR CUTLERY

FULLY LINED DECKHEAD

CABIN TOP WINCH

VIEW AT 'A' ENLARGED

FLANGED PERSPEX MUG HOLDERS ~ FOUR MUGS EACH

GIMBALLED COOKER

4-BOLT EYEPLATE FOR GALLEY STRAP. LARGE RUBBER WASHER STOPS HOOK FROM CLANGING

HIGH FAUCET MAKES IT EASY TO FILL DEEP PANS

4-BOLT EYE-PLATE

WOOD FIDDLE

SINK

SHALLOW SHELF

RECESSED LOCKER

LARGE ICE-BOX OUTSIDE SINK

SHELF WITH DEEP FIDDLE

BOTTLE RACK

FULL LENGTH DOOR HINGE

MOULDED PLASTIC SHELF UNIT

FOOT PUMP FOR FRESH WATER

DEEP FIDDLE ACROSS BOTTOM OF LOCKER

French galley design

No one is surprised that French yachts often have excellent galleys. Here is one packed with delightful ideas which can be incorporated in many yachts. This view is looking outboard to port, the galley being at the aft end of the cabin, on the port side.

The four mini-lockers for the knives, forks and spoons are made the correct depths for the implements, with the smallest one nearest the locker door for maximum convenience. Though the fiddle for the bottle rack on the inside of the locker door looks low, it is adequate as the bottles fit firmly, but not tightly, in the rack.

That full length door hinge is so sensible because galley locker doors get a lot of use and abuse. Common hinges too often fail . . . and this invariably happens in bad weather.

One of the reasons for using Perspex for the mug racks is that it never needs painting or varnishing or other finishing; also it is light, strong enough for the job, and easy to clean.

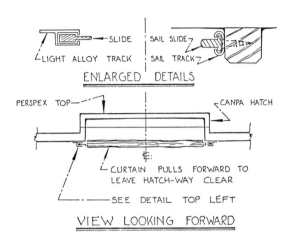

SLIDE

LIGHT ALLOY TRACK

SAIL SLIDE

SAIL TRACK

ENLARGED DETAILS

PERSPEX TOP

CANPA HATCH

CURTAIN PULLS FORWARD TO
LEAVE HATCH-WAY CLEAR

SEE DETAIL TOP LEFT

VIEW LOOKING FORWARD

For privacy and insulation

A blind which slides across under a hatch has two purposes. It gives privacy and it keeps in the warmth (or shuts out the too-hot sun). This type of blind is used in forward cabins and under those hatches fitted amidships as modern-style skylights.

The blind or curtain can be made of any material which is tough enough to stand up to the rigours of life afloat, and a double thickness of coloured spinnaker cloth has advantages. It is attractive, hard-wearing and easy to get from a sail-maker.

At the top of the picture are two types of slide for the curtain. The one on the right is common sail track, available from a mast-maker. The one on the left is sold in hardware shops, and is less strong but may be cheaper.

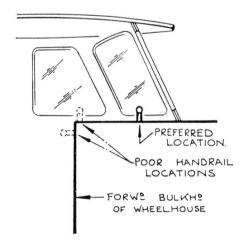

PREFERRED LOCATION.

POOR HANDRAIL LOCATIONS

FORWᴰ BULKHᴰ OF WHEELHOUSE

Wheelhouse handrails

Any power yacht that goes to sea needs plenty of handholds. Be she large or small, she will pitch and roll. Indeed the only known way of stopping a boat from rolling and pitching is to put her firmly aground.

This means every motor yacht should be well equipped with hand-grips for all the crew. Most people aboard will spend a lot of time in the wheelhouse, once under way, so this is a space which should be especially well equipped with handrails. Handrails should be located where they will not protrude and bruise anyone. They should also be set so that they fall conveniently to hand and are comfortable to grip even for long, tiring watches. Anyone standing at the fore end of the wheelhouse will want a handhold which is forward somewhat and not right up against the chest. If the handrail is set forward of the bulkhead it will also leave space aft of it convenient for chart-work.

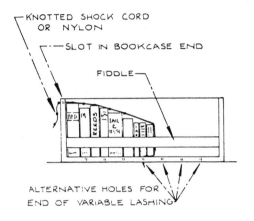

KNOTTED SHOCK CORD OR NYLON

SLOT IN BOOKCASE END

FIDDLE

ALTERNATIVE HOLES FOR END OF VARIABLE LASHING

A secure book-case

Every yacht's cabin needs a book-case. There are not only the navigation books, but also that vital selection of reading matter needed to while away the time when weather-bound in harbour or hove-to offshore. Also most well-conducted cruisers have a cookery book aboard, even if it is only as an *aide-mémoire* and guide to more adventurous forays around the supermarket.

Books should be well cared for. If one of them spends only half an hour on the cabin sole in wet, rough weather the chances are that it will be ruined. So the book-case must be designed to hold its contents regardless of which way the boat tumbles. This simple technique has much to recommend it because so many existing book-cases can be adapted. The front fiddle must be set at a carefully judged height to avoid obscuring titles. It is a good idea to use thick Perspex for the fiddle. The shock cord is adjusted easily to prevent the books falling.

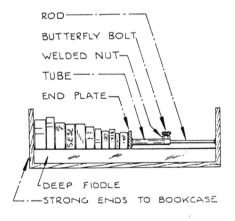

ROD

BUTTERFLY BOLT

WELDED NUT

TUBE

END PLATE

DEEP FIDDLE

STRONG ENDS TO BOOKCASE

Sea-worthy book-ends

There is no cabin decoration to beat a couple of well-filled book-racks. In fact there are some owners who go to sea just to get peace and quiet so that they can read without distraction!

This sliding clamp device is ideal to keep books safe and tidy, since it is so easy to use one-handed, so reliable, and yet simple to make. There are several variations on the basic idea. For instance, the sliding tube can travel on a fixed tube which also doubles as the front fiddle. A disadvantage of this is that the fiddle must be rather higher than is desirable. The sliding part cannot travel back to the right-hand side of the case, but this leaves a small space for stowing miscellaneous items.

An important detail is that the butterfly bolt must be large, otherwise it will need a spanner to loosen the traveller.

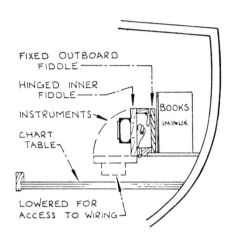

FIXED OUTBOARD FIDDLE
HINGED INNER FIDDLE
INSTRUMENTS
CHART TABLE
BOOKS
LOWERED FOR ACCESS TO WIRING

Easier access

All the instruments we put in our yachts these days need wires led to them, from masthead and under-water, to tell us how fast we are going and how soon we are going to run aground. But electric wiring is seldom pretty, and most owners prefer it out of sight. Instruments need attention at least once every twenty-four months so that it is desirable, indeed usually essential, to be able to get at the back of the instruments quite often.

By fitting all the instruments on a facia, set inboard of the book-case over the chart table, a space is left for the wiring. If this facia is then hinged along the bottom, and retained with a clip or slip bolt each end, it is very much easier to keep the instruments working.

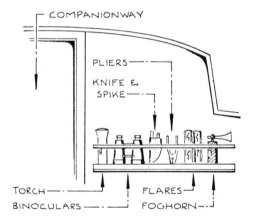

COMPANIONWAY
PLIERS
KNIFE & SPIKE
TORCH
BINOCULARS
FLARES
FOGHORN

For every crisis

Any yacht, big or small, power or sail, mono- or multi-hull, needs a rack just inside the companionway. Here is the handiest position for all the things needed in a hurry. This sort of equipment must be stowed out of the weather yet as near to the helmsman and crew in the cockpit or wheelhouse as possible.

Not every owner will agree with the list shown, because experience, sailing grounds, yacht size and other factors make different demands. Also each owner will have different priorities. The man who sails with small children and seldom finds himself under way after dark will not put the torch nearest the doorway.

Some owners will not put red flares on the rack, but white flares for steamer-scaring are strongly recommended.

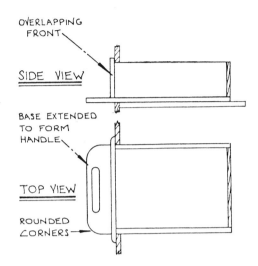

OVERLAPPING
FRONT.

SIDE VIEW

BASE EXTENDED
TO FORM
HANDLE.

TOP VIEW

ROUNDED
CORNERS

Drawers of character

It is not surprising that people are looking around for ways of making their identical mass-produced yachts a little different. When adding a drawer or two, this interesting design is worth considering.

The base is made of a piece of attractive wood extended to form a strong handle. Though only one hand-hole is shown, on a wide drawer a pair of slots might be preferable. The base also forms the runners, which is appropriate as it will be fairly thick, probably ¾ inch or more, and almost certainly of hard wood. It will probably have to be made up of pieces glued edge to edge.

Both top and ends are set on the base, being glued and screwed to it. The front overlaps the front of the main casing so that the drawer need not be a very exact fit. This will appeal to beginners and shipwrights short of time. Though no drawer fastener is shown one should be fitted, to prevent the drawer coming open in bad weather.

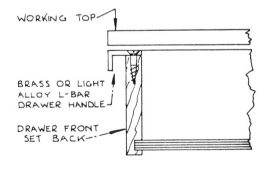

WORKING TOP

BRASS OR LIGHT
ALLOY L-BAR
DRAWER HANDLE

DRAWER FRONT
SET BACK

Drawer handle

Anyone wishing to give his yacht furniture an up-to-date appearance might adopt this feature. The drawer stows with the front set back from the edge of the working surface whilst the handle finishes flush with this edge.

The handle is made from a length of brass or light alloy angle which is screwed to the top of the front. For the best appearance the angle should extend right across the top of the drawer, but the weight-saving fanatic will shudder at this.

There should be sufficient screws – say a minimum of four, as they will have to be of a fairly small gauge to avoid splitting the drawer front. The angle must stand at least ¾ inch away from the drawer front to enable fingers to get an easy grip, and all sharp edges must be rounded off.

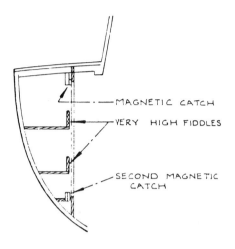

MAGNETIC CATCH

VERY HIGH FIDDLES

SECOND MAGNETIC CATCH

Door fastenings

Some of the door catches used in houses are attractively finished, light and cheap so that there is a temptation to use them afloat. Magnetic cupboard door catches have been used on some boats but this type of fastening needs careful thought. It only holds the door closed lightly so that if the boat rolls or heels the contents of the locker may fall against the door and push it open. The trouble can be circumvented by fitting high fiddles on the inboard edge of each shelf. This is a good practice regardless of the type of door catch since it enables the door to be opened safely even when the boat is rolling heavily. If the door is at all heavy it may fly open through its own inertia but this can often be prevented by fitting a second magnetic catch at the bottom. Among the advantages of this type of door holder are the ease of fitting, the fact that no exact lining up is needed and the low cost. For severe weather conditions a turn button or barrel bolt is needed on all but the smallest doors.

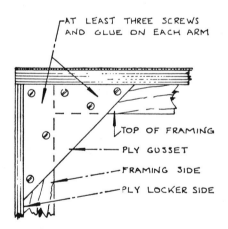

AT LEAST THREE SCREWS AND GLUE ON EACH ARM

TOP OF FRAMING

PLY GUSSET

FRAMING SIDE

PLY LOCKER SIDE

Furniture framing

Amateur boatbuilders often have to make up components at home in the evening during the week and take them down for fitting aboard at the weekend. Some of these builders lack the knowledge, equipment and skill to make proper joinery corners such as tenons. For them this idea can be a tremendous help.

Where a framing has to be made up, perhaps for a galley bench, the corners are joined by triangular ply gussets. These are cut easily and accurately to shape. They are carefully screwed on to the horizontal and vertical framing members, on the back faces of the frame parts. Great care is taken to get the horizontals exactly at right angles with the verticals.

The screws are taken out and the components are then easily carried down to the boat where they are re-assembled and glued.

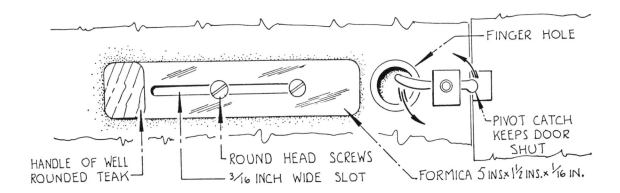

HANDLE OF WELL
ROUNDED TEAK

3/16 INCH WIDE SLOT

ROUND HEAD SCREWS

FINGER HOLE

PIVOT CATCH
KEEPS DOOR
SHUT

FORMICA 5 INS x 1½ INS. x 1/16 IN.

Toilet door lock

This door lock has all the virtues of simplicity and cheapness with strength. The door is secured by any one of the standard 'finger-hole' type locking arrangements which are sold by chandlers. So that anyone using the toilet compartment can prevent anyone else bursting in, there is a blanking-off plate which slides over the finger hole. The sketch shows the view from inside the compartment, and the Formica sliding plate which shuts off the finger hole is seen to be easily made. This sliding plate can also be of metal or even of wood.

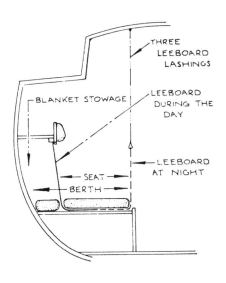

THREE
LEEBOARD
LASHINGS

BLANKET STOWAGE

LEEBOARD
DURING THE
DAY

LEEBOARD
AT NIGHT

SEAT

BERTH

Lightweight berth backs

Human beings vary in size and shape which, among other disadvantages means they require varying widths of seat and bed. A settee berth is liable to be too wide for sitting comfortably or too narrow for sleeping. One way to get round this conundrum is to use a strong fabric berth-back when serves as a leeboard at night. It means that a berth cushion must be divided longitudinally which is a pity but not serious provided the cushions fit tightly in the width of the berth. During the day the leeboard is fastened by closely spaced clips to the underside of the berth back-rest. Before turning in, the intending sleeper unclips the leeboard, passes it inboard of the big cushion and clips the lashing lines up to the eyebolts at the deckhead. A coloured Terylene fabric makes an attractive, long-lasting berth-back-cum-leeboard.

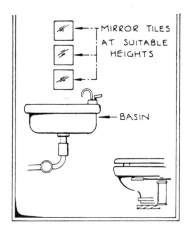

Bulkhead mirrors

Most cruisers are fitted with a mirror but this aid to feminine vanity and masculine shaving more often than not is unsuitable for the purpose. Most mirrors on the market are designed for the suburban bathroom; they tend to be of the wrong dimensions, too thick and heavy, difficult to secure and too expensive. An ideal solution to the problem is to use self-adhesive wall tiles with a mirror finish. These tiles are cheap, weigh a matter of ounces and are easy to secure. The mirror area need not be continuous; one tile can be fixed at a suitable height for shaving, another for feminine make-up and a third for younger crew members. Another advantage of this system is that if one tile gets broken it is cheap and easy to replace.

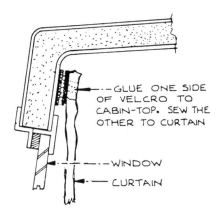

Screwless curtain-rail

On a glassfibre yacht it is difficult to add fittings once the boat is complete. For instance there are all sorts of problems facing anyone who tries to fix an ordinary curtain-rail to a glassfibre cabin top.

It is seldom advisable to put in screws or bolts. Apart from the fact that leaks are likely to be started, the nuts will show and the bolts cannot be tightened if the cabin top is foam filled. Velcro is useful under these conditions because it can be glued to the cabin top above the windows. The opposite mating strip is sewn to the top of the curtain. Pressing the top of the curtain in place fixes it.

Naturally the curtains cannot be drawn back, as they can on conventional runners. But this is a small disadvantage, if it is one at all.

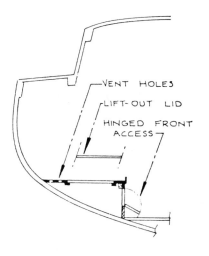

VENT HOLES
LIFT-OUT LID
HINGED FRONT ACCESS

Locker access

Builders and owners are often undecided on whether the lockers beneath berths should have front or top access. The answer is that on the ideal cruiser both will be provided. The front opening can be used for obtaining small items without disturbing anyone sitting or lying on the berth. The hatch should be hinged at its lower edge and should be provided with a strong and positive catch to prevent it flying open when the boat is heeled. The top hatch is useful when stowing big items in the locker, it makes cleaning and painting easy and ensures good ventilation during the winter lay-up period. It is advisable to have ventilation holes apart from the hatches to encourage air circulation and reduce weight.

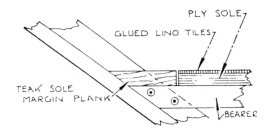

PLY SOLE
GLUED LINO TILES
TEAK SOLE MARGIN PLANK
BEARER

Toilet compartment sole

Modern synthetic tiles make a good surface for the sole in the toilet compartment. They are easy to buy, to fit and to clean. They wear well and are available in a variety of colours.

To give the sole a professional finish it is a good idea to fit a scrubbed teak border all round, recessed round structural parts. Inside this is a portable panel of marine ply, slightly thinner than the teak. The lino tiling is glued to the ply to bring the surface up flush with the teak.

This panel can be lifted out for scrubbing during the season and left out all winter to keep a flow of sweet air through the yacht. It is important to make the panel of *marine* ply; other grades eventually fail at the glue lines if they remain damp for long periods.

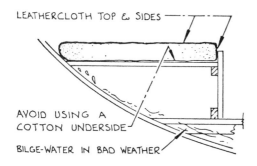

LEATHERCLOTH TOP & SIDES

AVOID USING A
COTTON UNDERSIDE

BILGE-WATER IN BAD WEATHER

False economy

For offshore conditions it is best to use a leathercloth covering for cushions.

Covering material comes in a variety of styles all of which are relatively costly though the expensive ones often pay for themselves in the long run. However, some builders try to save on the first cost by making the cushions with a cheap cotton cloth on the underside.

This practice has two disadvantages: the cotton rots very quickly, especially in small shallow craft where the bilge water slops up and wets the underside of the cushions. Secondly, where the bunks are so shaped to permit the cushions to be turned over and changed from port to starboard to give a long life, the cotton underside prevents this economy.

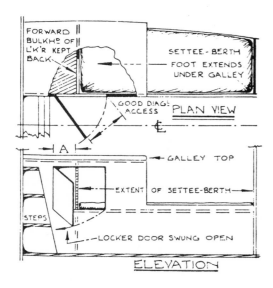

FORWARD
BULKHD OF
L'K'R KEPT
BACK

SETTEE - BERTH
FOOT EXTENDS
UNDER GALLEY

GOOD DIAG
ACCESS   PLAN VIEW

─ A ─

GALLEY TOP

EXTENT OF SETTEE-BERTH

STEPS

LOCKER DOOR SWUNG OPEN

ELEVATION

Locker access

It is often the case in small cruisers that the foot of a settee berth in the saloon must be tucked under part of the galley bench. This leaves some space under the aft end of the bench, which makes a most valuable locker. However, companionway steps often come just where the locker door is needed. It is no good putting the access to the locker through the bench on top as the stove or sink is in the way.

Here is an idea which seems to be a particularly good answer to the problem. The locker door is made to extend into the area at the foot of the berth. At the bottom of the berth there is a bulkhead shutting off the locker but the inboard half of this bulkhead is omitted. There must be deep fiddles on the locker shelves to prevent the locker contents spilling out, but this is usual anyway. Access to the locker is now easy – diagonally from inboard and forward.

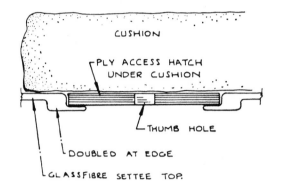

CUSHION

PLY ACCESS HATCH
UNDER CUSHION

THUMB HOLE

DOUBLED AT EDGE

GLASSFIBRE SETTEE TOP.

Getting into glassfibre lockers

Where a yacht has her settee berths made of glassfibre, the access into the lockers beneath can be awkward. It is always slightly undesirable to join metal hinges direct to fibreglass and it is necessary to provide a number of recesses on the settee top to take such hinges. On many boats the technique is to use ply lift-out panels. These are made an easy fit into a recessed flange so that the settee top is flush when the panel is in place. When the cushion is raised the ply can be lifted and slipped sideways, making the whole opening free. With a hinged lid the cushion has to be lifted so much higher even to provide moderate access. In winter the panels can be taken home for revarnishing.

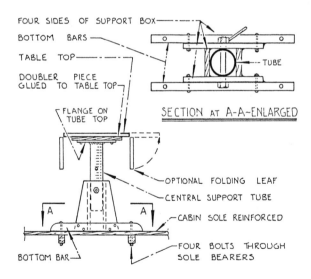

FOUR SIDES OF SUPPORT BOX

BOTTOM BARS

TABLE TOP

DOUBLER PIECE
GLUED TO TABLE TOP

FLANGE ON
TUBE TOP

SECTION AT A-A-ENLARGED

TUBE

OPTIONAL FOLDING LEAF

CENTRAL SUPPORT TUBE

CABIN SOLE REINFORCED

A   A

FOUR BOLTS THROUGH
SOLE BEARERS

BOTTOM BAR

Variable height cabin table

What makes this table special is that it has no difficult joins. There are no rebates or dovetails, so no special tools or skills are needed to complete it. In addition, the height of the table is easily changed by withdrawing the horizontal bolt through the tube and refitting it after lowering the table so that the bolt goes through a

different hole in the tube. In practice it will often be best to have two horizontal bolts, and each should have the short bar (shown top right) welded to the nut to make undoing easy without a spanner.

The bottom wood box and bottom bars should be glued together, as should the table top and its doubler.

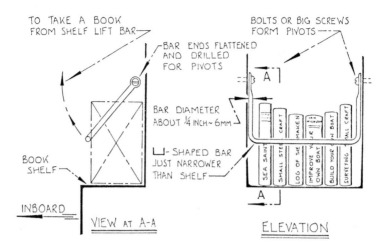

Book holder

Camper and Nicholson put this type of simple foldable fiddle on the book shelves of one of their yachts. Its only weakness is that it needs the book shelf to be full but not over-full to be a success. The pivoted bar can be made of solid rod or tube, and the material may be stainless steel or polished brass. It could be made of wood which in turn could be laminated with bent corners or made from solid strips with glued corners.

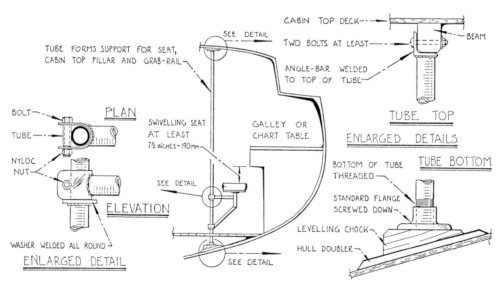

Adjustable stool

A seat which can be swung out of the way when not in use suits various locations in many boats. This stool can have a threaded stem under the wood base which holds the top cushion, and by rotating the base the cushion height above the cabin sole can be varied. This feature is not shown in the drawing, but the way the support pole terminates at top and bottom and the way the seat support tubes link onto the pillar are detailed. To prevent a metal to metal contact, the fork arms on the seat supports may be lined with a self-lubricating material such as nylon.

Chain-plates

Chain-plates have to be strong, but that alone is not enough. They must resist sideways movement otherwise they will cause deck leaks. They must look smart or they will detract from the general appearance of the yacht which may have been carefully built up with expensive deck-fittings. They should not be obtrusive, except perhaps on a long-range cruiser where a degree of massiveness makes for a high morale. They should wear well, because no one ever thinks of renewing them, though it is regular practice to change keel bolts, standing rigging and crosstrees (well, it is on a well conducted yacht, which of course is by no means every one).

Galvanised steel is the material to use if costs count most. But to improve the looks, the plates should be double-coated with epoxy paint all over before installation. This means that the bolt holes should be over-size. But then the holes have to be slightly over-size to allow for the galvanising anyway.

Stainless steel is the fashionable material, but it is not easy to work, which is discouraging for the small yard, or the amateur. Bronze is much easier to work, is a traditional sea-going material, is reliable, and for many situations is the best choice. Where the total weight of material is small, the cost will not be significant, but otherwise bronze is expensive. *Never* use brass. There are no exceptions, no excuses. It is treacherous, but it gives itself away because it is very easy to cut and drill, almost as easy as aluminium alloys. Aluminium alloy is seldom used, and when it is the holes for the rigging should be bushed.

Three fastenings is the absolute minimum because one might come loose, and then there is a fair chance that the other two will hold on and prevent the chain-plate coming loose. It is better to have four fastenings, even on a boat only 20 ft long. On any craft over 35 ft there should be five fastenings in each plate and six in a yacht over 50 ft. Ocean cruisers need one or two extra. I'll not forget the occasion when we discovered our main chain-plates were coming loose on *both sides*. We were something like 40 days out of Panama, and had another 41 days to landfall, though merciful providence hid this fact from us. It was the constant rolling and jolting that did it, also the boat was built fisherman style, with massive dumps to hold the chain-plates. They had held well for 40 years but this was no consolation at the time.

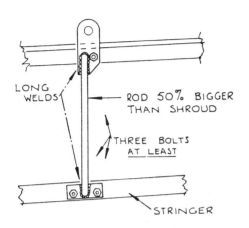

LONG WELDS

ROD 50% BIGGER THAN SHROUD

THREE BOLTS AT LEAST

STRINGER

Lightweight shroud plate

The pressure mounts monthly on the racing circuits. Ultra lightweight boats are the ones that pick up the prizes and any trick to shave off a few pounds is of interest.

This design of chain-plate is based on simple principles. First there must be about twice as much strength in a chain-plate as in the shroud it holds. Secondly every chain-plate should have at least three fastenings. Thirdly the fastenings should be well spread.

One attraction of this chain-plate, made from a length of rod and two short pieces of flat bar, is that it is very economical in material.

The welding must be above suspicion but the welds are purposely made extra long to ensure a perfect bond. In the sketch the chain-plate is shown for a vertical pull but for a forward (or aft) lower shroud it can be lined up with the wire.

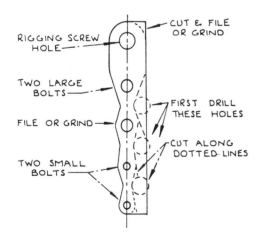

RIGGING SCREW HOLE

CUT & FILE OR GRIND

TWO LARGE BOLTS

FILE OR GRIND

FIRST DRILL THESE HOLES

CUT ALONG DOTTED LINES

TWO SMALL BOLTS

Lightened chain-plates

Probably the best way to reduce the weight of any boat is to lighten her metal fittings.

The chain-plate must be stronger than the rigging it holds, but not excessively so, unless ocean cruising is intended. It needs at least three bolts, and four or more if the yacht is bigger than 30 foot overall. But round each bolt there need be only the equivalent cross sectional area of metal that there is in the bolt itself, plus 20%.

The lower bolts can usually be smaller than the upper ones, which must be about the same diameter as the shroud. By first drilling, then cutting away the excess metal, a parallel sided strip of bar can be made into a delicate yet strong chain-plate. There must be no sharp changes of section, and of course a little extra thickness is infinitely preferable to a fracture.

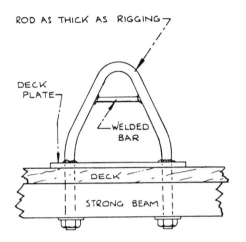

ROD AS THICK AS RIGGING

DECK PLATE

WELDED BAR

DECK

STRONG BEAM

Hair-pins

It was probably the advent of glassfibre which gave this type of chain-plate its first impetus and maintains its popularity. It is neat and light and there should not be leaks at the deck provided that the plate is large enough, thick enough and adequately bedded and that the shrouds are not exerting too much inward pull on the hooped bar. For lower shrouds which are angled inwards the fitting should be tilted inwards above the deck plate. It is vital that this style of chain-plate is fitted at a strong point and not just bolted through a thin deck and delicate half-beam. Indeed it is not rare to see the deck of a glassfibre boat lifting in places when going hard to windward with this kind of chain-plate.

One attraction of this type of fitting is that such gear as the spinnaker boom can conveniently be clipped to it when not in use. It is also light in weight and not difficult to make.

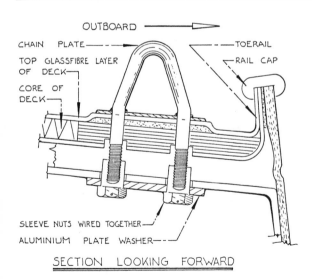

OUTBOARD

CHAIN PLATE

TOP GLASSFIBRE LAYER OF DECK

CORE OF DECK

TOE RAIL

RAIL CAP

SLEEVE NUTS WIRED TOGETHER

ALUMINIUM PLATE WASHER

SECTION LOOKING FORWARD

Camper and Nicholson chain-plate – view looking forward or aft

This design of chain-plate caters for shrouds which extend up over crosstrees, or tilt in at an angle, to tangs on the mast at the inner ends of crosstrees. It also spreads the load over a fair width of deck, can be easily replaced if worn or damaged, can be tightened down after the first few hours of sailing, and is not expensive to make or fit.

It is essential that the ply pad is large, and the under-deck plate washer should be quite a sixtieth of the boat's overall length in width and length.

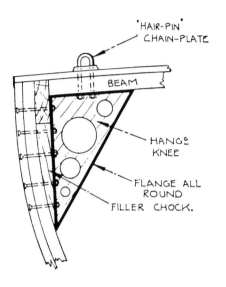

'HAIR-PIN' CHAIN-PLATE

BEAM

HANGᴱ KNEE

FLANGE ALL ROUND

FILLER CHOCK.

Hair-pin shroud plates

If genoas are to be correctly sheeted, then shrouds must be set inboard of the deck-edge of most yachts. The thought of sheeting *between* the shrouds is not to be considered.

Inboard fixings for the shrouds need careful planning since the angle between shroud and mast is likely to be reduced to a minimum. This means that the shroud tension will be high and the loading on the shroud plate will match it.

The 'hair-pin' type of shroud plate has many attractions, partly because it is quickly fitted, partly because it is made as a stock item. However it cannot be fitted to a beam or half-beam without some substantial backing. A metal hanging knee, carried well down the topsides, flanged on each edge and thoroughly bolted, is an excellent fitting in the location. It serves the additional purpose of stiffening the yacht athwartships in the region of the mast, where she needs extra strength.

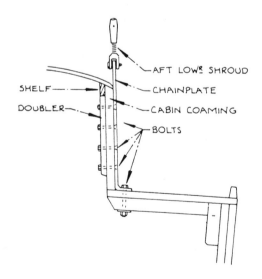

SHELF

DOUBLER

AFT LOWᴱ SHROUD

CHAINPLATE

CABIN COAMING

BOLTS

Rigging for sheeting

If the shrouds are carried down to the deck edge of a modern cruiser they hamper the correct sheeting of the headsails, because many boats are so beamy these days. Though this sketch shows a boat built of wood the technique can be used on craft made of other materials. The aft lower shroud chain-plate is bolted to the cabin coaming, with provision to take very high stresses which occur in these shrouds. The coaming itself acts as a deep web, held at the bulkheads. There is a toe at the bottom of the chain-plate which is bolted to the half-beam, and of course the side deck is well fastened to the coaming and the bulkheads.

An incidental advantage of this shroud location is that going forward is easier, since it is not necessary to duck under the wire.

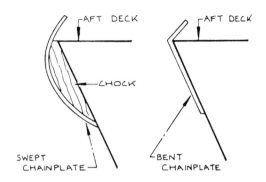

Unstressed chain-plate

The backstay plate is usually fitted right aft, or taken down through the deck to the forward face of the transom. Either way there is a sharp bend. This sudden bend is highly stressed and a natural place for weaknesses, as shown on the right. The one sketched on the left has many advantages, not the least being the absence of a sharp bend. It is set on a chock which should be wider than the plate with bevelled aft edges. The chock should be of hardwood and it must be drilled carefully as a split here would be serious. The bolts need to be spaced well, as the curve of the plate will tend to make them converge as they pass through the chock and transom. If they are too close they may meet inboard.

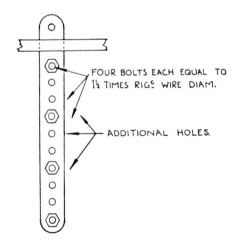

Chain-plate refinement

Every chain-plate needs bolts through it and bolts need holes. As a result the weakest part of the chain-plate is in way of each bolt-hole. All this is common sense and the obvious conclusion is to cut away surplus metal by drilling extra holes. These lightening holes can be the same size as the bolt-holes and should not be placed too closely. As a rough guide there should be at least as much metal between each hole as the diameter of the hole. There should be a minimum of four bolts through each plate. They can be as light as the rigging wire on the chain-plate, but for ocean cruising they should be twice as thick.

Anyone buying a mass-produced cruiser should use these rough rules to see how well she is constructed since there are sad modern tendencies to skimp such fittings as chain-plates.

Deck Fittings

There is scope indeed for anyone who wants to design equipment to go on yachts' decks. For instance the standard chandlers' stem-head fittings are seldom acceptable. Often enough these mass-produced fittings are designed more with an eye to economical production than to the best sea-going efficiency.

An amateur who wants to make his own deck fittings may feel that a drawing is a waste of time, or too difficult. In practice the drawing is well worth a bit of effort, especially if it is made full size and used to make a cardboard or plywood mock-up. This crude model of the final fitting is put in place on the deck, and will almost certainly suggest improvements. It should be considered from every angle. How will it be when the deck is pitching, heeled, at night? Will it be inconvenient for a left-handed man, is it too near a stanchion, does it need a pad to raise it off the deck, should the pad be bevelled to improve accessibility?

Where possible fittings should be sited low down, off the side decks, and not in the middle of decks which are in any case usually short of foot-room. And anything which is going to catch the genoa or main sheet should be altered or given some sort of guard.

The fitting itself should be designed with reserve strength, but just as important is the fastening. Last time I saw a sheet winch involved in real drama, was coming alongside a quay. The aft warp was made fast to a bollard ashore, but the yacht still had way on. The warp was being surged round a sheet winch, and it looked as if the yacht would soon lose way before she hit anything. Then a knot in the warp came up to the winch barrel, so that surging stopped suddenly. The rope went thin with strain. There was a shuddering creaking noise followed by a crash. The winch held on to its pedestal, which also kept hold of the cockpit coaming. But the coaming and a section of the deck tore off, hung suspended by the warp for a long second, then plunged overboard. The cost of replacing the winch was nothing compared with the expense of a complete new coaming and new deck section, as well as the new winch base.

What was needed in this and every other case was proper bolting through a strengthened deck with substantial doubling under the deck.

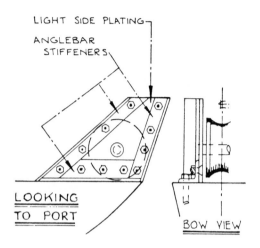

LIGHT SIDE PLATING
ANGLEBAR STIFFENERS
LOOKING TO PORT
BOW VIEW

Stem fitting without welding

Few amateurs have welding equipment. They might go round to the local garage with the components of a fitting to get it welded up, but who can be sure that the work done will be to the highest standards? For yacht fittings only the best welding is adequate. This is not only because of the high stresses but also because of corrosion and appearance.

Sketched here is the basic layout of a stem-head roller assembly which is fabricated from light plating and small size angle-bar. The advantage of using fairly thin plating is that it is easier to obtain and much easier to cut. For a 27 foot boat ⅛ inch side plates with 1 inch by 1 inch by ⅛ inch angle-bar will suffice. After bolting the sides to their stiffeners and drilling the fixing down bolt-holes, send the steelwork to be galvanised.

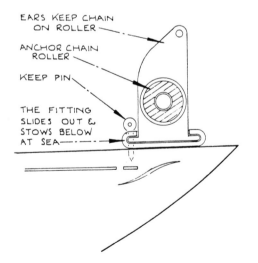

EARS KEEP CHAIN ON ROLLER
ANCHOR CHAIN ROLLER
KEEP PIN
THE FITTING SLIDES OUT & STOWS BELOW AT SEA

Portable stem-head roller

Once the mooring has been dropped, the roller at the stem-head is a nuisance. It is weight and windage badly located. It lurks wickedly awaiting a spinnaker to snarl. It should be removed, and stowed below while under way. This is not so difficult on a boat of less than 40 feet. The roller is made with a base flange which mates into an arthwartships slide, and a simple dowel pin (perhaps with its end threaded) keeps the fitting from sliding out.

Naturally the slide must be very tough, and it needs bolting rigidly to the deck. In practice most of the force is down on to the deck, even when the yacht sheers sideways or tide-rides round her anchor. Another essential is a safety line, which must be kept secured when the fitting is being taken off or refitted.

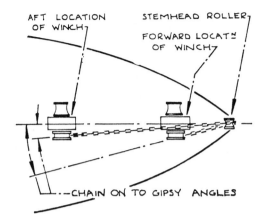

AFT LOCATION OF WINCH

STEMHEAD ROLLER

FORWARD LOCAT OF WINCH

CHAIN ON TO GIPSY ANGLES

Gipsy line-up

Hauling up an anchor can be hard work even when conditions are favourable. Short-handed, in bad weather, it can be such hard work that it leaves the crew prostrate. To reduce the work the equipment should be designed so that there is the minimum friction and the chain gipsy on the winch should be in line with the stem-head roller. This may mean fixing the winch off-centre. It almost certainly means the winch must be at the aft end of the foredeck. It may be that the winch has to be located so that the handle only just clears the fore end of the cabin top. This will mean that the crew will have to stand to one side.

In an extreme case a chain which leads diagonally to a gipsy can ride off or simply fail to grip. To avoid this situation it may be necessary to fit the winch on the top of the coachroof.

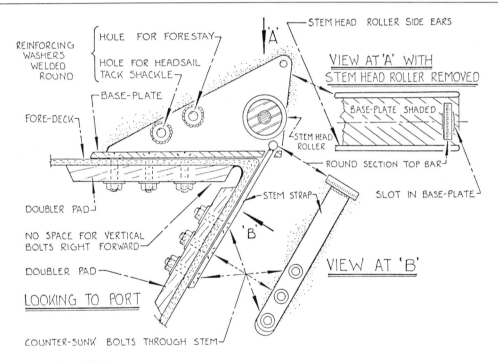

'Universal' stem-head fitting

The angle between the deck and the fore side of the stem varies from one type of boat to another. This gadget fits a wide variety of boats because the tang which extends down the fore side of the stem is in effect hinged to the deck plate.

As a result this fitting can be made with only the most primitive of drawing or template, and there is no doubt

that it will fit. The way the bolts are kept clear of the inaccessible space right at the very forward end of the boat is important.

The stem strap can be made as long or as short as needed. For ocean cruising this strap will go one third of the way down to the water-line; for racing it will be short, light, and drilled full of lightening holes.

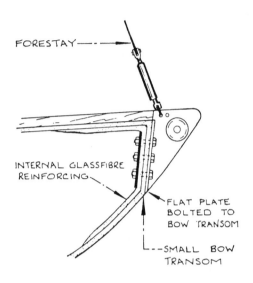

Glassfibre bow design

Many design headaches associated with glassfibre are in connection with bolted-on fittings. The glassfibre structure does not like high local stresses so that the load should be well spread. Metal fittings are expensive if they have to match a curved surface. This bow unit tries to eliminate common undesirable features. The bow of the mould (and hence all the boats taken from it) is cut back to give a little transom, like a pram dinghy. However the depth of this transom is quite small, perhaps 6 inches on a 30 footer and 12 inches on a 40 footer. There is a slight slope to the transom, so that the forestay has a tendency to pull the vertical flat plate of the stem-head on to the hull.

The lowered stem-head roller is easier to use than one flush with the deck.

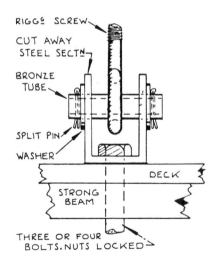

Forestay fitting

This steel forestay fitting was made recently for a fast cruiser. It was cut from a length of Structural Hollow Section, which is available in a variety of sizes. It is a standard section which provides a U-shaped fitting with the uprights close together.

With fittings of this type the weakness is often in the fastenings. There must be at least three bolts, however five are preferable. If each is as thick as the rigging-screw shank then all should be well. Naturally the bolts must have washers under their nuts and should be spaced at least four diameters apart. The bracket should not be fitted down to any deck, be it glassfibre, wood, or metal, without a bedding compound. This serves the double purpose of excluding the water and forming a flush, flat seating for the fitting.

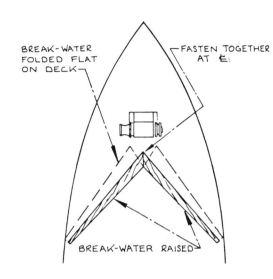

BREAK-WATER
FOLDED FLAT
ON DECK

FASTEN TOGETHER
AT €:

BREAK-WATER RAISED

Foldaway breakwaters

A displacement motor-cruiser pitching into a head sea
will sometimes take water green on the foredeck. The risk
can be reduced by slowing down, but there are limits to
this, when punching a tide for instance. Water running
deep along the deck is frightening, and also wetting.

One traditional way of dealing with the situation is to
fit a pointed breakwater across the foredeck. This idea
was popular in the days of fine-bowed cruisers, but it has
rather gone out of fashion. One reason why breakwaters
are not popular is that they take up a lot of space.

However there is no reason why the breakwater has to
be permanently upright. It can be made to fold flat, or
even hinge at each end to swing out to the guard-rails.

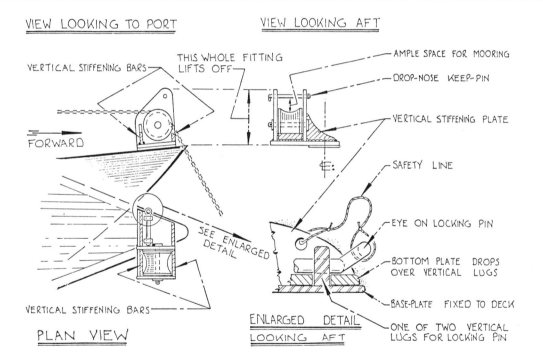

VIEW LOOKING TO PORT

VIEW LOOKING AFT

VERTICAL STIFFENING BARS

THIS WHOLE FITTING
LIFTS OFF

FORWARD

SEE ENLARGED
DETAIL

VERTICAL STIFFENING BARS

PLAN VIEW

AMPLE SPACE FOR MOORING

DROP-NOSE KEEP-PIN

VERTICAL STIFFENING PLATE

€:

SAFETY LINE

EYE ON LOCKING PIN

BOTTOM PLATE DROPS
OVER VERTICAL LUGS

BASE-PLATE FIXED TO DECK

ONE OF TWO VERTICAL
LUGS FOR LOCKING PIN

ENLARGED DETAIL
LOOKING AFT

Portable stem-head roller

No racing yacht should have inessential fittings on deck
when there is a race to be won. Weight and windage is
reduced by taking off all surplus gear, and once clear of
the moorings the stem-head roller is just a potential
spinnaker-ripper.

To make the stem-head roller portable a very strongly
secured base-plate is fitted on deck right forward, with a

pair of metal loops standing up from it. The framework of
the roller drops over these loops, and a locking pin slides
through the loops. This pin must be a firm push fit, and
must be secured with a lashing so that it will not come out
accidentally. The end of the pin may be threaded to
match a thread in the starboard upstanding metal loop.

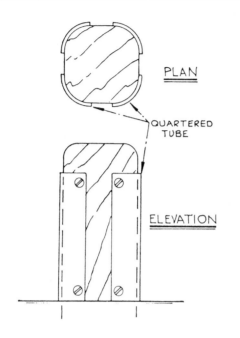

PLAN

QUARTERED TUBE

ELEVATION

Protecting posts

Come in to a mooring rather too fast, let go the anchor while still going ahead and what do you get? A lot of frightened owners on the yachts all round, for a start. You also get a sampson post chafed almost right through if you anchor like this often. As the chain whirls out of its pipe, if it is allowed to belt round the post, it will act like a saw. Of course you can just let the chain run free from pipe to stem-head roller but then how are you going to check it when enough is out?

It is common though not universal practice to fit coping strips vertically at the sampson post edges. These are called whelps and they take chafe well. But if chafe occurs before they are fitted it is not easy to get them to lie properly, or if the edges of the sampson post have been previously well rounded coping may be too narrow.

A sensible scheme in such cases is to fit slices of pipe over each edge.

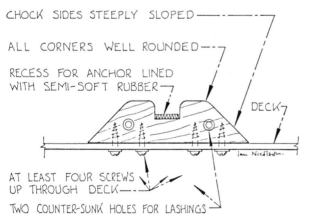

CHOCK SIDES STEEPLY SLOPED

ALL CORNERS WELL ROUNDED

RECESS FOR ANCHOR LINED WITH SEMI-SOFT RUBBER

DECK

AT LEAST FOUR SCREWS UP THROUGH DECK

TWO COUNTER-SUNK HOLES FOR LASHINGS

Ian Nicolson.

Anchor securing

Anchor chocks should be made from fault-free hardwood. It is customary to bolt them down, but this means the bolt ends have to be dowelled over or they show and may look 'industrial'. A neat trick is to secure the chocks from below with a row of screws which should normally be round-headed, probably with semi-hard washers under the heads to bed into the glassfibre. The chock sides are sloped so that ropes do not catch in them and to give a broader base for more screws widely spaced.

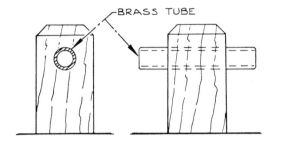

BRASS TUBE

Sampson post pin

There are few things more essential on a yacht than a really good mooring point. If one consistent criticism can be levelled at the modern mass-produced cruiser it is that there is no totally reliable strongpoint for securing warps and tow-ropes. Even when a sampson post is fitted there is a sad tendency to make it of a relatively soft wood without whelps and to provide only a flimsy pin through the top. This last fault at least can be altered without much difficulty.

Instead of the thin rod, what is needed is a piece of stout non-ferrous tube which will neither rust nor bend even when it is scoured by a fast-surging rope. The ends of the tube need not be blanked off but this does add to the finished appearance.

The tube should be a tight drive fit and should not need any fastening to hold it in place. Before boring out the post for its new cross-bar a trial should be made in a piece of scrap wood to ensure that the bit is the right size for the tube.

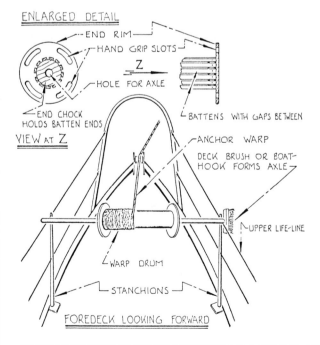

ENLARGED DETAIL
- END RIM
- HAND GRIP SLOTS
Z
- HOLE FOR AXLE
- END CHOCK HOLDS BATTEN ENDS
- BATTENS WITH GAPS BETWEEN
VIEW AT Z
- ANCHOR WARP
- DECK BRUSH OR BOAT-HOOK FORMS AXLE
- UPPER LIFE-LINE
- WARP DRUM
- STANCHIONS
FOREDECK LOOKING FORWARD

Anchor warp stowage

It is so important that the anchor warp runs out smoothly, without kinks or snarls. The best way to ensure that hurried anchoring is completed safely is to have the warp on a drum. A drum also helps the wet warp to dry quickly when it is hauled in.

No one wants a lot of special tackle for the anchor warp so it is sensible to use an existing piece of gear as the axle of the drum. On some boats it may be better to tie the axle onto the lower life-line fore end brackets, on the pulpit, or even onto the top bar of the pulpit. Once the warp has been run out, it must be secured to the mooring cleat in the normal way as no drum will take the load.

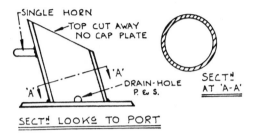

SINGLE HORN
TOP CUT AWAY
NO CAP PLATE

'A'
'A'
'A'
DRAIN-HOLE
P. & S.

SECT⁵
AT 'A-A'

SECT⁵ LOOKS TO PORT

Ultra-light bollard

Just how light is it possible to make a mooring post?
Some designers have used a large wood cleat to get a
lightweight anchoring point on the foredeck, but this
type of fitting cannot withstand the chafe and grind of an
anchor chain running out fast round it. A sampson post
can be well tapered below deck to lighten it but it needs
sheathing with metal, or whelps, to protect it and is not
all that light.

This drawing shows a mooring bollard with no excess
material. The top is cut at an angle to keep down the
weight of the length of tube. No cover plate is welded on,
to save more ounces, and there are drains to let out
accumulated spray. Only a single horizontal horn is
welded on to retain the mooring chain on the bollard. The
idea of raking the upright tube is to lengthen the weld
round its base, where it joins the base-plate. This whole
fitting might be fabricated from ¼ inch thick plate and
5 inch diameter tube for a 33 footer.

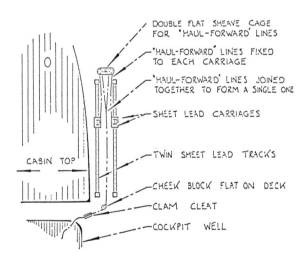

DOUBLE FLAT SHEAVE CAGE
FOR 'HAUL-FORWARD' LINES

'HAUL-FORWARD' LINES FIXED
TO EACH CARRIAGE

'HAUL-FORWARD' LINES JOINED
TOGETHER TO FORM A SINGLE ONE

SHEET LEAD CARRIAGES

TWIN SHEET LEAD TRACKS

CABIN TOP

CHEEK BLOCK FLAT ON DECK

CLAM CLEAT

COCKPIT WELL

Sheet lead carriage adjuster

Moving sheet lead carriages when they are under load is
often hard work. Getting them to shift aft is sometimes
fairly easy, but the upward lead of the sheet makes it
almost impossible to ease them forward. What is needed
is a rope from the carriage to a block at the front of the
track then back to a winch.

The layout in this picture minimises the number of
fittings and ropes, but it is only suitable for a boat up to
about 35 feet. A touch of grease on the track helps, but it
must be applied lightly otherwise it will lubricate the
bottoms of the crew's shoes.

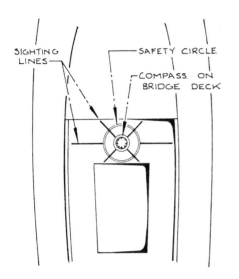

SIGHTING
LINES

SAFETY CIRCLE

COMPASS ON
BRIDGE DECK

Compass embellishment

A simple way to reduce the risk of steel objects being left by the compass is to paint a red line round the area where the compass is fitted. This red warning line is a constant reminder to the crew to keep beer cans, knives, belts with metal buckles and so on well away from the compass.

If the compass is set on the bridge deck it is easy to paint the line round. If the instrument is mounted on a binnacle it is more difficult to paint a red circle in a conspicuous place. However, a circle can be painted round the base with half circles on the cockpit seats each side.

Another useful guide is the painting of bold lines athwartships and at 45 degrees in each direction. These will be found useful when taking bearings and before tacking, to help decide if an objective can be laid.

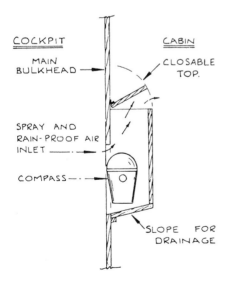

COCKPIT

CABIN

MAIN
BULKHEAD

CLOSABLE
TOP.

SPRAY AND
RAIN-PROOF AIR
INLET

COMPASS

SLOPE FOR
DRAINAGE

Compass cubby hole

In some yachts the steering compass is fitted in such a manner that it takes up a lot of room and may even obstruct the crew. This will not do the compass any good and it may tear an oilskin, or at least bruise one of the crew. It is good design practice to locate the compass in its own recess, where it is easily visible from almost anywhere in the cockpit, yet out of the way of passing traffic. A small fully or partly boxed recess in the bulkhead between the cockpit and saloon is a good place, especially if a few refinements are included. The bottom of the recessed casing should be sloped so that it drains effectively and is easy to clean. It can be used also as a handy place for lodging notes like the next course to steer and time of high water.

There is much to be said for leaving the top of the casing open to form a vent into the cabin. This also enables anyone in the cabin to see the course.

For offshore boats a bad weather closure is needed.

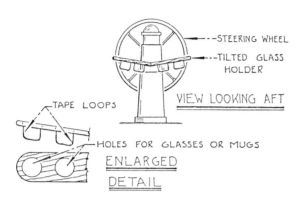

STEERING WHEEL

TILTED GLASS HOLDER

VIEW LOOKING AFT

TAPE LOOPS

HOLES FOR GLASSES OR MUGS

ENLARGED DETAIL

Safe stowage for drinks

Sitting in the cockpit, sipping long cool drinks in hot weather, or hot soup in chilly conditions, is what makes sailing bliss. But if there is nowhere to put down mug or glass then any work on jib sheets can result in spilt fluid.

This rack for mugs or glasses is shown on a binnacle, but it could as easily be fitted to the aft coaming of the cabin top or perhaps to the forward end of the cockpit well. Only two lengths of wood are needed, with holes cut to suit the crockery on the ship. The tapes can be made from toe-strap material.

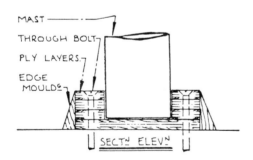

MAST

THROUGH BOLT

PLY LAYERS

EDGE MOULDᶢ

SECTᴺ ELEVᴺ

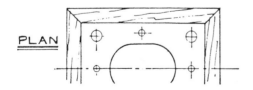

PLAN

Simple mast step

Just about the most economical way of making a step for a mast standing on deck is to use layers of marine ply. One or two layers form the base and the next three or four are built up to form a secure wall around the foot of the spar. As a rough guide, the depth of the recess should be about half the major axis of the spar. For example, a mast which is 4¼ inches by 3 inches requires a recess 2⅛ inch deep. In this case a couple of layers of 1 inch ply with a third layer for the base would be a minimum. It might be better to go for two bottom layers of ⅝ inch and four layers of ⅝ inch for the walls. The layers should be glued together after the hole for the mast has been cut, though this gluing is not essential. Efficient bolting is vital.

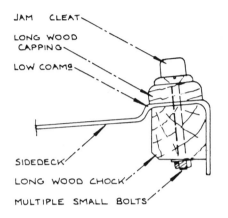

JAM CLEAT
LONG WOOD CAPPING
LOW COAMg
SIDEDECK
LONG WOOD CHOCK
MULTIPLE SMALL BOLTS

Fittings on glassfibre

To attach deck fittings on to a glassfibre deck can be expensive. There must be no points of high local stress and the structure must be reinforced to take loads on the fitting. Glassfibre itself is costly so most builders avoid building up great thicknesses of it. Shown here in section is a scheme to use wood in conjunction with glassfibre. The top wood capping, perhaps of varnished teak to delight the hearts of the traditionalists, will spread the load on the cleat through a row of fairly closely spaced bolts.

The chock underneath is not encased so that if it gets wet, it can dry easily and is thus unlikely to rot. It will not only take the deck fittings but also add rigidity to the cockpit coaming. It should be well bedded in a firm but compressible material so as to lie snugly under the deck.

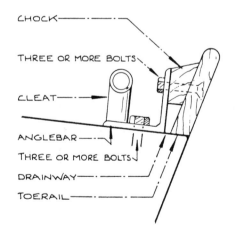

CHOCK
THREE OR MORE BOLTS
CLEAT
ANGLEBAR
THREE OR MORE BOLTS
DRAINWAY
TOERAIL

High toerail

Whether a boat is built of wood or glassfibre a difficulty arises when the toerail is relatively thin yet high. If it also flares out, in line with the topsides, then the problem can be acute. This is because the toerail needs plenty of support, yet it is so located that stiffening is not easy to introduce.

The type of support used on commercial ships, steel bulwark stanchions, and suchlike are ugly and obtrusive. What is needed is something that helps the toerail without being too obviously the item which is holding it up.

A length of stainless steel angle-bar, with a cleat of the same material fastened to it, can be used. Cleats are needed anyway up forward, just where the toerail is most likely to be tilted out.

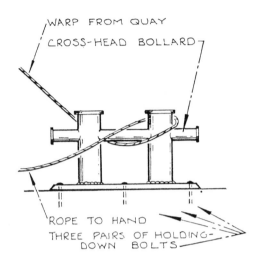

Cross-head bollard

Any boat which frequently is tied up to a high quay wall or goes through locks requires special bollards. The ordinary tubular type of bollard will not hold a rope which leads upwards from the anchorage point.

In theory all that has to be done is to weld lugs, ears or horizontal top plates on to the tubular bollard. But warps are like babies; leave them in peace for long enough and they will untie themselves even when the job looks impossible. For this reason it is well worth-while fitting cross-head bollards on to boats which operate through canals or are moored so that their warps extend above deck.

The cross-head has additional advantages too. For instance it is easy to surge warps round it without squatting awkwardly on deck. It normally has at least three pairs of holding-down bolts and when more than 16 inches long may well have four sets.

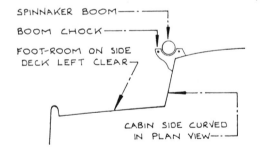

Boom stowage

It is always a problem trying to find a suitable place to stow the spinnaker boom. Where twin booms are carried, the problem is even greater. One solution is to put the booms in chocks bolted to the edges of the cabin top. In this position they leave the decks clear, are convenient when needed and fit snugly. The chocks must fit the booms exactly, otherwise it will be difficult to lash down the spars securely.

This stowage position will not suit every yacht but works very well on yachts built with long cabin tops which extend well forward.

The boom should not extend forward of the cabin top unless some sort of guard is fitted to prevent the jib sheet catching round the boom end.

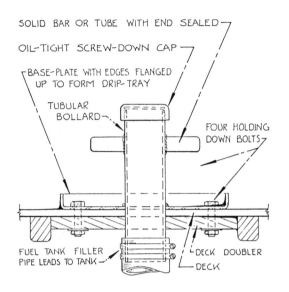

SOLID BAR OR TUBE WITH END SEALED

OIL-TIGHT SCREW-DOWN CAP

BASE-PLATE WITH EDGES FLANGED
UP TO FORM DRIP-TRAY

TUBULAR
BOLLARD

FOUR HOLDING
DOWN BOLTS

FUEL TANK FILLER
PIPE LEADS TO TANK

DECK DOUBLER

DECK

Bollard and filler fitting

Though the sketch shows a fuel filler fitting, the same idea can be used for a water tank filler. However the latter will not need the upturned flanges on the base plate to form a drip-tray. When refuelling the drip-tray should be filled with paper or old rags to catch spilt diesel.

Because the top of the filler pipe is high there is little chance of sea-water getting into the tank until waves are very deep on deck.

One or two short stubs of bar or tube may be welded to the side of the cap to make it easy to remove by hand. The whole fitting may be made of stainless steel, or if the owner wants to make his boat distinctive he can use bronze and keep the fitting well polished.

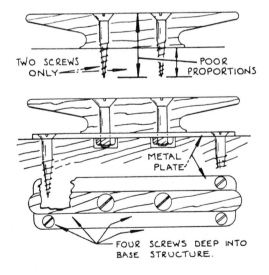

TWO SCREWS
ONLY

POOR
PROPORTIONS

METAL
PLATE

FOUR SCREWS DEEP INTO
BASE STRUCTURE.

Reliable cleat fastening

At the top of this sketch is a badly fastened cleat. For the first season or two this cleat will probably remain firmly secured. Once it has been subjected to sideways load, however, the screws will move very slightly because they have insufficient grip. Water can then enter the wood and soften it, so weakening the attachment until the cleat pulls out.

The same length of screw used through a bronze or even a brass plate would be much more effective.

The cleat shown in elevation and plan at the bottom of the picture is not just twice as strongly fastened as its luckless cousin at the top. There are four screws, but what is more important, these are virtually all embedded in the base structure. As a rough estimate, the bottom cleat will hold ten times the load of the top one.

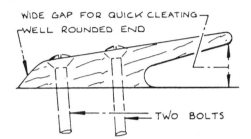

WIDE GAP FOR QUICK CLEATING
WELL ROUNDED END
TWO BOLTS

Thumb cleat

In the dark ages, before dinghies planed, before the invention of the jam cleat, it was an inflexible rule that 'the main sheet is never cleated, in a centreboard boat'. This was all very fine, but in heavy weather hanging on to the sheet was a trial. So somebody invented the thumb cleat. This is a half cleat, which has to be located with special care. It is used to hook the sheet round, so that quite a useful percentage of the pull is taken by the cleat instead of the helmsman's hand.

It is almost impossible to make a sheet fast to a thumb cleat, so that it is unlikely to be misused. It cannot seize, the way some modern jam cleats do, and it lets the rope go quickly and surely. Even a knot in the rope is quickly cleared. It is very cheap to make, but it must be bolted in place, never screwed.

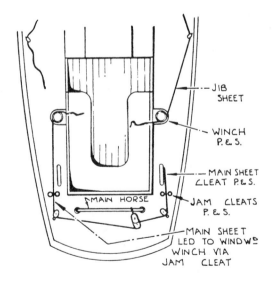

JIB SHEET
WINCH P. & S.
MAIN SHEET CLEAT P. & S.
MAIN HORSE
JAM CLEATS P. & S.
MAIN SHEET LED TO WINDW.d WINCH VIA JAM CLEAT

Poor man's main sheet winch

Many small cruisers have a pair of winches for the jib sheets but none for the main. This is because of the cost of an extra winch. It has to be admitted that a main sheet winch is not usually needed all that often so many builders take the chance to save money here. All this is very fine until the owner is cruising single handed or is out in a stiff blow and wants a bit more power on the main sheet. He then 'has to grin and bear it and put up with a badly setting mainsail. With very little adaptation the windward jib sheet winch can be used to haul in the main sheet. The most important alteration is the addition of a couple of jam cleats so that once the sheet is hauled taut it can be taken off the winch and cleated in the usual way without losing tension. It is necessary to use a double-ended main sheet arrangement but often a single-ended system can be adapted by using extra blocks.

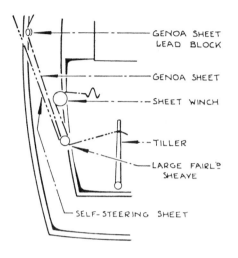

GENOA SHEET
LEAD BLOCK

GENOA SHEET

SHEET WINCH

TILLER

LARGE FAIRL'D
SHEAVE

SELF-STEERING SHEET

Large flat sheet sheaves

Look on any modern sailing yacht and the chances are
there will be large deck blocks at the aft end of each side
deck. These sheaves are fitted in addition to the normal
adjustable sheet leads which are generally on lengths of
track on each side deck. They are positioned so that
riding turns on the winch are avoided.

For an owner planning a long cruise it is sensible to
locate these sheaves so that they can be used both to give
the desirable lead to their winches and for taking the
twin self-steering headsail sheets to the tiller. Anyone
who has cruised short-handed knows the bliss of being
able to leave the helm to a self-steering device.

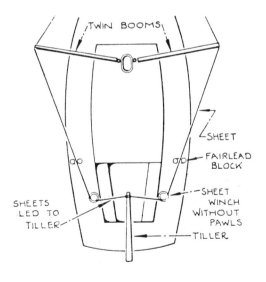

TWIN BOOMS

SHEET

FAIRLEAD
BLOCK

SHEET
WINCH
WITHOUT
PAWLS

SHEETS
LED TO
TILLER

TILLER

Self-steering gear

Owners of coastal cruisers are following the ocean
cruising self-steering technique of using twin headsails
for down-wind sailing. The idea is so simple with twin
booms having sheets linked to the tiller. It is reliable and
needs very little extra equipment.

What is essential is a pair of good sheaves each side to
lead the sheets fair and square to the tiller. Some people
just take the pawls out of the sheet winches, and use the
barrels as sheaves. This only works where the barrels are
the right height, and the correct distance fore-and-aft.

When building a boat to self-steer down-wind under
twins, this will influence the location of the winches.
Anyone adopting this idea should study the assembly of
the winches in harbour and have spare parts on board.
On some models the springs holding the pawls leap
overboard when released!

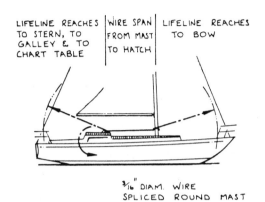

LIFELINE REACHES TO STERN, TO GALLEY & TO CHART TABLE | WIRE SPAN FROM MAST TO HATCH | LIFELINE REACHES TO BOW

3/16" DIAM. WIRE SPLICED ROUND MAST

Safety harness anchorage

One reason why many people will not wear a safety harness is because of discomfort to the wearer when working on deck. One of the drawbacks is the necessity of transferring the lanyard hook from one point to another. To overcome this problem the 'tethered goat' principle may be used.

A wire of about 3/16 inch diameter is spliced to the mast and led to an eye plate which is bolted securely to the top of the doghouse. The length of the wire plus the length of the safety harness lanyard is critical. It should be possible for the crew to work anywhere on deck with the safety harness hook attached to the central wire. It usually does not matter too much if the crew cannot get right aft but they must be able to reach the forestay.

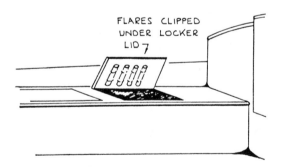

FLARES CLIPPED UNDER LOCKER LID

Flares please

There is an increasing realisation that white flares are the best 'steamer scarers'. Owners used to flash powerful torches on their sails, and on the bridge of the approaching ship. However, there have been plenty of narrow escapes, and it is being appreciated that the long range torches sometimes have a beam which is too narrow.

A white flare gives a great burst of brightness which even a sleepy watchkeeper should notice. Admittedly it ruins the night vision of everyone on the yacht, but under the circumstances this is hardly significant. All this means that a convenient stowage is now needed for white flares, as well as red rockets. The stowage needs to be near the helmsman and clear of the usual clutter of warps, fenders and petrol cans which litter every deck locker.

One good location for the flares is on the underside of the cockpit locker lids, in Terry clips. Each flare needs at least two clips, preferably three, of the sort that are sheathed in plastic, or made of stainless steel.

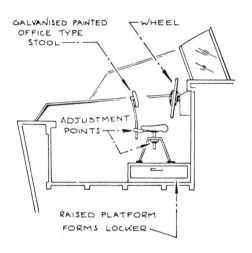

GALVANISED PAINTED
OFFICE TYPE
STOOL

WHEEL

ADJUSTMENT
POINTS

RAISED PLATFORM
FORMS LOCKER

Helmsman's chair

On a number of powerboats the centrepiece of the
cockpit or wheelhouse is the helmsman's chair. It is often
an elaborate affair, beautifully chromed, with deep foam
plastic cushions covered with rich leathercloth.

It so happens that some models of office chairs can be
well adapted to suit yacht needs. The components come
apart without difficulty, and most of the parts can then be
galvanised. It is a mistake to hope that a good coat of
paint will suffice. Even a seat kept under cover should be
galvanised if possible.

This sort of chair is likely to be expensive and does not
always have facilities for adjustment, so the height will
only suit a few people, and the lack of alteration of the
posture results in tired backs.

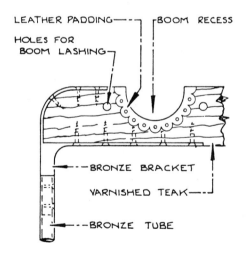

LEATHER PADDING

BOOM RECESS

HOLES FOR
BOOM LASHING

BRONZE BRACKET

VARNISHED TEAK

BRONZE TUBE

Traditional permanent boom gallows

We are in danger of forgetting how things were done in
the grand manner, before the days of mass-production
factory built craft, so it is worth studying this sketch of
traditional yacht-building.

Three recesses would be made for the boom, one each
side and one amidships. The side ones would be angled
to allow for the fact that the boom would not cross the
plank at right angles. Each recess is lined with a thick,
soft, white leather, scalloped to fit round the curve and
nailed exactly in the middle of each scallop.

Countersunk holes each side of each recess take the
lashing to hold the boom and all the edges of the teak are
carefully bevelled before the six coats of varnish.

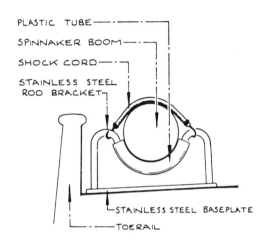

PLASTIC TUBE
SPINNAKER BOOM
SHOCK CORD
STAINLESS STEEL ROD BRACKET
STAINLESS STEEL BASEPLATE
TOERAIL

Spinnaker pole stowage

A stowage fitting is needed at each end of a spinnaker pole. Each bracket bolts to the deck with a flat base-plate of stainless steel bedded down to prevent water seeping through the holes in the deck.

Since the poles will be dropped hurriedly into their racks when dropping the spinnaker as the yacht rounds the lee mark, the brackets are padded. This will ensure that poles are not dented when dropped in place, but also keep them lodged quietly and snugly when the yacht pitches and rolls. Holding the poles in place are short stout lengths of shock cord secured at one end and with hooks on the other.

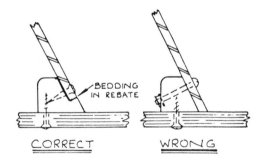

BEDDING IN REBATE

CORRECT   WRONG

Fitting a windscreen

Perspex windscreens are fitted to every sort of boat from outboard launches to ocean cruisers. They are so easily made since Perspex can be worked with wood-working tools and is light to handle.

The bottom edge should be fitted in a rebated moulding. This moulding should first be made to fit the deck which is likely to have both camber and sheer, or maybe reverse sheer. The fit must be exact even though there will be bedding between the moulding and the deck, otherwise there will be leaks at the screw holes.

Once the moulding has been fixed, the Perspex should be lodged in the rebate and fitted carefully. It should be screwed at about 4 inch centres.

The sketch on the left is an indication of the correct procedure.

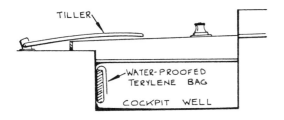

Cockpit stowage

The ideal cockpit for an offshore yacht is completely watertight. This means that conventional cockpit lockers are out as they almost always let driblets through – usually right onto the quarter berths!

All this is very sad for every helmsman and jib sheet hand wants somewhere in the cockpit to stow vital gear. This equipment varies from person to person. It may be pipe tobacco or chocolate biscuits, a paperback book or a spare towelling scarf. A convenient dry stowage near the helmsman's hand is required. This can be provided by fastening a waterproof bag to the aft end of the cockpit beneath the tiller.

The container should be made of some material like PVC-impregnated nylon. The flap should extend well down and have sides to keep out the spray. As water often swills about in the cockpit, the bag should be fixed a few inches up so that there is no chance of it filling with water.

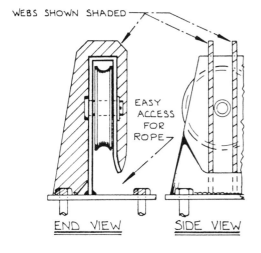

Mast foot snatch block

It is a feature of modern yachting that sail changing has to be snappy. Where the halyard winches are mounted flat on deck, to save windage and keep weight low, it is necessary to lead the halyards through blocks at the foot of the mast, to change their direction from vertical (down the mast) to horizontal (along the deck). This is done with blocks. An ordinary block is no good, as the rope cannot be taken out quickly to let it run fast. A normal snatch block needs an extra second or two to open or close.

Sketched here is a permanently open snatch block. When lowering the tension is taken off the rope and it is immediately unhooked from the block, so that it can snake swiftly aloft, unhampered.

Pulpits, Stanchions and Guard-rails

If ever there was a case where prevention is better than cure, this is it. It is vastly better to keep people on deck than to have elaborate equipment for recovering them from the water. In bad weather, even in daytime, the chances of recovering someone from the sea are frighteningly small.

So the clever thing is to spend lots of time, trouble, and money on a good fence all round the yacht. The lifebuoys and heaving lines, floating quoits and their ropes are important, but it is much better to ensure they never need using.

It is important to appreciate that the fence round a yacht is in fact primarily a handrail. It is for steadying the reeling deck-hand as he moves about. To keep him aboard he has his personal lifeline, clipped round his chest and strongly made fast to a jack-wire or eye-plate (not eye-bolt) on deck. But human nature being contrary and inclined to take the easy way out, we find that very often personal lifelines are made fast to guard-rails or pulpits. So these defences must have a big enough factor of safety to withstand this abuse easily.

At the foot of each stanchion or pulpit leg the plate onto the deck should have three or four bolts. In this location screws will last no time at all, even on a 20 footer used up-river. By the same token a bolt needs a good backing plate and big washer under the nut. The tension on each bolt can amount to over a ton when someone falls against the top wire, so it is no wonder screws pull out easily.

This tremendous loading on the bottom bolts is so serious that it is important to keep stanchions inboard a little. This prevents them being forced over when lying alongside another yacht or quay wall. Each stanchion has to stand up to heavy work, but if they are spaced 5 ft or at most 6 ft apart they should survive many seasons.

It is seldom a reasonable economy to fix the guardrails to shrouds because this puts an unfair strain on the stanchions adjacent to the shrouds.

Anyone who blanches at the cost of a set of stanchions plus a pulpit at each end of a yacht should approach the problem from a new angle. Either the equipment can be made up at home, instead of being bought from a chandler, or the pulpits may be omitted, by resiting the stanchions. This will call for some skill, since the bow stanchions will almost certainly need angling outwards, and the two on the transom will need struts to keep them upright.

If there are children on the yacht then the normal two lifelines will be inadequate. Three lifelines, as fitted on some ocean cruisers may be the answer, but netting is probably best. It needs thorough securing along the bottom, and a mesh size of about 5 inches (12 cm).

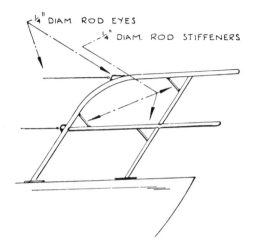

¼" DIAM ROD EYES

¼" DIAM. ROD STIFFENERS

A strong pulpit

Pulpits on yachts of less than 35 feet are quite often too flimsy. This is hardly surprising when it is remembered how many are fabricated in cramped workshops and garages, at the bottom of owners' gardens and during the coldest winter months. Added to this, most people try hard to save weight and economise on materials. It is small wonder that quite a few pulpits will not tolerate a man standing on them.

There is one simple way to toughen up the bow railings. Using quite thin rod, say ¼ inch diameter, or even light pipe, the whole structure can be made much stronger. Short lengths of this material are welded in to triangulate the joins.

Though they are shown here at the junctions of the horizontal and vertical tubes they can also be used with great effect to anchor the verticals more strongly to the base plates.

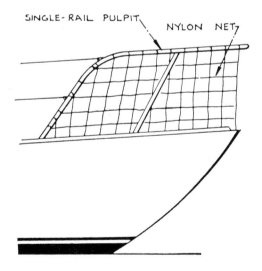

SINGLE-RAIL PULPIT

NYLON NET

A safer pulpit

The dilemma of the designer of a pulpit is this: if there are two or more rails the pulpit is safe, but more than a single top rail makes the recovery of the anchor very awkward, and sometimes almost impossible.

To try to get the best of both worlds a single-rail pulpit may be fitted with a wide gauge nylon net. Lashed to the pulpit along the top at close intervals, the bottom is secured every 6 inches or so to eye-bolts or similar local strong-points. Screw eyes and suchlike flimsy contrivances are no good here. The net is kept in position except when the anchor is to be lowered or brought back on deck. Then the bottom is unlaced or unhooked and the anchor can easily be pulled in under the rail.

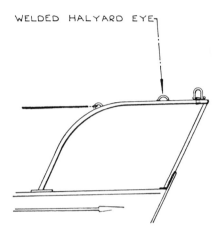

WELDED HALYARD EYE

Pulpit embellishment

A man working in a pulpit is usually either hanking on a sail, getting it off, or putting the boat to bed on Sunday evening. Whatever he is doing he will want to fix down the halyard ends. This is for two reasons: he will not want to loose a halyard end aloft and he will want to secure the halyard where it is handy when next needed.

If there is a metal eye at each side on top of the pulpit, it is easy to clip the snap shackle straight on. The eye should not be too light; even on a 24 footer anything *under* 3/16 inch diameter metal rod is likely to be too flimsy.

It will not be easy to weld eyes onto pulpits already in place so an alternative is to seize shackles to the top rail. Though a conventional shackle is shown in the sketch it might make better sense to use snap shackles fitted with their mouths upwards.

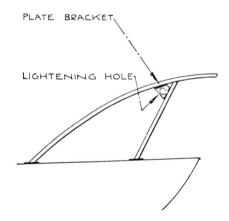

PLATE BRACKET

LIGHTENING HOLE

Pulpit gusset

A lightly made pulpit consisting of a main curved rail and two forward legs can be very limber. If two massive toughs have to wrestle with a wind-filled genoa inside this type of pulpit the whole affair may collapse overboard in a welter of arms, oilskins, sails and metal tubing. All very funny till the swimmers have to be recovered! It may be hard to get light rod or smaller size piping to make corner struts in order to strengthen the joins. Instead, pieces of plate may be used as gussets to strengthen the joins. The plating should be thick enough to weld well and can be lightened by a pattern of neatly drilled, carefully spaced holes. This same plate can also be used to make lugs to take the life-line end shackles.

A variation on this theme is to use narrow strips of plate, widening the ends to a fish-tail shape.

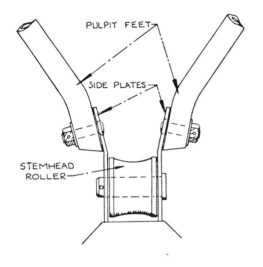

A pulpit variation

It is usual practice to fasten the feet of a yacht's pulpit to the deck. As the foot plates are often small, and the loadings on them high, it is not unusual to produce deck leaks. Sketched here is a technique which not only avoids this risk, but also saves the weight of the plates and the bottom four or six inches of the forward legs. It has to be admitted that the anchor itself will probably not be easy to take in, between the pulpit legs. In most cases the best plan will be to haul the anchor up till it is high enough to grasp, then take it aboard to one side, aft of these two feet, leaving the chain running out through the roller and round one pulpit foot to the anchor. One detail: notice how the bolt heads are countersunk, and do not obtrude in the way of the anchor chain. Also of course, the nuts are locked on.

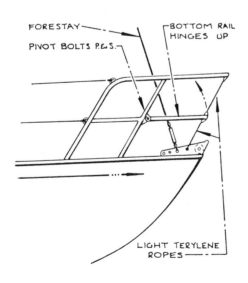

Pulpit improvement

Pulpits with double rails provide a high degree of safety but the lower rail makes life difficult for crew members who have to lug a heavy anchor aboard. If the anchor is a 60-pounder and there is only room for one person right forward, slipped discs and crushed fingers will be the order of the day.

It is not difficult to make up a pulpit with the forward part of the lower rail hinged. The hinge pin each side should be a bolt with its nut locked on, passing through a plate welded to the upright. The end of the lower rail can either be flattened or have a welded plate to take the pivot hole. To keep the pivoting rail in place all that is needed is a piece of ⅜ inch diameter Terylene spliced round the two rails and tied at the stemhead.

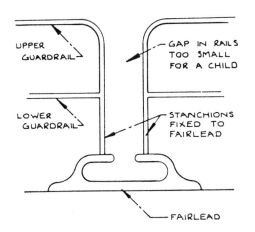

Big ship style

Coming alongside in a yacht when short-handed can pose its problems. On a big yacht with heavy warps, the job of feeding the warps out under the guard-rails can be laborious. If the sea is rough it is sometimes necessary to leave this job till the yacht is inside the harbour.

'On some big ships the guard-rails are stopped at the fairleads, then started again after a gap of about 4½ inches. This space is too small for a child to fall through, yet large enough to drop the warp down. In the sketch the stanchions are shown on top of the fairlead, but if this is not easy to achieve, the stanchions can be set clear of the fairlead. The guard-rails are carried past the stanchions and the top one swept down to the bottom one, almost filling the gap.

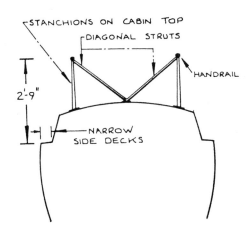

Motor yacht stanchions

On a small power cruiser it is not unusual to have narrow side decks. This is seldom a disadvantage, since it is easy to get on to the foredeck via the forehatch. Besides, just about the only time anyone wants to go forward is when coming into moorings, when the boat will normally be in sheltered waters.

But even on a calm river the crew need something to hang on to when they are on the side deck.

Stanchions on the outboard edge would make the deck space almost unusable so the place to put them is on the cabin top. They can be stiffened with diagonal struts of light tubing.

The stanchions and struts will all be located in line athwartships, on a beam, and through bolted. Even if someone holds the handrail and leans right outboard, they will not uproot a strutted stanchion.

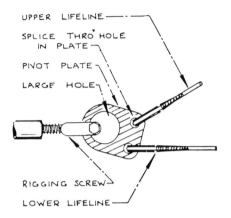

UPPER LIFELINE
SPLICE THRO' HOLE IN PLATE
PIVOT PLATE
LARGE HOLE
RIGGING SCREW
LOWER LIFELINE

Lifeline tensioner

It has become fashionable to use a single rigging screw to tighten both upper and lower lifelines on cruisers. It is not unusual to see the fore end of the top lifeline led round a thimble, then aft to form the bottom line. This is an unsatisfactory solution to the problem, for if one line should break, the other will be released.

By using a simple pivot plate, it is possible to overcome these difficulties. The plate will probably be made from 3/16 inch thick plate, non-ferrous metal or galvanised steel.

A pivot plate not only saves money, it means that there is only one rigging screw to adjust, grease and wire up instead of two.

However, it will not make a big difference in lifeline lengths. As a result they must be carefully measured when making up.

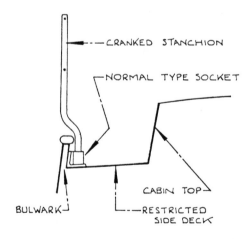

CRANKED STANCHION
NORMAL TYPE SOCKET
CABIN TOP
BULWARK
RESTRICTED SIDE DECK

Swan-neck stanchion

Some owners are tempted to fit stanchions outboard of the toerail or bulwark to give an uncluttered side deck. This makes the side decks easier to walk along especially on the windward side when heeled. In practice stanchions mounted outboard are too vulnerable.

Using standard pattern stanchion sockets, it is possible to fit specially cranked stanchions amidships, or from the sheet winches forward, leaving the others straight. If only a proportion of the stanchions are given this set to their socket ends, there will be a small saving in overall cost.

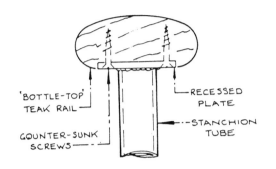

'BOTTLE-TOP' TEAK RAIL

COUNTER-SUNK SCREWS

RECESSED PLATE

STANCHION TUBE

Handrail detail

A teak handrail should not be shaped like a thick narrow plank with the edges rounded. That sort of section dubs a boat as one built by a keen but inexperienced amateur. The professional uses what is called a 'bottle top' shape. This looks just right and is practical as it throws off water quickly so that it dries fast after rain.

The flange plates of the stanchions should be recessed to give a good grip so that the screws have little work to do. These screws should be as long as possible extending to within ¼ inch of the top of the rail so as to provide the maximum grip. The stanchions should not be much more than 6 ft apart, a distance which does not vary with the size of yacht. To look solid and luxurious the teak rail should almost be massive, even on quite a small boat.

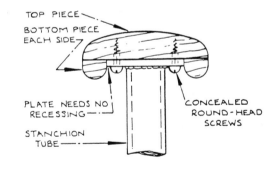

TOP PIECE

BOTTOM PIECE EACH SIDE

PLATE NEEDS NO RECESSING

STANCHION TUBE

CONCEALED ROUND-HEAD SCREWS

Simple teak rail

While there is nothing to beat a smart teak handrail the high price of teak makes it an expensive feature. This design uses teak economically since a deep rich-looking rail is made up from a fairly thin plank and two small mouldings. The lengths should be glued together; it is usually necessary to apply a degreasing agent to the wood before gluing. The careful shipwright will stagger the butts of the upper and lower pieces and carefully match up the timber so that after finishing the joins will be hard to detect. As the top plate for the stanchion is recessed well into the hollow of the handrail it can be fastened with round-headed screws because they will not show.

Only short screws may be used with this construction; these will be adequate since sideways loads are borne by the lower pieces of teak.

Spars

It might be thought that there is no longer scope for the amateur or professional yacht designer in the spar-making world because the vast majority of masts come from specialist companies who do nothing but churn out thousands of light alloy masts.

In practice the situation is not so simple. For a start the designer should know what to ask the spar-maker. He should specify steps on a mast of a yacht intended for offshore cruising, as a general rule. He should insist on a reversible topping lift on the same spar, so that if the headsail halyards both fail the topping lift can do as a substitute.

Also it so happens that a few yacht yards and plenty of amateurs make their own light alloy spars. I have designed lots of masts for owners to make in their own gardens, after the success of the original pair I made myself for our *St Mary*. As this mast-making was described in detail in the book *Building the St Mary* and this book was subsequently included in *The Ian Nicolson Omnibus* the idea has spread.

The firms specialising in mast-making started off with relatively simple products. But the widening demands and increasing competition, both commercially and afloat, has meant that mast-making is now more complex.

In a few cases it is still advisable to select a wood rather than a light alloy mast. The amateur making his own mast, and not counting his own hours, would probably save a little, but not much money building in wood. The man who lives a long way from a spar-making company will almost certainly save, possibly 50% or more, because alloy spars are expensive to move and vulnerable to damage in transit. The owner who wants a specialised mast such as one with a bend in it, or one with a very deep chord to breadth, may find it best to have a wood mast.

The field of glassfibre spars is just opening, and it could become as big as light alloys. Here professionals with limited facilities and amateurs will find they could steal a march on the rest of the sailing world by using ingenuity. One or two of the ideas here may act as a guide or stimulus. And of course there are possibilities that other materials will be found useful for spar-making. Titanium comes to mind, or mild steel skinned over with stainless steel for inexpensive spars.

Whatever is used, it is worth remembering two basic principles:

For racing: the mast is very much part of the rig, which is the engine, and it is horse-power which wins races. But you will not win if your 'engine-bearer' fails.

For cruising: if the mast fails it's going to cost a lot more to get back into commission than the few pounds saved by skimping on the spars and rigging.

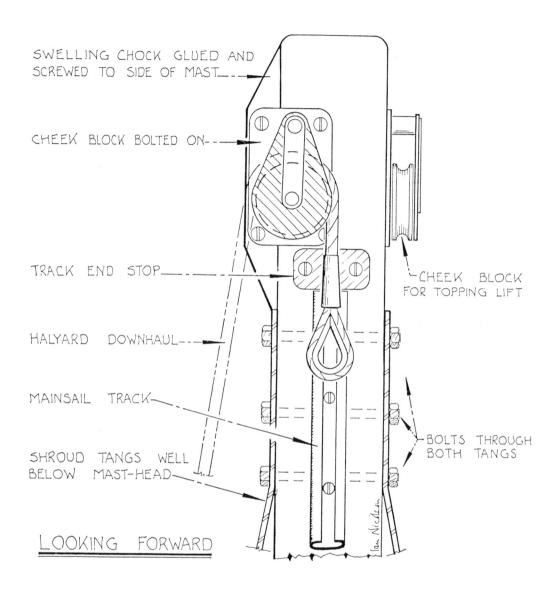

SWELLING CHOCK GLUED AND
SCREWED TO SIDE OF MAST

CHEEK BLOCK BOLTED ON

TRACK END STOP

HALYARD DOWNHAUL

MAINSAIL TRACK

SHROUD TANGS WELL
BELOW MAST-HEAD

CHEEK BLOCK
FOR TOPPING LIFT

BOLTS THROUGH
BOTH TANGS

LOOKING FORWARD

Masthead halyard sheave

This arrangement was originally designed for an amateur who was making his own wood mast. He was unsure that he could make a slot through the masthead for the main halyard sheave. He thought that his skill might not be up to achieving that tight fit which is essential if the halyard is never to ride off the sheave and jam between the sheave and the side of the slot.

A standard 'cheek' block is secured to the mast, located to one side so that the halyard pulls exactly up the middle of the mast track. This scheme can be used for head-sails, and on alloy spars as well as wood ones. Anyone who finds himself with a defective masthead sheave and no facilities to have the repairs carried out by a mast-maker can use this technique. Where possible bolts rather than screws should be used to hold the block. If screws are used they must be long and thick. The appearance of a 'cheek' block from one side is shown on the right of the picture.

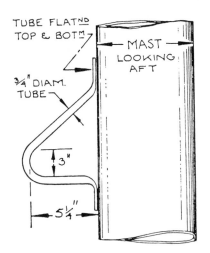

TUBE FLATND
TOP & BOT^M

MAST
LOOKING
AFT

¾" DIAM.
TUBE

3"

5¼"

Offshore cruising asset

Now that ratlines have virtually disappeared from the face of the seas, owners of offshore cruising yachts are finding that they need an easy method of going aloft. The use of a multi-part tackle and bosun's chair is tedious, often dangerous and usually very slow. A chair and winch presupposes there is someone to wind the winch, whereas most owners want to be able to get up unaided.

Various forms of mast foot hold have been devised in the past few years and the one drawn here has many advantages. It is cheap, easy to make, fairly light and easily fastened to a metal mast with pop-rivets. It forms a very fine hand hold, though some care must be taken not to tug forwards or aft and strain the rivets. Perhaps its greatest asset is the safety it provides.

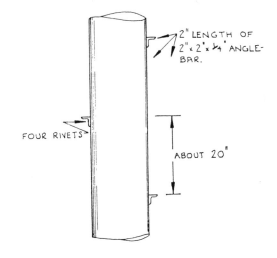

2" LENGTH OF
2" x 2" x ¼" ANGLE-
BAR.

FOUR RIVETS

ABOUT 20"

Especially for deep sea sailing

The care of the mast and its gear is essential. Without a halyard, or with a jammed halyard, the boat is partly or completely incapacitated. If she is offshore the chances are that the failure will occur when the boat has too far to motor home. This means that the crew have to remedy any defects themselves, on the spot.

Over the ages this problem has been well recognised, and owners used to fit ratlines up the rigging to make it easy to go aloft.

The modern form of ratlines are a set of little steps fitted to the side of the mast. They are located as far apart as convenient to reduce weight and windage to a minimum. However, they must be close enough for the smallest (and perhaps lightest and most athletic) member of the crew to go aloft to deal with the trouble.

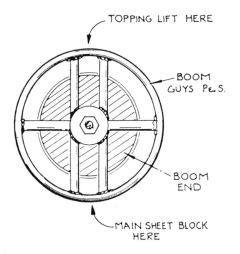

TOPPING LIFT HERE

BOOM GUYS P&S.

BOOM END

MAIN SHEET BLOCK HERE

Boom guy attachment

One way to lose a man overboard is to ask him to clip on a main boom guy while the yacht is running and rolling heavily. The unlucky fellow hangs out over the rail trying to get the snap shackle into a puny little hole in a metal lug. One moment the boom skies, the next moment it is under water. It can be very difficult.

Sketched here is the sort of fitting which avoids unnecessary frustration for crews. The boom end has an outsize metal loop which extends well beyond the diameter of the boom. It positively invites snap shackles to wrap themselves round it. There is plenty of room for a big shackle for the main sheet block. If you favour twin topping lifts (American style) to bunch the mainsail onto the boom after it has been lowered, this fitting has much to commend it.

It looks very smart fabricated from welded polished stainless steel, and if the main sheet block shackle wears part of the fitting it can be reversed to even up the wear top and bottom.

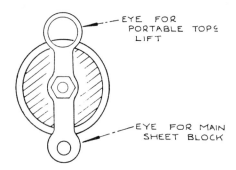

EYE FOR PORTABLE TOPS LIFT

EYE FOR MAIN SHEET BLOCK

Topping lift fitting

On those small cruisers where the topping lift consists of a short line secured one-third of the way up the back-stay, this type of boom end fitting is best. This idea of using a fixed length topping lift which offers just about the minimum possible windage is favoured for racing boats. But when working in a rough sea, it can be very hard indeed to latch the topping lift on to the boom end.

The sting can be taken out of this situation if a good-sized snap shackle is fitted to the lower end of the topping lift and the eye on the boom fitting is extra large. Its opposite number for the main sheet needs to be much more massive to allow for the inevitable wear of the shackle on the main sheet block. Another important detail is that the eye at the top must stand well clear of the top of the boom. Of course the swivelling plate should automatically lie the correct way up.

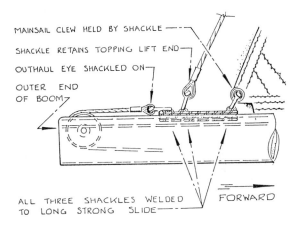

MAINSAIL CLEW HELD BY SHACKLE

SHACKLE RETAINS TOPPING LIFT END

OUTHAUL EYE SHACKLED ON

OUTER END OF BOOM

ALL THREE SHACKLES WELDED TO LONG STRONG SLIDE

FORWARD

Boom outer end

This fitting is made up using common stainless steel shackles and a standard slide, all items bought at a chandler's. The long slide spreads the big upward pull of the sail over a good length of track, and avoids the risk that the clew of the sail may pull up out of the boom track.

Each shackle is welded to the slide at the correct angle for its particular job, and each shackle pin should have its own little safety line.

To double the purchase of the outhaul the line is made fast at the boom end and led forward to a single block held by the aft shackle then aft round the sheave in the boom.

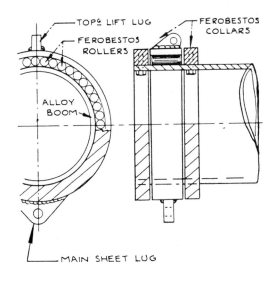

TOPᴱ LIFT LUG

FEROBESTOS ROLLERS

FEROBESTOS COLLARS

ALLOY BOOM

MAIN SHEET LUG

Roller boom fitting

This outer end fitting is made like this: two collars are machined up from Ferobestos or Tufnol or light alloy. These collars hold the rotating band which carries lugs for the main sheet and topping lift. There may also be lugs each side for the boom guys.

The rotating band must be thick enough not to distort when under load and when the lugs are welded to it. This means a section of about 1 inch by ¼ inch thick for a 4 inch diameter boom. As the band does not touch the alloy boom, it could be of bronze, but it is best to chrome plate it to make sure that no electrolytic action occurs.

The rollers are made last, then they can be turned down to fit the gap between the band and the boom.

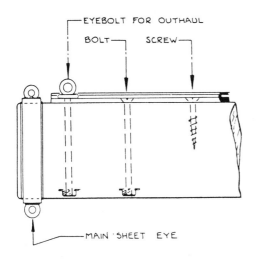

EYEBOLT FOR OUTHAUL

BOLT — SCREW —

MAIN SHEET EYE

For ocean cruising

Successful long range cruising consists largely of taking four times as many precautions as are required inshore. This treatment of the boom end is typical. It is normal to screw the sail track on to a wood boom. Sometimes an owner will double up the screws at the aft end, because the stresses here are high. However, if the last screw fails this will throw the strain on the next, which in turn will probably fail and so on.

A through bolt is a much better insurance so an eyebolt can be fitted to take the clew outhaul, or the outhaul tackle. The ocean cruising owner will not trust the eyebolt alone. For a start he knows that they are not available in a tested version, like his shackles, so he puts a second bolt in for good measure.

The same technique can be used on aluminium booms, where there is a risk that the rivets in the aft end of the track may fail.

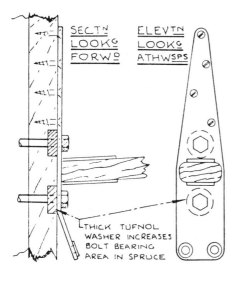

SECTN LOOKG FORWD   ELEVTN LOOKG ATHWSPS

THICK TUFNOL WASHER INCREASES BOLT BEARING AREA IN SPRUCE

Tangs on a wood mast

Tangs are normally screwed on, with a large number of heavy gauge screws, but bolts are needed to stop lower shrouds from pulling the tangs from the spar surface. Naturally no one wants to put large bolts through the tangs, since the tensile strength needed is not high.

Small diameter bolts tend to pull down through the wood, therefore splitting it. To get the best of both worlds, put on short lengths of thick-wall tube, like thick Tufnol washers, under the tangs.

They must be very carefully recessed, so that they fit exactly. They take the load on the bolts and spread it on a wide area of wood. Because of their relatively large diameter they do not split the grain downwards, yet they need not be very thick.

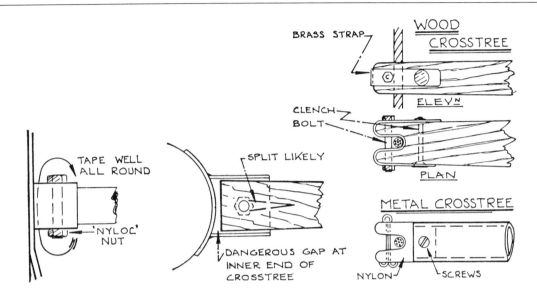

Crosstree vital details

There is nothing so calculated to give trouble as a crosstree. It sits half way up the mast, too high for man to see and evidently too low for guardian angels to care for. When the boat pitches into a head sea it wobbles back and forth just very slightly, working itself and its fastenings loose.

When making crosstrees there is only one principle to follow: take every possible precaution and double it. On a wooden crosstree both ends should be clenched to prevent splitting. On a big wood one, double the clenches and do them both vertically and horizontally.

The inner end of any 'tree', but especially a wood one, must lie hard up against the mast, otherwise it will split at the inner end bolt or break the bolt, or both. The inner

end should be a firm fit and, though only one bolt is shown here, a pair or three are better.

Never trust any part, but especially the outer fork. Make sure it is well rounded, bolt the shroud in, tape it over, add padding then inspect weekly. The reason for this fanatical mistrust is the awfulness of the consequences if the shroud hops out of the fork. A retaining bolt is needed since wire will chafe sails and work harden, then fracture. Any form of lashing will chafe through.

Wood crosstrees are best made of oak because it is tough. It is heavy, so if you are racing in such a way that risks are acceptable to give you that extra fraction of a second, go for spruce.

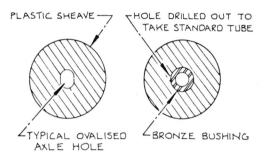

PLASTIC SHEAVE

HOLE DRILLED OUT TO
TAKE STANDARD TUBE

TYPICAL OVALISED
AXLE HOLE

BRONZE BUSHING

Worn sheaves

It is sometimes difficult to tighten a mainsail luff after reefing and one cause of this may be found if the halyard sheave is examined. Even though the sheave may be made of Tufnol or some self-lubricating material, the pivot hole sometimes wears to an oval.

There are several ways to rectify this defect, including buying a new sheave, which *may* be the cheapest solution. Another way is to fit a bush. It can be stainless steel but this is hard to cut and work, so it is probably better to use bronze or even brass. Buy a length which will do for the majority of sheaves on board and cut off lengths as needed. Obtain a drill to suit the outside diameter of the tubing, so that it is easy to drill out for the bushing. In time all the sheave pins can be changed to a common size using the same drill and same piece of bronze bushing, so simplifying the spares and repairing problem.

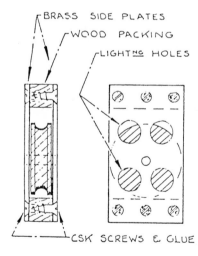

BRASS SIDE PLATES

WOOD PACKING

LIGHTNG HOLES

CSK SCREWS & GLUE

Reliable sheave cage

Probably the most common rigging failure today is a jammed halyard. With the current tendency for thin wire halyards and big sheaves, we find that if there is quite a small gap between sheave and casing side the wire will contrive to squeeze into it. Shown here is one way of preventing the trouble. The casing sides are made of brass or, better still, bronze. They must be fairly thick to prevent bending, but can be reduced in weight by drilling a pattern of lightening holes.

The top and bottom of the casing are of a hard wood, which is planed down till it is just fractionally thicker than the sheaves. This is the whole secret and it is because wood is so easy to finish to an exact thickness that it is used. The casing is assembled first without gluing to make sure it is accurate and then reassembled using glue.

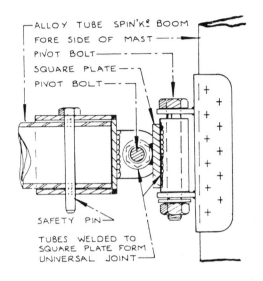

ALLOY TUBE SPIN'K⁰ BOOM
FORE SIDE OF MAST
PIVOT BOLT
SQUARE PLATE
PIVOT BOLT
SAFETY PIN
TUBES WELDED TO
SQUARE PLATE FORM
UNIVERSAL JOINT

Spinnaker boom fitting

Here is another fitting that the handyman can make using standard steel tube and plate. It may be necessary to get the parts professionally welded.

The alloy tube is left unplugged and the end is thrust into a short length of steel tube pivoted on a plate on the fore side of the mast.

To make the pivot, which is a simple form of universal joint, just take a square plate and weld a small tube on each side. The tubes are at right angles and each holds a bolt which also passes through a pair of plates, one at each end. One pair is welded to the mast plate, the other to the socket end blanking plate.

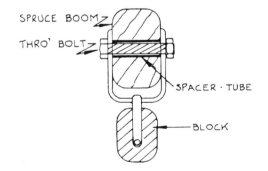

SPRUCE BOOM
THRO' BOLT
SPACER·TUBE
BLOCK

Fittings on spruce booms

Virtually all wood booms are made of spruce because it is a light-weight timber with a reasonably high strength factor. However it is a timber which is easily crushed, so that when a fitting is attached to a spar, certain precautions are advisable.

For instance, a typical method of fitting a main sheet block on to a boom is by making up a U-shaped stainless steel strap which is bolted through to the boom. On a dinghy a single bolt is probably adequate, but the further offshore the boat goes, the more bolts are needed.

If the nut is tightened hard, the metal strap will dig into the wood, crushing the fibres badly. To avoid this the bolt hole should be bushed with a metal tube.

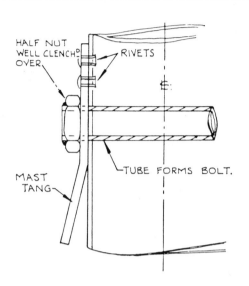

HALF NUT
WELL CLENCH?
OVER

RIVETS

MAST
TANG

TUBE FORMS BOLT.

Tang fastening

Whether a mast is made of wood, light alloy, glassfibre, steel or any other material, there is a need to join the fittings with light but strong fastenings. As the load is usually entirely in shear, the bolts or rivets used need to be of the necessary strength to resist this force and need little strength in tension or twisting.

In addition, the fastenings must not tend to split the spar or crush it by high local loading. For this reason a tubular bolt has much to commend it. However, such a bolt is not readily available so it has to be specially made. This can be easy, since it is necessary only to take a length of tubing, thread each end and fit a half nut which is then clenched over. This type of bolt gives much strength for very little weight.

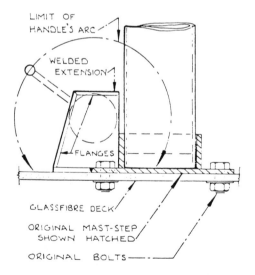

LIMIT OF
HANDLE'S ARC

WELDED
EXTENSION

FLANGES

GLASSFIBRE DECK

ORIGINAL MAST-STEP
SHOWN HATCHED

ORIGINAL BOLTS

Adding a halyard winch

Owners of glassfibre boats with alloy masts often find it hard to add even the smallest fitting. A bolt through glassfibre will cause cracking unless the load is spread correctly. An ingenious stratagem is to use the existing mast step fastenings. In this case the mast step is removed and either re-made with extra length to take the winch or an extension is welded on. This added part must be very rigid since the loads applied are often not in line with the holding-down bolts. Almost certainly the best way to make it rigid is to flange all the edges and weld the flanges at the corners where they meet. It has to be admitted that a winch fitted this way cannot be high off the deck, so the handle will not have space to rotate right round.

But there will be plenty of room to pump the handle and so tighten the halyard on the ratchet.

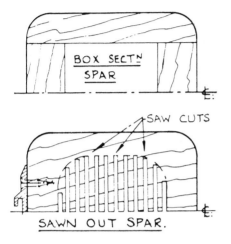

Hollow spar-making

In spite of the popularity of alloy spars there are still plenty of people requiring wooden masts.

One way to make a mast is to use two lengths of wood and have a single fore and aft seam. This reduces gluing to a minimum though it may be more expensive on wood than the procedure which consists of assembling a long, hollow box.

The bottom half of the drawing shows the fabrication technique favoured by some shipwrights. A circular saw is used to rout out a series of cuts along the length of the spar, leaving solid sections where required at the crosstree and gooseneck level. The final routing out is done with a chisel. Side fastened track is needed otherwise the track screws will all be in the glue line.

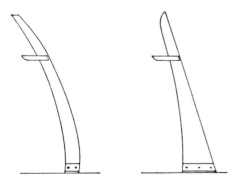

Smart masts

An ill-contrived signal mast always spoils a boat. It is so obtrusive that even if the rest of the boat is attractive the overall effect is wrecked. There are many rules for designing good masts for power boats. Some insist that the spar should always stand well clear above the level of the heads of those on board. Others consider that the location fore and aft is the dominant factor.

The thing to avoid at all costs is a spar which tries to be streamlined by bending backwards. One such is shown on the left and the result is pitiful. The mast on the right manages to convey the impression of speed without being pseudo-streamlined and has the practical advantage that the bottom is long enough to provide a secure base.

The temptation to cut out sections of the mast should be avoided as this is both costly and unsightly. The simple spar looks better in nearly every case.

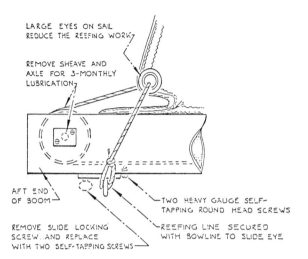

LARGE EYES ON SAIL
REDUCE THE REEFING WORK

REMOVE SHEAVE AND
AXLE FOR 3-MONTHLY
LUBRICATION

AFT END
OF BOOM

REMOVE SLIDE LOCKING
SCREW AND REPLACE
WITH TWO SELF-TAPPING SCREWS

TWO HEAVY GAUGE SELF-
TAPPING ROUND HEAD SCREWS

REEFING LINE SECURED
WITH BOWLINE TO SLIDE EYE

Improved jiffy reefing

Even with good winches, jiffy reefing can be hard work. To make it easier, all the sheaves and their axles should be greased regularly, and the reefing lines should be no more than one third the diameter of the eyes in the sail.

The reefing line must lead well back, roughly 45 degrees from the leech eye in its tight down position. Once the correct lead has been found by trial and error, the slide eye on the bottom or side of the boom should be locked with two large self-tapping screws driven into the aluminium walls of the boom. Those hand-tightened thumb screws in the slides seldom work reliably, and should be jettisoned.

Sails and Rigging

Yachts became simpler aloft with the passing of the gaff rig. Now the pendulum is swinging back to greater complexity. The aim now is to get greater efficiency from each sail. Naturally everyone wants speed, and since this cannot normally be done by increasing sail area, it has to be achieved by making better use of the available air-flow.

Crews want to be able to move the position of maximum camber of each sail, vary the amount of camber, alter within quite fine limits the angle of attack of each sail and the distances between sails. They need to be able to do this in all weathers, and to repeat a successful setting weeks later without fumbling around and wasting time achieving an optimum.

A big influence is the variety and power of winches now easily available. Compact winches can be bought by those with enough money, to give a lone man a pull of several tons. This sort of power has helped transform the current situation, but it does mean that stresses are now very high.

This of course is a situation which mostly interests the racing world. On a cruising yacht it is good design principle to keep the loadings low to get reliability and reduce maintenance.

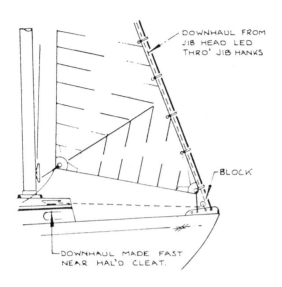

DOWNHAUL FROM
JIB HEAD LED
THRO' JIB HANKS

BLOCK

DOWNHAUL MADE FAST
NEAR HAL'D CLEAT.

Safety for singlehanders

Once the halyard has been cast off, a headsail will sag part of the way down the forestay. If the sail is large and the wind strong, it can be difficult to muzzle the sail down and keep it quiet.

This ocean cruising technique is worth adopting for sails which are too big for the available crew to handle in rough weather. A downhaul is made fast to the head of the sail and led down through the hanks to a block at the tack then aft to a point near the halyard cleat. A good jolt on this downhaul will bring the sail down and if the downhaul is made fast to a convenient cleat, the sail will remain subdued as it cannot ride up the forestay.

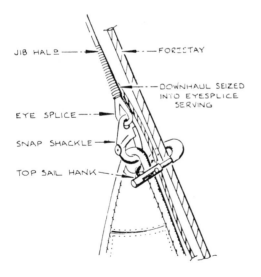

JIB HAL⊵

FORESTAY

DOWNHAUL SEIZED
INTO EYESPLICE
SERVING

EYE SPLICE

SNAP SHACKLE

TOP SAIL HANK

Downhaul detail

When reeving a downhaul from the head of a foresail the downhaul line should pass through all the jib hanks both to prevent it blowing off to leeward and to reduce wind resistance. The top should be made fast to the serving of the jib halyard wire, since this by-passes two vulnerable points. If either the halyard snap-shackle or the eye splice fails, the halyard is not lost aloft. Either of these breakages is likely on a long voyage where a halyard may sometimes be in use non-stop for fifty days, including a couple of full-blooded storms.

The downhaul can be quite light; ¼ inch diameter Terylene is suitable for most ocean cruisers up to about 35 foot long. Its great advantage is that it will reduce the need to go aloft at sea, as well as make sail handling easier.

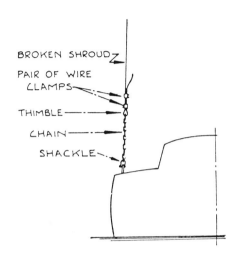

BROKEN SHROUD

PAIR OF WIRE CLAMPS

THIMBLE

CHAIN

SHACKLE

Emergency repair

A broken shroud or bottle-screw cannot safely be repaired with rope, not even a heavy gauge of Terylene. For a start the Terylene stretches and may do so enough to cause mast failure. On boats under 25 feet long it is possible to use multiple windings of Terylene to replace a broken bottle-screw, but for bigger boats something substantial is vital.

A piece of chain is useful for jury rigging. The short length of chain fitted to a kedge will do. Or the main anchor chain can be used. It is not necessary to cut the chain, just get the jury rigging set up quickly before the mast comes down. Later, when more time is available, the chain might be cut, though this will often be unnecessary as the main bulk of the anchor chain can remain stowed below.

Every well-found cruising yacht will carry a pair of wire clamps to pin back the shroud. A thimble at the turn prevents fatigue fracture of the wire.

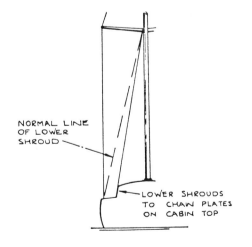

NORMAL LINE OF LOWER SHROUD

LOWER SHROUDS TO CHAIN PLATES ON CABIN TOP

Struggling forward

Small yachts are easier to handle than their bigger sisters because the gear is lighter, but a bigger boat provides compensations. There is a steadier working platform, and usually it is easier to move about on the deck.

Typical of the facets of this problem is the way the shrouds hamper access up the side decks. On a small cruiser it can be a regular battle to get through or round the wires holding the mast up. By putting the lower shrouds on to the cabin coamings, the situation can be much improved. However, careful measurement must be made before going for this idea as it can make matters worse.

The lower shrouds must be linked on to a strong structure such as bulkheads well fastened to the cabin coamings and topsides with additional vertical internal stiffeners. In some instances it is possible to carry the chain-plates down the cabin top and continue them below to meet the shell.

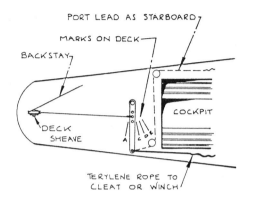

Precise backstay adjustment

The difficulty with any tuning on a yacht is to measure exactly how much a piece of rigging is tightened. Sketched here is a convenient method of adjusting a backstay so that the same amount of tension can always be applied.

The backstay wire comes down from the masthead round a sheave on the deck and forward to a lever with a vertical pivot. There are alternative attachment points for the backstay on the lever while the outer end of the lever has a line leading forward to a cleat. For extra power this line may be led to a winch and for adjustment from either side of the yacht another line is rove to port.

Marked on deck are various angles, suitably labelled, so that after experimenting the crew will know what setting to use for different wind strengths. There must be stops to prevent the lever going right aft. The whole contrivance may be below deck, with a Perspex panel over the lever.

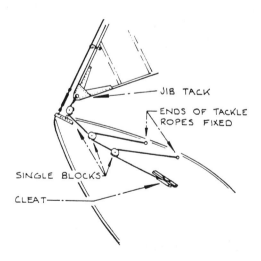

Poor man's tackle

Tuning a boat is not a matter of miracles. Beginners tend to think that successful helmsmen tinker with one rigging screw and then sail off twice as fast as the rest of the fleet. In practice tuning is a lengthy process involving a vast number of adjustments. One thing which has considerable effect is the tightening of the headsail luff, so that it holds straight.

To get a headsail luff really tight a tackle or winch is needed. A powerful winch is often best, but a multiple tackle is nearly as good. The cheapest way to make a four part purchase is to rig two single blocks as shown, with a single block to take the tack pennant down and along the deck. This simple arrangement can be multiplied again with another single block but it then becomes cumbersome.

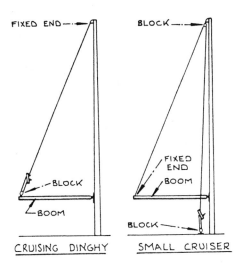

FIXED END

BLOCK

BLOCK

BOOM

CRUISING DINGHY

FIXED END

BOOM

BLOCK

SMALL CRUISER

Simple topping lifts

Some small mass-produced cruisers are offered without topping lifts. This can be most inconvenient. The topping lift is so handy when coming in to moorings, especially when on one's own. For jiffy reefing it may not be essential but it helps, especially if the mainsail is one which has a tendency to pucker, wrinkle and snarl up. For roller reefing there must be a topping lift.

For a very small boat, like a cruising dinghy, a piece of ⅛ inch diameter nylon or Terylene is made fast at the masthead. The other end passes through a block, or even a bull's-eye, and back up to a simple bowsie which is just a strip of wood with two holes drilled in it. This layout gives low weight and windage but on a small cruiser it is handy to be able to adjust the topping lift from near the mast so the system shown on the right can be used.

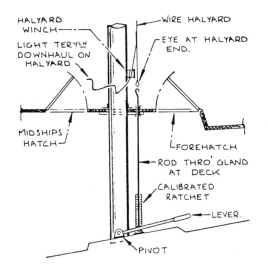

HALYARD WINCH

LIGHT TERYL⁼ DOWNHAUL ON HALYARD

WIRE HALYARD

EYE AT HALYARD END.

MIDSHIPS HATCH

FOREHATCH

ROD THRO' GLAND AT DECK

CALIBRATED RATCHET

LEVER.

PIVOT

Accurate halyard tensioning

This arrangement will suit racing yachts up to about 32 feet overall. It can be used for headsails or mainsail and it has the advantages that it can be amateur made, it is mostly low down and offers no windage on deck, and above all, the correct tension found during a successful race can be reproduced for subsequent races.

The halyard is hauled by hand, the down-haul being of light Terylene, which may be taken to a small winch in heavy weather. To get the final tightening correct, the end of the wire part of the halyard has an eye which slips over the hook at the top of a vertical rod. This rod is forced down the correct distance with the lever located near the mast foot. A safety line on the fore end of the lever is worth having. When the lever is tight down this line will be secured to a nearby cleat.

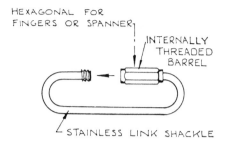

HEXAGONAL FOR FINGERS OR SPANNER

INTERNALLY THREADED BARREL

STAINLESS LINK SHACKLE

Deserves to be better known

The stainless steel link shackle has a variety of applications and its virtues especially suit halyard-to-sail attachment.

This type of shackle has no loose parts and can be worked with one hand only. It consists of a loop of stainless rod which is swollen and threaded at each end. On one end is a hexagonal barrel – threaded inside. This turns up to close the gap and engage the threaded section shown on the left.

It is a tool for the weight-saver since the $^{3}/_{16}$ inch size with a breaking load of $7^{3}/_{4}$ cwt tips the scales at under 1 oz. A common make of snap shackle which breaks at 7 cwt weighs 5 oz.

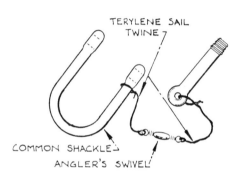

TERYLENE SAIL TWINE

COMMON SHACKLE

ANGLER'S SWIVEL

Retaining a shackle pin

The multiplicity of snap shackle designs owes much to the fact that common shackle pins so often drop overboard. If it were not for this, it has to be admitted that a normal shackle has much to commend it. It stands up to high loading, does not distort often and is cheaply and easily obtained. Anyone who has tried tying the shackle pin to the main body of the item will know that trouble occurs when screwing the pin home. The linking twine soon tangles up. Lengthening the twine makes an untidy awkward mess. However with a little swivel in the line there is no trouble winding the pin in.

A suitable swivel is made for anglers. It is non-ferrous, cheap and has eyes each end quite large enough for sail thread. A little experimenting with different sizes of shackle will determine the best minimum length of line at each side of the swivel.

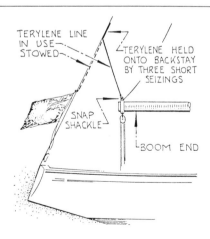

TERYLENE LINE IN USE
STOWED

TERYLENE HELD ONTO BACKSTAY BY THREE SHORT SEIZINGS

SNAP SHACKLE

BOOM END

The lightest cheapest topping lift and boom gallows

To support the boom in harbour, nothing is simpler than a short length of rope secured to the permanent back-stay. The bottom end has a stainless steel snap shackle which engages in the eye at the top of the boom, or into a shackle which is through this eye if the eye is too small.

This type of gallows has been used as a topping lift on small yachts during reefing, when the traditional style of reefing was in vogue.

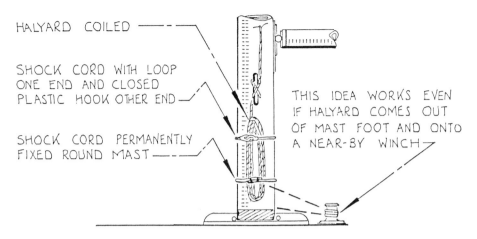

HALYARD COILED

SHOCK CORD WITH LOOP
ONE END AND CLOSED
PLASTIC HOOK OTHER END

SHOCK CORD PERMANENTLY
FIXED ROUND MAST

THIS IDEA WORKS EVEN
IF HALYARD COMES OUT
OF MAST FOOT AND ONTO
A NEAR-BY WINCH

Stowing coiled halyards

A halyard which is not neatly and safely stowed may slip overboard. When the engine is started the propeller will maliciously suck the rope to itself. The next thing anyone knows is that the engine stops suddenly with the rope solid round the propeller, and the sail cannot be lowered because the halyard end is all too well secured . . . under water.

This arrangement of halyard stowage fits every size and type of yacht and means that the halyard can be let go quickly. For large halyards it may be best to have three or even four loops of shock cord round the mast. New shock cord will be needed every year or two as this material perishes in sunlight.

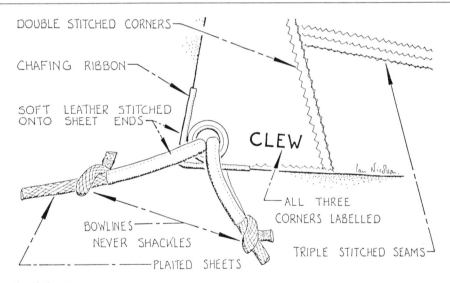

DOUBLE STITCHED CORNERS

CHAFING RIBBON

SOFT LEATHER STITCHED
ONTO SHEET ENDS

CLEW

ALL THREE
CORNERS LABELLED

BOWLINES
NEVER SHACKLES

TRIPLE STITCHED SEAMS

PLAITED SHEETS

Securing headsail sheets

No one has ever found a better way of securing headsail sheets than tying a bowline in the end of each one. Shackles on the ends of sheets too often cause crew injury when the sails lash backwards and forwards in windy conditions, or even in light weather.

To make the sheets last, they should have soft leather stitched to the fore ends, and when wear starts to show –

at the winches, for instance – the sheets should be turned end for end.

Other good ideas shown here are the triple stitching of the sails, which is recommended for all far ranging boats, and the naming in thick black ink lines of all three corners.

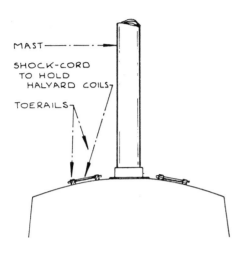

MAST

SHOCK-CORD
TO HOLD
HALYARD COILS

TOERAILS

Halyard stowage

There are two types of yacht which need quick access to the halyards – racing yachts and multi-hulls. The former must be able to change sails with the minimum of delay, while the latter may have to reduce or drop sails quickly in a squall.

These two breeds are having an increasing effect on other types and classes, so this idea is likely to spread. It consists of toerails each side of the mast, probably made of teak or perhaps well varnished mahogany. These rails give the crew a good grip when working round the mast, but their primary purpose is to hold sets of shock-cord straps beneath which the coiled halyards are stowed.

It might make sense to use alternate lengths of stout and light shock-cord, the former for a permanent stowing, the latter for a temporary job.

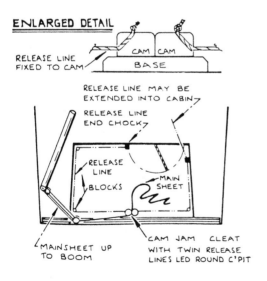

ENLARGED DETAIL

RELEASE LINE
FIXED TO CAM

CAM   CAM
BASE

RELEASE LINE MAY BE
EXTENDED INTO CABIN

RELEASE LINE
END CHOCK

RELEASE
LINE

BLOCKS

MAIN
SHEET

MAINSHEET UP
TO BOOM

CAM JAM CLEAT
WITH TWIN RELEASE
LINES LED ROUND C'PIT

Multi-hull safety

There seems general agreement that the way to stop cruising multi-hull yachts from capsizing is to have an alert crew constantly on the job. This sketch shows how to give this crew a choice of positions in the cockpit, yet keep them in full control.

So that they can let the mainsheet fly from any part of the cockpit, the sheet is led through a cam jam cleat. Each cam has a light Terylene line made fast to it, possibly by drilling a hole through the cam, with the line threaded through the hole. This light line, the release line, is led round the cockpit via bull's-eyes or blocks, so that anyone in any part of the cockpit can release the hold on the main sheet.

The release lines can be taken anywhere in the ship. It is important that the bitter end of the line is very firmly secured and that the blocks are all tough.

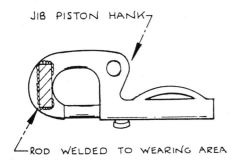

JIB PISTON HANK

ROD WELDED TO WEARING AREA

Hank repair

The top piston hank on any well used headsail will show wear after a couple of seasons. It is best to keep changing the hanks around so that the one at the top does not remain long in that position. In this way the hanks should last as long as the sail since they will receive equal wear. In ocean cruising yachts the wear may be intensive and it is not always convenient to change the hanks around at sea. For this sort of sailing the top hanks should be doubled up with short lengths of rod to increase the wearing surface.

In the same way hanks which have become worn can be repaired but they should not be used on hard weather sails after repair. Nor should repaired hanks be put at the top or bottom where the strain is greatest, but used in between.

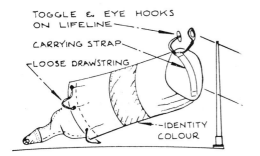

TOGGLE & EYE HOOKS
ON LIFELINE

CARRYING STRAP

LOOSE DRAWSTRING

IDENTITY
COLOUR

Sail bag improvements

When a foresail is being bent on to a forestay at sea it is essential that the sail bag is secured to the boat to prevent it falling or blowing overboard. If the bag is secured to the lifeline by the drawstring the opening is restricted and the sail difficult to get out. If a lanyard and toggle are fitted to the bottom of the sail bag cold fingers can quickly secure the bag to the lifeline and the opening will be at deck level. The sail is thus easy to remove.

Each sail bag should bear a band of colour for easy identification. Some owners work on the principle that the sky is darker in bad weather, so the darker the colour of the band the smaller the headsail.

SECTION AT 'A-A'

A.

A

More efficient headsails

This is not a new idea, in fact it certainly dates back to the later days of the 6 metre class and probably goes back to the early Egyptians.

It is well known that in order to make a sail efficient, measures must be taken to keep the high pressure air on one side from flowing round to the lower pressure area on the other. With a genoa a good scheme is to arrange the foot of the sail to drape along the deck so that no air can dodge under the bottom of the sail. New sails may be specially made and old sails can be adapted to this idea. Without breaking the rules, it is often allowable to fit a soft light flexy skirt of thin material along the foot, to hang down to the deck and lie snugly inside the toerail.

The main part of the sail extends in a straight line from tack to clew, and the skirt sweeps down in a bight between these two points. Certain classes prohibit or penalise this idea.

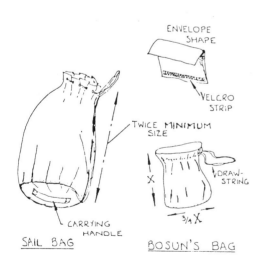

ENVELOPE SHAPE

VELCRO STRIP

TWICE MINIMUM SIZE

X

DRAW-STRING

¾ X

SAIL BAG

BOSUN'S BAG

CARRYING HANDLE

For sail repairs

In days gone by, sails were made of cotton and were torn quite easily, but now that synthetics are used tears occur less frequently. As a result it is unusual for an owner to carry spare sail cloth aboard.

In small cruisers there is relatively little space for spares. However, emergencies still occur so it is best to be prepared for them. One ingenious idea is to have each sail bag made of the same material as the sail it carries. This way there is always a good piece of spare material aboard. As sail bags should be very roomy – big enough for two sails – the bag is still adequate even after a piece has been chopped out. Bosun's bags for shackles and so forth can also be made of sail cloth and used for patching in an emergency. The envelope shape is not so good as the kit bag shape but can be improved with a Velcro fastener. The kit bag shape must be wide-mouthed to provide good accessibility.

Engines and Electricity

One fascinating aspect of yachting history concerns the unreliability of the machinery. From the time that engines were put into yachts till about 1950 there was a continuous tale of woe. Engines failed in droves every weekend, all weekend, all summer, in every harbour and off all the coasts of the world. When the majority of yachts changed over to diesel the number of breakdowns dropped vastly. Diesels tend to be reliable, so that it is quite usual for a yacht yard to have only a trickle of engine troubles through the summer.

However the ancillaries are not all that reliable, partly because too many of them are made to the same pattern as motor car equipment. Also of course many of these auxiliaries are electrical equipment.

All electrical gear on yachts gives trouble out of all proportion to its size, cost, weight or importance. Again the trouble stems partly from the use of motor car or household equipment. Proper yacht electric equipment is often very expensive, and by no means thoroughly reliable.

This would seem to be a field where designers might exercise their brains to advantage. Owners who like to potter in their workshops should not have much difficulty in beating the industry in this field.

When installing anything connected with the engine or electrical equipment, the cardinal rule is to keep everything out of the weather. Nothing should even be sited near, let alone under a hatch. When a ship rolls, the drips through the hatches do not fall straight towards her keel; they fall under gravity plus the force of any local draughts. As a result it is not unusual to find trickles of water several feet offset from directly below a hatch. This means that electrical equipment and machinery which is below decks should be as well protected from the weather as if it was out in the open. This encasing or protection does not mean that a location below a hatch is tolerable, it is simply that we need belt *and* braces here.

Reverting to the reliability of diesels, this must not blind us to the vulnerability of stern gear and other parts of the machinery. Just because an engine can stand a lot of neglect does not mean that the stern gland never needs tightening or repacking. A few years ago a puffer* sank in the Sound of Mull. She had been taking water for weeks through her stern tube, and during a spell of bad weather this leak increased. The engineer tried to tighten the gland by hardening up the nuts. The leak continued, so he tightened harder, till one of the studs broke and the water gushed in to sink the ship. Of course the nuts did not need all that force to tighten them, it was just that the gland had not been repacked for months. The cost of new packing would be less than £10, and for this a ship was lost.

* A puffer is a small coaster used in Scotland. It has a vertical stem and stern-post with outside rudder. The intention here is to get the biggest ship which would fit into the locks in the Crinan and former Forth-Clyde canal. The early models were tiller steered, the bridge being behind the funnel. They got their name from the puff-puff of steam which came out of the funnel from the non-condensing steam engine.

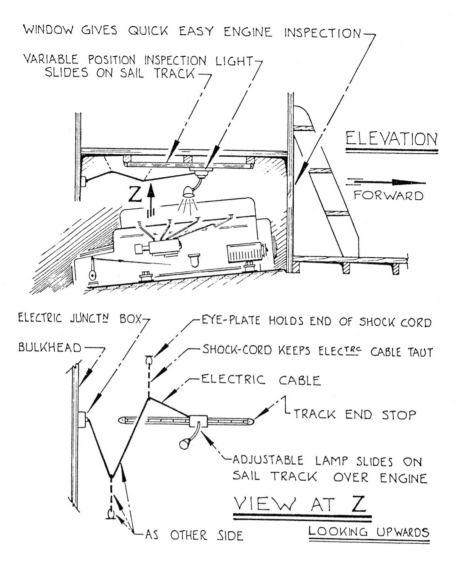

WINDOW GIVES QUICK EASY ENGINE INSPECTION

VARIABLE POSITION INSPECTION LIGHT
SLIDES ON SAIL TRACK

ELEVATION

FORWARD

Z

ELECTRIC JUNCT$\underline{N}$ BOX

BULKHEAD

EYE-PLATE HOLDS END OF SHOCK CORD

SHOCK-CORD KEEPS ELEC$\underline{TRC}$ CABLE TAUT

ELECTRIC CABLE

TRACK END STOP

ADJUSTABLE LAMP SLIDES ON
SAIL TRACK OVER ENGINE

VIEW AT Z

AS OTHER SIDE

LOOKING UPWARDS

Light in engine compartment

If an engine compartment has a bright light and a window which gives a good view of the machinery it is easy to check the engine frequently without opening up the compartment.

This regular inspection is good seamanship and engineering, and gives peace of mind. It is only possible if the space is so well lit that all the auxiliaries such as generator, water pump and drive belts are clearly visible.

The light shown in this sketch has the advantages of a wandering lead, which the Americans like to call a

'trouble lamp'... how right they are. A length of ordinary sail track extends over the engine, or along one side, and running on this is a carriage with the lamp base bolted to it. The lamp is on an arm which is adjustable, and the flexible cable leading to the light is always tight because it is pulled outboard by two or more lengths of shock cord.

In practice it may be best to have two lights, or even two pairs of lights, depending on the size and complexity of the space and machinery and the available wattage.

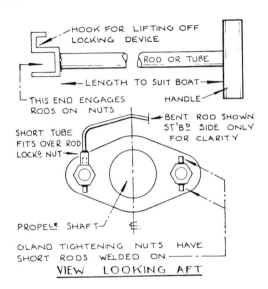

HOOK FOR LIFTING OFF
LOCKING DEVICE

ROD OR TUBE

LENGTH TO SUIT BOAT

THIS END ENGAGES
RODS ON NUTS

HANDLE

BENT ROD SHOWN
ST'BD SIDE ONLY
FOR CLARITY

SHORT TUBE
FITS OVER ROD
LOCKG NUT

PROPELR SHAFT

GLAND TIGHTENING NUTS HAVE
SHORT RODS WELDED ON.

VIEW LOOKING AFT

Inaccessible stern gland

What do you do if you cannot reach the stern gland to tighten it every month? Let it leak? Train a monkey to climb in behind the engine to tighten the nuts? One solution is sketched here. The nuts are removed (if need be by taking the engine out, since this is a vital matter) and on opposite faces small rods are welded. To tighten the nuts a long rod or tube is made up with a C-shaped end to engage on the nut and a handle at the opposite end. This long rod is used from a position forward of the engine.

Remote locking is achieved by welding two short lengths of tube to a bent rod. The tubes drop over the rods sticking up from the nuts, effectively preventing the nuts from turning under vibration. This scheme would not work on a lively leaping offshore powerboat.

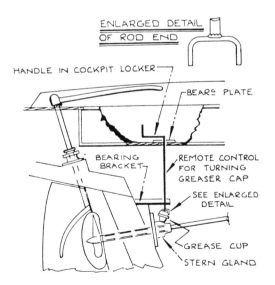

ENLARGED DETAIL
OF ROD END

HANDLE IN COCKPIT LOCKER

BEARG PLATE

BEARING
BRACKET

REMOTE CONTROL
FOR TURNING
GREASER CAP

SEE ENLARGED
DETAIL

GREASE CUP

STERN GLAND

Saving shaft wear

Every owner *thinks* about giving the cap of the greaser at the stern gland a turn each weekend. Those that *do* something about it are the owners who can reach their stern glands without inverted contortions. Owners who cannot get anywhere near the stern greaser just sigh and frequently have to buy new propeller shafts. This small modification will cost less than renewing the shaft.

A long rod, made up perhaps of ½ inch diameter brass tube, is extended from a cockpit locker down to the greaser. A flat brass plate about 1 inch high and 3/16 inch thick is brazed right across the top of the greaser cap. The end of the shaft is fitted with a two-pronged fork which engages over the greaser cap plate to turn it. The shaft needs a pair of simple bearings to hold it, and the top is bent twice at right angles.

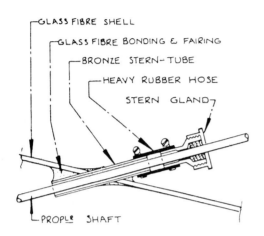

GLASS FIBRE SHELL

GLASS FIBRE BONDING & FAIRING

BRONZE STERN-TUBE

HEAVY RUBBER HOSE

STERN GLAND

PROPLE SHAFT

Stern tube through glassfibre

A simple way to take a propeller shaft out through a glassfibre hull is through a conventional stern tube which is glassed in place. The sketch shows a particularly useful type of stern tube, which does not have to be lined up precisely, as the short length of hose accommodates minor misalignments.

One attraction of this arrangement is that the glands can easily be bought, and the tube needs no machining. Just pop it through the aperture in the hull and glass it up. It needs glassing inside and out; the latter must be well faired for best effect.

One small risk with this type of gland is that if it seizes, there is every chance that the rubber will be torn free and water will pour in. This danger is eliminated by having lugs on the gland which fit loosely in slots at the fore end of the tube like a dog clutch.

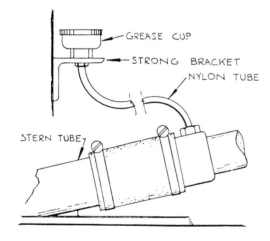

GREASE CUP

STRONG BRACKET

NYLON TUBE

STERN TUBE

Remote stern gland greaser

It is quite usual on the best engineered yachts to find that the grease cup of the stern gland has been shifted. The cup is located somewhere high up and handy, so that there is every temptation to give it a twist daily, and hence ensure an easy turning, leak-free shaft. The mechanics of fitting the remote grease cup are interesting: use nylon tubing from the cup to the gland, so that when the grease is first introduced, it can be seen moving down the pipe. Fit the cup clear of bulkheads because it needs a strong fist working hard to force even warm grease down six feet of winding ¼ inch diameter tube. For the same reason make sure the bracket holding the cup is strong and able to withstand reversing loads. The nylon piping should on no account be kinked, but should be supported at say 8 inch intervals and of course the grease must be the right grade to makers' recommendations.

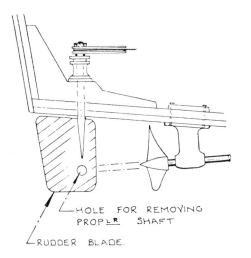

HOLE FOR REMOVING PROP**LR** SHAFT

RUDDER BLADE.

Propeller shaft renewal

A power boat which is used hard all through the season may seriously wear a new prop shaft within a year – especially if she is operating in shallow, gritty water. Even in less arduous conditions the shaft will need renewing every three seasons if the annual mileage is high or if the boat can flex, which will produce high loading on the shaft at times.

The rudder stock is not likely to need attention anything like so often. This means that where the prop shaft is right in line with the rudder a time-wasting job of removing the rudder is necessary in order to fit the new shaft. To get round this a hole may be drilled in the rudder, dead in line with the shaft. Once the propeller is removed and the shaft uncoupled at the fore end it is an easy job to turn the rudder athwartships and slide the shaft out.

The loss of rudder turning efficiency will be relatively small and very seldom matter.

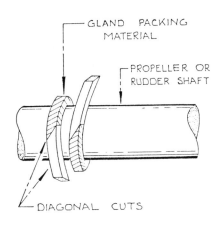

GLAND PACKING MATERIAL

PROPELLER OR RUDDER SHAFT

DIAGONAL CUTS

Cutting stern and rudder gland packing

When repacking a gland the correct diameter of that greasy string called 'gland packing' is bought from a marine engineer. The packing is cut in short lengths which fit neatly and exactly round the shaft, using the shaft as a gauge to get the correct length.

Each length of packing has tapered ends which mate together; each join is located at a different point round the shaft to avoid leaks, and a very sharp knife is needed to cut gland packing.

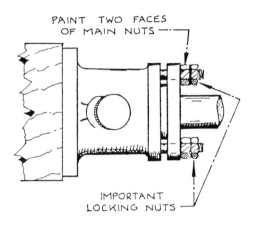

PAINT TWO FACES
OF MAIN NUTS

IMPORTANT
LOCKING NUTS

Locking nuts

Throughout every yacht there are many nuts which should be locked. It is true to say that every nut needs some form of safety catch, either clenching (which is virtually permanent) or a split pin (which is renewable every season). As the stern gland is subject to vibration it is especially important that its retaining nuts are locked since they will be greasy and could easily work loose. If they come right off the inflow of water might be very serious. It is a nuisance having to release then tighten the locking nuts every time the gland has to be tightened, but the inconvenience should remind the owner of the importance of correct shaft installation and alignment. If two opposite faces of the main nuts are painted contrasting colours it will be easy to tighten port and starboard nuts the identical amount.

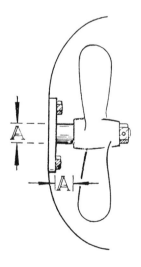

Shaft overhang

One dimension never given in any of the technical books is the allowable shaft length between the forward face of the propeller boss and the aft face of the stern bearing.

Ideally the shaft would continue a long way aft, to keep the propeller so far from the bearing that a good flow of water to the blades would be ensured. There are snags to this arrangement, though. For instance the propeller would tend to whip, especially if slightly off balance. Wear in the bearing would probably induce whirling, and this would quickly worsen the wear.

If the shaft overhang is very short there is no allowance for tiny errors in measuring and the engine cannot be moved even slightly forward during installation. A good compromise is to make the aft overhang about equal to the shaft diameter.

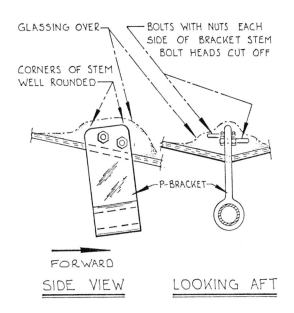

GLASSING OVER

BOLTS WITH NUTS EACH
SIDE OF BRACKET STEM
BOLT HEADS CUT OFF

CORNERS OF STEM
WELL ROUNDED

P-BRACKET

FORWARD

SIDE VIEW   LOOKING AFT

A well-secured P-bracket

It is not enough to push the stem of a P-bracket up
through a slot in a glass fibre hull, and glass over on the
inside. If the propeller fouls a rope the bracket will tend to
become loose. So before the bracket is fitted it should be
drilled for at least two athwartships bolts. These are fitted
after the bracket has been lightly glassed in. The bolts
must have their heads cut off and ends rounded to allow
the glass to bond on well. Each bolt is held by a nut on
each side of the bracket stem.

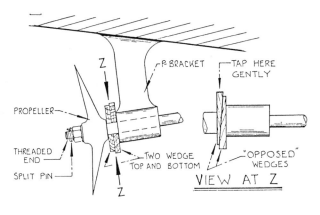

Z

P-BRACKET

TAP HERE
GENTLY

PROPELLER

THREADED
END

SPLIT PIN

TWO WEDGE
TOP AND BOTTOM

"OPPOSED"
WEDGES

Z

VIEW AT Z

Tap gently please

To get a propeller off its shaft the ideal tool is a 'propeller
puller', because it hooks round the prop blades and
pushes against the end of the shaft. Not everyone has
such a specialised tool, and the following trick can be
used *but only very carefully*.

Two pairs of wedges are tapped – not bashed – in
between the prop boss and the P-bracket. If too much
force is used the P-bracket will be tilted forward, causing
damage to the hull if it is a glassfibre one.

Before using the wedges, freeing oil is applied each
side of the boss where the shaft passes through, and this
is left for a week. Ideally three applications of oil at
weekly intervals should be used. Another safety
precaution is a clamp on the shaft forward of the
P-bracket.

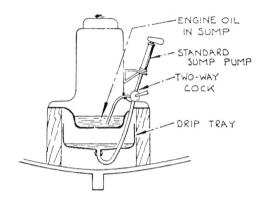

Emptying the drip tray

Engines in boats are often inaccessible. It is also common for drip trays to be hard to see, let alone reach. Cleaning out a tray is seldom attempted because it is such awkward mucky work and results in splashes of oil all over the engine space. As a result the drip tray gradually fills with a mixture of oil, water, rust, soot and dirt. This horrible concoction slops out of the drip tray and soon the whole bilge is contaminated.

To avoid this trouble all that is needed is a two-way cock below the sump pump. One suction leads to the pump in the ordinary way and the other to the drip tray. A strum box with a fine mesh is needed in the drip tray suction, and it must have a big area since the tiny mesh may become partly clogged.

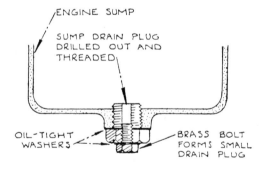

Modifying the sump plug

On many small marine engines the only way to change the oil is to undo the sump plug. This allows the oil to pour into the drip tray, where it has to be bailed into a bucket, and then taken ashore for burning or other disposal. Getting the oil out of the drip tray is often a slow and extremely messy procedure, so here is a short cut to easier maintenance.

Before installing the engine take out the sump plug, drill a hole through it, tap this hole, clean it well, and screw in a brass, or better still a bronze bolt which naturally must be quite small. Now when the oil is to be changed the little bolt is removed instead of the main plug. This lets the oil out slowly, into a small cup put under the plug. When the cup is nearly full a finger over the hole stops the flow while the cup is emptied and put back under the plug. In theory it should be possible to follow this procedure using the sump plug itself, but they are always too large and the oil flows out too fast.

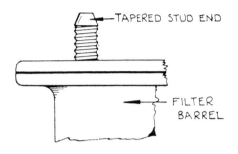

TAPERED STUD END

FILTER BARREL

Tapered studs

This is one of those small safety details which may not come into play for many years. Then, one wild wind-struck night it could make all the difference between a heap of shattered yacht on a pile of rocks and safety in harbour. Many bolt ends and studs are located in awkward places. The cover of a filter and seacock where the engine cooling-water comes through the hull is a good example. This cock is always situated well down in the bilge, so when the cover is taken off, it is usually a bit of a struggle to get it back on again. If the nuts are dropped in the bilge during the job, it is a fair bet there will be no spares on board.

To make the nuts easy to put on, the stud ends should be machined to a blunt point.

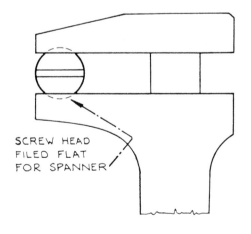

SCREW HEAD FILED FLAT FOR SPANNER

Engineer's trick

A well known type of yacht's w.c. has brass metal-threads (bolts threaded to the head) to hold on the inlet valve. If seaweed is sucked into this w.c. it jams at this valve and a minor dismantling job is called for.

Taking the bottom of the valve off is the work of half a minute *provided* a stubby screwdriver is available. If such a tool is not to hand, the job is murder.

To avoid the trouble it is worth filing a pair of flats on the heads of the screws so that a spanner can be used as an alternative to the screwdriver. Of course these flats should be filed *before* the w.c. is installed.

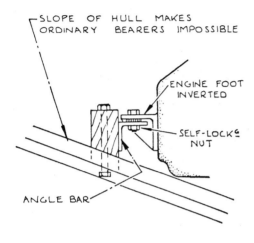

A low-slung engine

It is a regular problem in every design office to install engines low enough. Engines must be kept down to avoid steep shafts which in turn mean sloping sumps and oil starvation.

Even if the engine can be fitted with the sump right down on the planking there are occasions when this is impossible as the engine feet would foul the hull shell. On some engines this dilemma can be overcome by inverting the engine feet. They are held to the engine casing by two or four bolts so that there is no problem to refastening the feet upside down.

In the sketch the feet have been set on steel angle-bars inside the main bearers, otherwise the bearers would lack depth and hence rigidity. The use of a self-locking nut, such as the kind with a nylon insert, is recommended and is particularly worth using where access is awkward so that a locking nut would be difficult to get on.

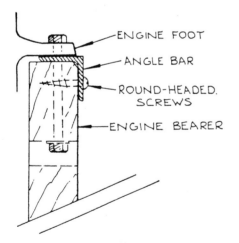

Avoiding misalignment

Any competent boat-builder will tell you that an engine must not be set direct on to wood bearers. He will explain that the weight of the engine crushes the wood so that the whole engine settles slightly and misalignment occurs. The trouble also occurs with glassfibre covered wood bearers.

He will show how the bearers must be capped with a steel or brass strip, or at least long plate washers, to prevent this crushing of the wood. What he may not realise is that flat bar is no good if the engine is a very heavy one. The reason is that the flat bar will flex, admittedly very slightly, so that some misalignment can still occur.

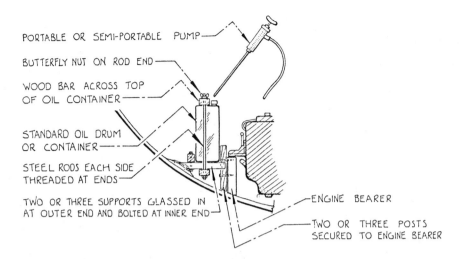

PORTABLE OR SEMI-PORTABLE PUMP

BUTTERFLY NUT ON ROD END

WOOD BAR ACROSS TOP
OF OIL CONTAINER

STANDARD OIL DRUM
OR CONTAINER

STEEL RODS EACH SIDE
THREADED AT ENDS

TWO OR THREE SUPPORTS GLASSED IN
AT OUTER END AND BOLTED AT INNER END

ENGINE BEARER

TWO OR THREE POSTS
SECURED TO ENGINE BEARER

Dirty oil out, clean oil in

Nothing spoils enjoyment afloat like a cup of dirty oil swilling around in the bilge. Just this small amount does untold damage. It gets into lockers, mucks up bedding, makes cabin soles dangerously slippery, and in time seems to spread through the whole boat.

If there are proper containers well secured close by the engine it can be a straightforward business sucking the old oil out and, using a different, clean pump, putting fresh oil in.

The containers must be semi-portable so that the dirty oil can be taken ashore when the drum is full and new cans of clean oil easily put in place of empty ones. Rods threaded their full length, called studding, can be bought to make into holding-down rods, one on each side of each container.

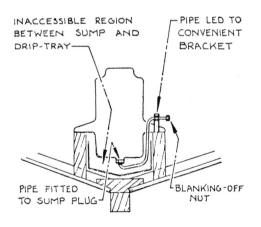

INACCESSIBLE REGION
BETWEEN SUMP AND
DRIP-TRAY

PIPE LED TO
CONVENIENT
BRACKET

PIPE FITTED
TO SUMP PLUG

BLANKING-OFF
NUT

Draining the sump

It is usual to find that the space under a boat's engine is smaller than a mouse's home. Trying to unscrew the sump plug to get rid of the oil often calls for a Houdini twelve inches tall using a spanner with three dog-leg bends in it. So before installing the engine, or next time it is out, this modification is worth making. The sump plug is drilled out and a copper pipe very carefully brazed on. This pipe is led up to a convenient point on the engine (so that it vibrates with the engine). A blanking off nut is fitted, making the end oil-tight. When the time comes to change the oil it is easy to take off the end nut, fit a small pump and suck the oil into an old tin for disposal. This is vastly easier than the dreary business of sucking the oil out of the dip-stick hole, or the castastrophe of opening the crankcase side and having all the oil in the drip tray and probably some of it overflowing into the bilge.

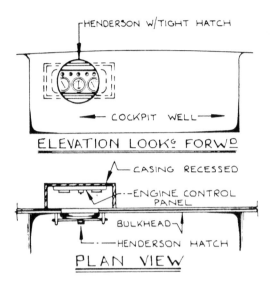

HENDERSON W/TIGHT HATCH

← COCKPIT WELL →

ELEVATION LOOK⁹ FORW⁰

CASING RECESSED

ENGINE CONTROL PANEL

BULKHEAD

HENDERSON HATCH

PLAN VIEW

Avoiding corrosion

It is often the practice to fit engine instruments which are quite unsuitable for sea-going conditions. Even on motor-cruisers with enclosed wheelhouses, the condition of the dashboard will often deteriorate over the season, starting with the panel light and ending with total failure caused by a gritty white powder which defies the passage of electricity. On a sailing yacht some designers put the instrument panel inside the cabin, to try to defeat this seizing up and electrical failure. This is a defeatist attitude, brought home when the oil pressure drops without being noticed because the gauge cannot be seen from the cockpit.

The instrument panel in this sketch has been fitted inside a watertight casing. The front of the casing is one of those truly watertight Henderson hatch covers.

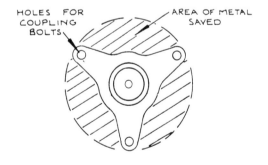

HOLES FOR COUPLING BOLTS

AREA OF METAL SAVED

Light-weight engine coupling

The weight of the engine forms a substantial part of the total weight of a boat, but it is hard to reduce the weight of the machinery. However some components can be lightened. For instance the shaft coupling need not be the usual type consisting of two thick round mating discs. That redundant area of metal between the bolt holes can be eliminated even on a diesel engine which puts much higher loadings on its coupling then a petrol one.

Other ways of reducing the total engine weight involve changing metal piping for plastic tubing, and perhaps reducing the bore, minimising the exhaust length, and making the drip tray of aluminium alloy.

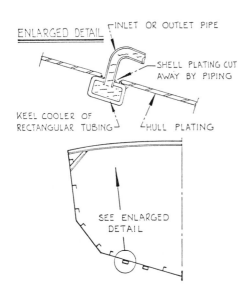

ENLARGED DETAIL

INLET OR OUTLET PIPE

SHELL PLATING CUT
AWAY BY PIPING

KEEL COOLER OF
RECTANGULAR TUBING

HULL PLATING

SEE ENLARGED
DETAIL

Keel coolers on a metal hull

The lower drawing shows a section through a steel or aluminium hull built with stringers extending fore and aft. The bottom plate is stiffened with rectangular hollow section tubes on the outside which also act as heat exchangers for the engine coolant. The outside tubes may be square in section, and the pipes leading into the tubing must be heavy duty. The hull shell is cut away by the inlet and outlet pipes, and at these points the shell is fully welded on the inside to the stringer tubes.

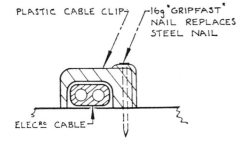

PLASTIC CABLE CLIP

16g 'GRIPFAST'
NAIL REPLACES
STEEL NAIL

ELECᴿᶜ CABLE

Wiring clips

There is a rather good type of electric cable holding device which comes in a range of sizes suitable for different thicknesses of cable. It is quickly and easily fastened, since it needs only one nail to hold it. The plastic bridge is provided with a hardened plated steel nail, which is intended for use in buildings but should not be used on yacht work. However the nail is easily removed. It should be replaced by a non-ferrous nail or panel pin. Among the advantages of this type of clip are its neatness, its freedom from corrosion and the ease with which it can be fixed. This will encourage the electrician to put them in at a close spacing; 6 inches apart is ideal for most jobs. These clips can also be used for holding small sizes of piping.

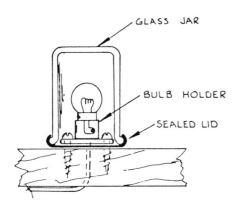

A light for a few pence

This light will appeal to anyone who lives a long way from a yacht chandler, or anyone boatbuilding on a shoestring. This is a watertight light fabricated from a bulb-holder and a baby-food jar. The bulb-holder can be bought from shops like Woolworths.

The jar is inverted and the lid pierced for the electric wire. The bulb-holder is fastened to the lid, and the lid held down on to whatever surface is to take the light. This may be a bulkhead or cabin top coaming, or a beam.

Some form of gasket or bedding material is needed to make the hole where the wire enters watertight. The glass jar screws into the lid tightly but a wipe of grease to ensure watertightness is worthwhile.

The metal parts like the lid must be fully painted, preferably with long-lasting epoxy paints.

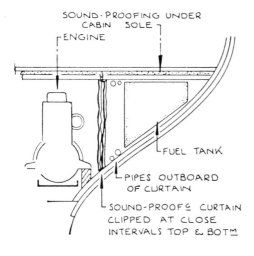

Sound-proofing without tears

Reducing the amount of noise which emanates from an engine into the cabin is difficult. The work can take hours, especially on a finished boat which has all the piping and wiring in place. If the sound-proofing is put on top of the piping, servicing and painting may be awkward. Yet getting the padding under the piping may entail re-running the pipes.

A novel approach is to make up semi-portable curtains of sound-proofing material. Common blanket in layers is surprisingly effective, though of course it needs fire-proofing and making moisture resistant.

The curtains must be secured all round to prevent them touching the machinery. As large a space as possible between engine and curtain should be left to make the sound-deadening effective. Also there should be no gap at the edges and ends of the curtains.

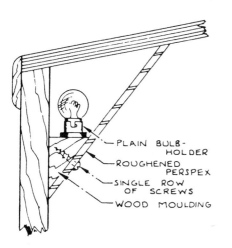

PLAIN BULB-
HOLDER
ROUGHENED
PERSPEX
SINGLE ROW
OF SCREWS
WOOD MOULDING

Novel light

This idea has the merits of simplicity and universality. To make up a cabin light which costs little, yet can be fitted in virtually any space, just mount a common holder behind a piece of Perspex. The essence of the trick is the way the Perspex is treated. It must be roughened with a piece of fine emery paper.

The bulb-holder is mounted on any convenient piece of wood, and shrouded by the Perspex. If the plastic is left clear, the bulb and holder can be seen, and this looks crude. It is best to put the rough side of the Perspex on the outside.

Since the bulb gets hot the Perspex must be kept back a little. However with typical yacht bulbs the heat is so slight that a clearance of ¾ inch is usually adequate.

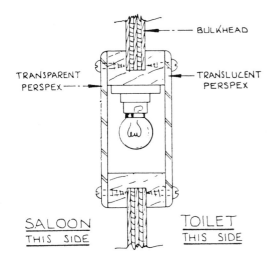

BULKHEAD
TRANSPARENT
PERSPEX
TRANSLUCENT
PERSPEX
SALOON
THIS SIDE
TOILET
THIS SIDE

Light in the loo

It is inconvenient if there is no light fitted in the toilet compartment of a cruiser, yet this light will be used for very few hours in total although there is a risk that it will be left switched on undetected for long periods. A 'do-it-yourself' light fitting can be made which lights both the saloon and the toilet compartment. A slot is cut in the dividing bulkhead and the bulb-holder is screwed to a chock fastened to the edge of the bulkhead. Transparent Perspex panels screwed to the side faces of the chock let light into the saloon and the toilet compartment. On the toilet compartment side the Perspex should be made opaque either by painting it with white paint or rubbing it with fine emery paper. This scheme could also be used between the galley and the saloon.

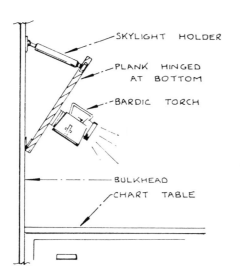

SKYLIGHT HOLDER

PLANK HINGED AT BOTTOM

BARDIC TORCH

BULKHEAD

CHART TABLE

Chart table light

Most yachts carry a powerful torch for steamer-scaring, flashing on the sails and as an emergency navigation light when the mains fail or fuse. It is best to get a torch with a bracket clip on the back, like a bicycle light. However, a bicycle light lacks the power or stamina for this sort of work. One wants a flashlight with a big battery, or set of batteries.

If the torch is just dumped in a locker, its glass may be broken by the other things sharing the locker. The adjustable bracket shown here in section not only holds the torch safely, it also makes it handy for studying charts at night. The Bardic torch has built-in filters, so that a coloured light can be used by the watch on deck to avoid losing full night vision.

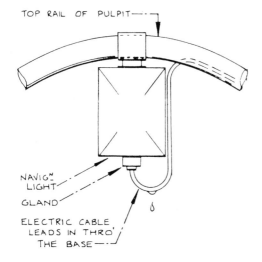

TOP RAIL OF PULPIT

NAVIGⁿ LIGHT

GLAND

ELECTRIC CABLE LEADS IN THRO' THE BASE

Navigation light position

Yacht navigation lights are among the more fallible of man's inventions. It is probably true to say that by mid-season, at least one boat in five is suffering from water in her lights.

Part of the trouble used to be the poor quality of the lights and their flimsy cases. Nowadays there are various types available, some heavy enough to withstand the thump of a spinnaker boom end, but it still pays to give the lights a fighting chance. For a start they should be put under, not on top of, the pulpit or on a special outrigger well ahead of the reach of the spinnaker boom.

If the cable is led in through the bottom, water cannot run down it and into the light. The point of entry needs sealing well.

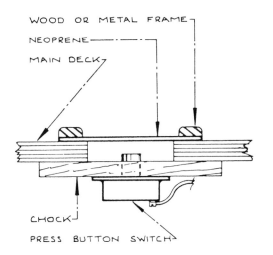

WOOD OR METAL FRAME
NEOPRENE
MAIN DECK
CHOCK
PRESS BUTTON SWITCH

Watertight switch

If an owner claims to have rounded the Fastnet twenty times, believe him. But if he claims to have watertight electric switches, he's a liar almost certainly. Because so many types of switch let in a seepage of sea-water, and because even a tiny drop is enough to cause wide-spread corrosion, few switches can be relied upon even when only a couple of weeks old. The best answer seems to be the oblique approach. Where a switch has to be available on deck, it should be fitted below deck with a waterproof cover. The most obvious type of switch to use is the press button kind, shown here in section. It is easily worked even though there is a flexible cover on top.

If a tumbler switch is chosen, the neoprene cover must be fitted with plenty of slack, or even a fold in it.

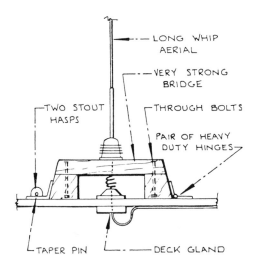

LONG WHIP AERIAL
VERY STRONG BRIDGE
TWO STOUT HASPS
THROUGH BOLTS
PAIR OF HEAVY DUTY HINGES
TAPER PIN
DECK GLAND

Aerial safety

Some folk think it smart and modern to have one or two or even more whip aerials sprouting from the cabin-top, suggesting masses of the latest electronic finery lurking below. But in a bad sea the whip aerials may live up to their name too much and eventually snap off. This is expensive, and may be dangerous, quite apart from the inconvenience of losing radio contact just when it may be most urgently needed.

For this reason it is worth devising arrangements for lowering the whip aerials in moderate weather, in case the sea gets really bad. This sketch suggests one very simple approach. There must be adequate length of wire under the bridge down to the deck to allow the bridge to fold back. Also at least two clips will be needed on deck to grip the lowered aerial.

Tanks, Piping and Plumbing

There are some ocean cruising yachtsmen who refuse to have a single piece of plumbing in their yachts. This is the measure of distrust which they have for the whole paraphernalia of piping and seacocks and suchlike. To be sure, their main dislike is for the ship's side valves because if one of these fails the ship is so easily lost. I know one case where a 45 foot boat sank because one of her lavatory seacocks developed a defect, and remember racing against a 62 foot boat which had to give up because a small pipe fractured, letting gallons of fuel into the bilge.

Probably the source of most troubles in this department at present come from the tendency to imitate house-building practice. There are plenty of good ideas and useful equipment used ashore which can be adapted for yachts, but much higher standards are needed on boats. The use of plastic valves is acceptable, provided they are not going to be asked to stand up to fire, but plastic piping without pipe clips is not acceptable afloat. Indeed a lot of minor leaks on boats stem from using single instead of double pipe clips. Those cheaply built craft which are sold without *any* clips are positively dangerous.

Another reason why this department is so important is the difficulty of making repairs at sea. Quite apart from the inaccessibility of the components, few yachts carry the tools and spares needed to cure a leak in the plumbing or tanks. I feel very strongly about this because on one voyage we had to sail miles off course to Cocos Island, in the hope that there would be someone living there who would have a blow-torch which we could borrow. But the island was deserted, apart from myriads of seabirds, and it was weeks later that the opportunity occurred to borrow the necessary equipment and put the engine back in commission by repairing one small pipe.

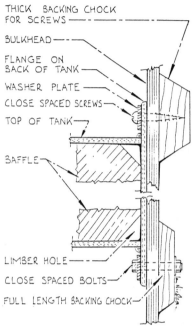

THICK BACKING CHOCK FOR SCREWS
BULKHEAD
FLANGE ON BACK OF TANK
WASHER PLATE
CLOSE SPACED SCREWS
TOP OF TANK
BAFFLE
LIMBER HOLE
CLOSE SPACED BOLTS
FULL LENGTH BACKING CHOCK

Tank fixing

There is nothing so unpleasant as a loose tank thumping around inside a boat which is being thrown about by severe seas. Tanks which are held by encircling straps too often work loose, so the method of securing tanks shown here is commended. The side of the tank, and ideally an end as well, is extended at top and bottom to form a continuous flange which is pierced at close intervals for screws, or better still bolts.

If screws are used they should be spaced typically every 5 inches, and there should never be less than five of them in any flange. Short screws, those under 1½ inches, are not to be trusted, nor are bolts under ¼ inch diameter.

The fastenings must not be put through a bulkhead which has no doubler or backing strap, and this doubler can be a metal angle-bar if bolts are used.

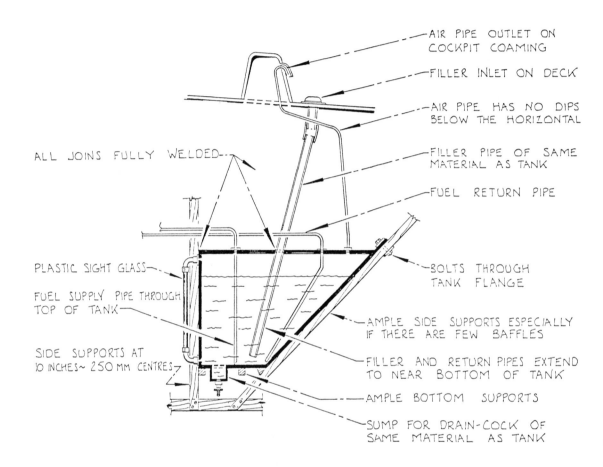

ALL JOINS FULLY WELDED

AIR PIPE OUTLET ON COCKPIT COAMING

FILLER INLET ON DECK

AIR PIPE HAS NO DIPS BELOW THE HORIZONTAL

FILLER PIPE OF SAME MATERIAL AS TANK

FUEL RETURN PIPE

BOLTS THROUGH TANK FLANGE

PLASTIC SIGHT GLASS

FUEL SUPPLY PIPE THROUGH TOP OF TANK

SIDE SUPPORTS AT 10 INCHES ~ 250 MM CENTRES

AMPLE SIDE SUPPORTS ESPECIALLY IF THERE ARE FEW BAFFLES

FILLER AND RETURN PIPES EXTEND TO NEAR BOTTOM OF TANK

AMPLE BOTTOM SUPPORTS

SUMP FOR DRAIN-COCK OF SAME MATERIAL AS TANK

Polypropylene and other tanks

Tanks made of polypropylene are becoming popular because they are light, never corrode, look smart, and are easy to clean. Since the material is not as strong as metal it is best not to rely only on fastenings through edge flanges to hold the tank in place.

The section through the tank illustrated here shows many details which apply to all types of tank. For instance the lead of the supply pipe through the top of the tank reduces the chance of leaks. Running the filler and fuel return pipes to the bottom of the tank cuts out a lot of bubbling and aeration, which can result in a bad fuel supply to the engine and just occasionally to an engine stoppage.

A sump to collect water and dirt is much to be desired, and can be made by using a short length of pipe with the bottom blanked off. There must be good access under the sump to allow a can to be put under it when drawing off water and dirt.

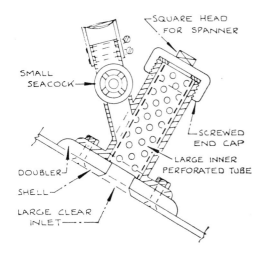

SQUARE HEAD FOR SPANNER

SMALL SEACOCK

SCREWED END CAP

LARGE INNER PERFORATED TUBE

DOUBLER

SHELL

LARGE CLEAR INLET

A money-saver

An amateur boatbuilder could make up this combined filter and inlet for his yacht's engine in an evening or two. The flange should be of bronze, square or round with four bolts. On to this is brazed a wide bore tube, with a standard plumber's blanking off cap on top and a watertight washer inside. Inside the main tube there is a slack-fitting length of tube which forms the filter element: this can have quite thin walls and is drilled all over with ⅛ inch holes. The skin is drilled with a hole slightly less in diameter than the filter element to stop the latter dropping out. Alternatively the hole in the base flange can be of slightly less diameter than that of the inner tube. The lead-off pipe would be of the same diameter as the connection on the engine and probably two or three sizes smaller than the main tube. As the seacock is on the small tube it will be far cheaper than if it had to shut off the large tube.

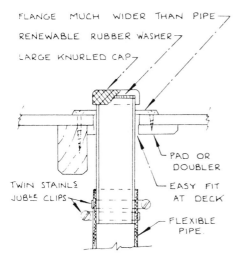

FLANGE MUCH WIDER THAN PIPE

RENEWABLE RUBBER WASHER

LARGE KNURLED CAP

PAD OR DOUBLER

EASY FIT AT DECK

TWIN STAINLS JUBLE CLIPS

FLEXIBLE PIPE

Deck filler

Perhaps because the standard deck filler pipe falls so far short of the ideal, a few people make up their own specials. The cap is large so that it can be tightened down or opened without a special tool yet remains watertight with the help of the flat rubber washer, which is so easy to renew. As the pipe extends well below the deck, it is easy to get at the bottom to slip on the flexible extension to the tank. Because this sort of pipe is so often tucked away, the Jubilee clips are stainless, so that the chances of corrosion are negligible.

Fitting is made easy by the large flange which is well bedded and seals the deck opening. As the flange is wide, the hole in the deck for the pipe can be oversize.

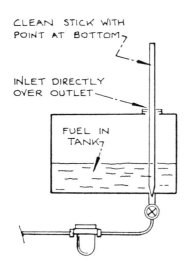

CLEAN STICK WITH
POINT AT BOTTOM

INLET DIRECTLY
OVER OUTLET

FUEL IN
TANK

No fuel spillage

One place where fuel leaks are found is at the cock right under the tank. This is because it is used often and therefore becomes worn.

Replacing this cock can be particularly awkward, because as soon as it is unscrewed, all the fuel in the tank splashes down into the bilge. If the filler cap of the tank is right over the outlet (and where possible it should be made this way) it is only necessary to get a stick, sharpen the end and force it into the fuel outlet pipe. This will stop leaks while the new cock is fitted.

On some small engines the tank is mounted on the engine and a cock may not be fitted. But when the filter element is being changed this pointed-stick trick can be used to stop fuel escaping.

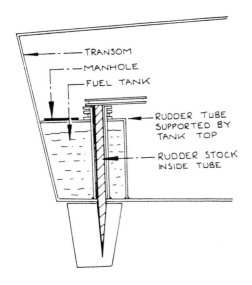

TRANSOM

MANHOLE

FUEL TANK

RUDDER TUBE
SUPPORTED BY
TANK TOP

RUDDER STOCK
INSIDE TUBE

Built-in tank

One of the advantages of building in metal is that tanks can be made part of the ship's structure. If the tank is up against the transom, only a front and top are needed, since the ship's shell provides the other boundaries. This saving in material, welding and cutting not only reduces weight but also saves time and money.

Where the trunk comes in way of the rudder stock, it is necessary to use a little ingenuity. One simple approach is to weld a rudder tube up through the tank, using the tank top as the tube's upper support. The tube stiffens the tank top and vice versa.

Among the advantages of this layout are the low position of the tank, the fact that it uses otherwise wasted space, and it avoids having to place the tank in the bilge.

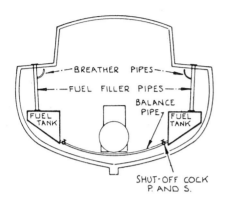

Not the best practice

Just occasionally this piping arrangement is used on yachts in a misguided attempt to keep the air pipes protected from the weather. It is true that the breather pipes are beautifully guarded but there are serious disadvantages. If either tank is filled so fast that excess fuel enters the filler both breathers will discharge fuel into the bilge. Also, if either of the cross pipe cocks is shut off the breathers are useless since they are dependent on the fact that one breather operates whilst the opposite filler is in use.

All breather pipes should terminate on deck in a swan neck bend, that is, one which starts as a vertical rise and turns down through 180 deg. This ensures that any discharge and fumes spill out on deck and so overboard. One good feature in the arrangement illustrated is that the filler pipes are straight which facilitates the use of dipsticks and reduces the chance of air locks.

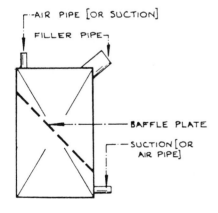

Tank design

This tank can be installed as drawn, or laid on the left side, so that it is a fairly shallow flat tank. Either way the filler will be on top, and the air pipes and the draw-off pipes are interchangeable being of the same diameter. Perhaps the least satisfactory feature is the baffle plate, which will not be fully effective either way. In practice tanks up to about 15 gallons seldom need baffle plates. But where a tank is being made to be suitable for alternative installations, if it does need baffling, the best bet would be to put in two plates at right angles to each other down the centre each way. One or two engine manufacturers already supply their power plants with this sort of fuel tank.

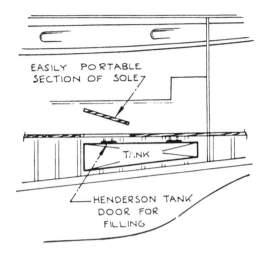

EASILY PORTABLE SECTION OF SOLE

TANK

HENDERSON TANK DOOR FOR FILLING

Plumbing simplification

The Henderson diaphragm pump has become one of the most popular pieces of yacht equipment in recent years. One of its assets is the easily removed back which lets even a ten-thumbed beginner clean out the pump in a matter of seconds.

This portable back, complete with its cam-type catch, is sold as a water tank door. It is just big enough for a man's hand to pass through, which is good for cleaning, yet small enough to ensure that the hole does not weaken the tank.

With a little cunning, this type of mini-manhole cover can be used both for access into the tank for cleaning, and also for filling the tank. The Henderson cover must be conveniently located so that the water cans and hoses can be brought to it. But unlike some of those tiny fillers, no funnel is needed to pour the water in. There is a saving of the deck filler, piping down to the tank and the usual bolt-on manhole. Naturally long tanks will need two or three of these covers.

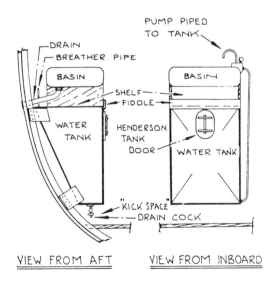

PUMP PIPED TO TANK

DRAIN
BREATHER PIPE

BASIN

BASIN

SHELF
FIDDLE

WATER TANK

HENDERSON TANK DOOR

WATER TANK

"KICK SPACE"
DRAIN COCK

VIEW FROM AFT

VIEW FROM INBOARD

Prefabricated toilet unit

It is not uncommon for the cost of installing a piece of boat furniture to exceed that of manufacture. This is because the interiors of yachts are such irregular shapes. Where possible components should be made off the boat. For the amateur this makes double sense for he can make his furniture at home and take it to the boat for fitting at the weekend.

This basin and tank unit is made up with pairs of lugs each side of the tank. The tank is exactly the same width as one or more frame spaces if the boat is of wood or metal. The tank lugs can then be bolted to the frames and the basin drain led to a skin fitting which should be fitted before installation. There is no other preparation work. Neither vertical heights nor position athwartships are critical.

As the tank is self-contained it acts as an emergency supply if the main tank leaks. The door in the front is for both filling and cleaning out.

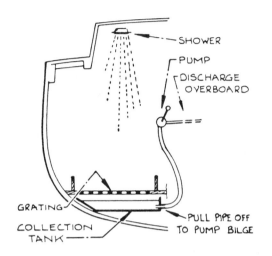

SHOWER

PUMP

DISCHARGE
OVERBOARD

GRATING

COLLECTION
TANK

PULL PIPE OFF
TO PUMP BILGE

Shower arrangement

Installing a shower is an easy and straightforward job.
The rose, as the top spray unit is called, should be small,
with very tiny holes to conserve water. It can be portable
with a flexible water pipe and a stowage hook set near the
deck-head.

To catch the water there must be a tank under the sole
made like a tray with high sides. This is a good place to
use glassfibre, as the tank can be shaped round awkward
projections. Over the tray there should be a teak grating.

To get rid of the used water some people fit an electric
pump, which is poor psychology. A hand pump which
has to be operated by the person taking the shower is a
most effective way of saving water.

This same pump can double as the number two bilge
pump.

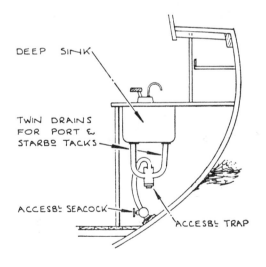

DEEP SINK

TWIN DRAINS
FOR PORT &
STARBᵈ TACKS

ACCESBᴸ SEACOCK

ACCESBᴸ TRAP

Sink drains

An ideal sink for a yacht has two outlets so that no water
is left in the bowl even when the wind is fresh and the
angle of heel is acute. Naturally this means two plugs and
two drain pipes. These should flow to a common trap,
which is easily made from a length of brass tube of about
2½ inch bore, or more. Its bottom end is threaded and
sealed with a pipe end blanking piece such as plumbers'
suppliers sell. The waste runs from the top of the trap.

There must be a seacock at the sink outlet and this
should be easily accessible so that there is no difficulty in
turning it off. It may pay to make the pad inside the hull
wedge-shaped to tilt the seacock handle in the most
convenient direction.

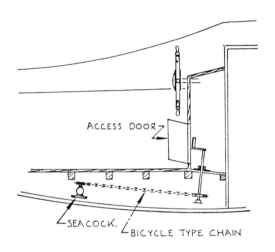

Remote control for a seacock

When leaving a yacht on Sunday night, wise owners shut off all the seacocks. At least they try to, but in this they are sometimes frustrated by those inaccessible taps which lurk under engine sumps. Even if they can be reached, no-one wants to sully his clothes with oil smears.

A designer who was faced with this problem thought out a simple solution. He bolted a chain sprocket to the handle of the cock and led a chain forward to a handle near the steering wheel. This handle was an ordinary car starting handle, set vertically (or nearly so, to take the correct line of the chain). It had a pair of simple bearings, and a chain sprocket fitted near the bottom carefully aligned with the seacock.

The sprockets and chain can be obtained from firms like Reynolds who specialise in this type of equipment and have a vast range. Ordinary bicycle chains and sprockets can be used provided they are heavily greased.

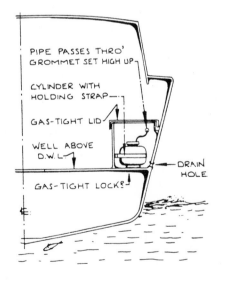

Calor safety

In glassfibre yachts it is particularly easy to make gas-tight lockers, draining directly overboard, for Calor cylinders. This is perhaps the biggest contribution to safety that a designer can work into a yacht. The technique can be used on any yacht, but it is easiest where the construction material is easily made gas-tight. A welded steel or alloy hull, for instance, is particularly suitable for this idea. The box containing the cylinder must be well above the water-line. If the boat is used outside very sheltered waters, the whole casing must be water-tight but for a river boat it is enough that the top is high above the DWL. An important detail is the way the piping is led from the cylinder. There must be no risk that the gas can trickle into the bilge through the hole for the pipe.

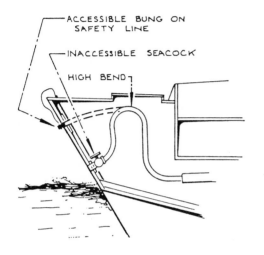

Confound convention

It is an established practice to fit exhaust pipes with a high bend just forward of the outlet and a seacock at the ship's skin, where the exhaust pipe ends. The thinking behind this arrangement is that the seacock is kept shut when the yacht is moored or under sail so that water cannot swill up the pipe. With the high bend right aft the chance of water flooding into the engine is minimised during the period when the yacht is not yet under power.

On a great many boats it is very hard, sometimes almost impossible, to open the seacock. Inevitably the seacock is left open permanently.

An unconventional approach is to lead the exhaust out high up and fit a wood bung. This is safe, cheap and reliable. The bung is near deck level so anyone can whip it out in a jiffy.

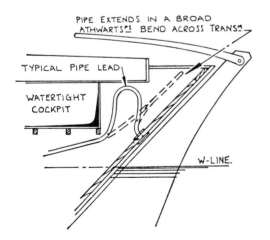

Exhaust pipe sense

One trouble with watertight cockpits is that there is seldom any way to get underneath them. At least on small boats, say under 30 feet, the space beneath is very cramped. Even when you can get under the watertight well, it takes many a long wriggling minute to achieve this access. As a result, there is seldom any way of turning off a seacock in the exhaust pipe. Engineers get over this by fitting the pipe with a large up-sweep just forward of the transom. This is only a half measure. A wave roaring up from astern swamps into the pipe with scarcely a pause. With the aft deck almost submerged, there is plenty of water pressure to force a mini-tidal-wave right up the exhaust into the engine.

The sensible thing to do is to sweep the pipe in a larger curve, but take it aft of the outlet, and turn it athwartships, across the top of the transom and down to the outlet. Every bend must be quite gentle. The dotted line shows the preferred path.

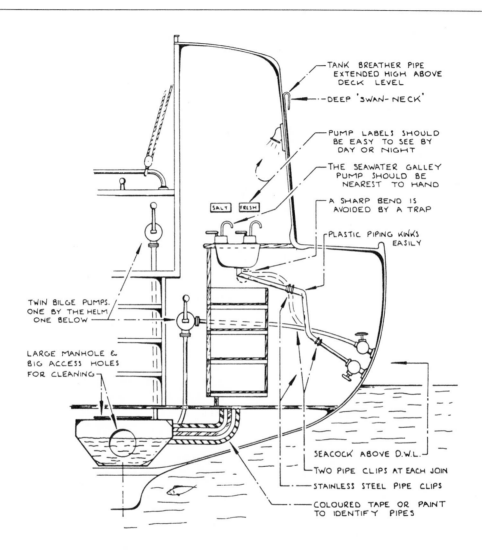

TANK BREATHER PIPE
EXTENDED HIGH ABOVE
DECK LEVEL

DEEP 'SWAN-NECK'

PUMP LABELS SHOULD
BE EASY TO SEE BY
DAY OR NIGHT

THE SEAWATER GALLEY
PUMP SHOULD BE
NEAREST TO HAND

A SHARP BEND IS
AVOIDED BY A TRAP

PLASTIC PIPING KINKS
EASILY

SALT   FRESH

TWIN BILGE PUMPS.
ONE BY THE HELM
ONE BELOW

LARGE MANHOLE &
BIG ACCESS HOLES
FOR CLEANING

SEACOCK ABOVE D.W.L.

TWO PIPE CLIPS AT EACH JOIN

STAINLESS STEEL PIPE CLIPS

COLOURED TAPE OR PAINT
TO IDENTIFY PIPES

Plumbing

Piping is mostly hidden away, ugly and unglamorous. During fitting out a lot can be done to make any yacht more comfortable and safer, by doing a little work on the piping. It is almost all the sort of work that can be done when it is too wet to paint, too windy for varnishing or too cold to be out on deck. Much of it costs very little, like the idea of marking pipes with paint or tape so that they are identifiable throughout their length. This is a particularly valuable idea for a big yacht. No pipe clip of galvanised steel seems able to resist rust for more than one season. It is best to fit stainless clips right away, and forget about them. They should be in pairs, to ensure a life-long seal. For safety, seacocks should be fitted above the water line, at boot-top level, except of course inlet pipes. However some people do not like the appearance of holes in the topsides, even though only just visible. But it is really better to be safe than sorry even if slightly less pretty. Where piping is installed in awkward places it is important to avoid sharp bends, as these cause partial or total blockages.

The reason for having two bilge pumps is that one may fail, seize, become choked, or break at the handle. If the pumps are identical, then one lot of spares will serve for both. A pump by the helm is best for cruising because in an emergency the helmsman can pump and steer while the rest of the crew try to stem the leak. A pump down below is best when hove-to in a gale. Another safety feature is the high breather pipe, well above any water swilling along the side deck, and turned over to a deep swan-neck so that it is virtually impossible to get dirt inside.

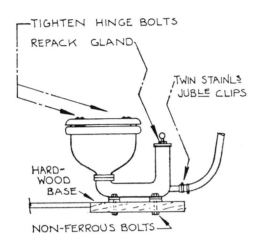

TIGHTEN HINGE BOLTS
REPACK GLAND
TWIN STAINL⁵ JUBLE CLIPS
HARD-WOOD BASE
NON-FERROUS BOLTS

Overhauling the toilet

'A stitch in time' is certainly the motto for anyone who owns a yacht with a pump type toilet. These machines will work efficiently for years if given a chance, but they can require yearly overhaul if they are not properly installed.

They should be mounted on a well-painted hardwood base, or a glassfibre or corrosion-proof metal pedestal. Through bolts that will not rust are needed to keep the bowl rigid, otherwise it is likely to get cracked. At almost any cost, avoid using coach screws, certainly never use ordinary screws.

When fitting out test all the bolts for tightness. If the Jubilee clips are crusted with rust, throw them away and fit a pair of stainless steel ones, with the screws at opposite sides of the pipe. After all, it would be ignominious to admit to having sunk your own yacht through a leaking loo.

Not every make has packable glands at the pump.

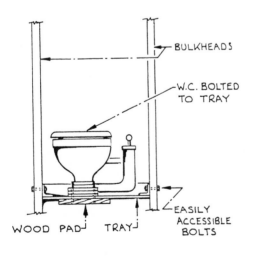

BULKHEADS
W.C. BOLTED TO TRAY
EASILY ACCESSIBLE BOLTS
WOOD PAD   TRAY

Securing the w.c.

A job which is difficult in any small yacht is the fastening down of the w.c. Whatever the type and construction of the boat, often it is difficult to tighten up the holding down bolts. These bolts are usually right under the machinery, two of them are at the back so that they are both out of sight and out of reach.

A different approach to this problem is shown here. A strong tray is made to fit between the bulkheads of the toilet compartment. Its up-turned flanges are bolted easily through the bulkheads. The tray is then removed from the boat and the toilet fitted to it. Probably a wood pad will be needed under the tray in way of the bolts for local stiffness.

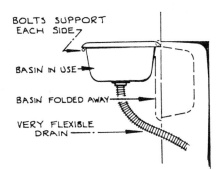

BOLTS SUPPORT EACH SIDE

BASIN IN USE

BASIN FOLDED AWAY

VERY FLEXIBLE DRAIN

Unobtrusive washbasin

The toilet compartment of most yachts is cramped. It is sometimes possible to steal a few inches from an adjacent compartment, to box this in and hinge the basin into the recess. The basin can then be located so that it swings out and drains straight into the lavatory.

Of course there is no reason why the basin should be in the toilet compartment. It could perhaps be in the forward cabin. In this type of installation the drain pipe must not be the usual relatively rigid plastic piping as this will not adapt itself properly to the stowed position. The basin can be either a simple plastic bowl or a purpose-made article bought from a chandler. In either case, two stout barrel bolts will be needed as supports in the raised position.

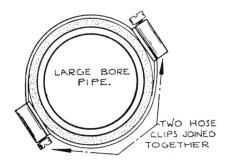

LARGE BORE PIPE.

TWO HOSE CLIPS JOINED TOGETHER

Emergency pipe clip

It is a basic law of yachting that the piece of equipment needed vitally, in a hurry, is out of stock in the chandlery and local hardware shop, nor is it to be found aboard friends' yachts on the same mooring. This is why yachtsmen are such versatile, inventive people.

Some nameless genius produced this idea to cover the absence of a big pipe clip. He found that if two clips are unscrewed and straightened out, the tail of one put in the mouth of the other and its tail put in the opposite mouth, a big pipe clip results.

Yacht Tenders, Dinghies and Liferafts

Stowing yachts' tenders has always been vexing. Plenty of designers have seen their best creation spoilt afloat by the awkward arrangement of the dinghy. When inflatable dinghies came on the market it looked as if our difficulties were cured, but we soon found out that it is a tedious job inflating and deflating every time we came into harbour and wanted to go ashore for a brief time. So we are still involved with stowage problems. A friend of mine, admittedly not a racing fanatic, has taken a bold line. He ties the painter to a halyard and hauls away, till the dinghy, which incidentally is a wood one, rises bow first up the mast. Then he lowers away a little, till the transom settles at the base of the mast. Finally he puts a couple of lashings round the mast and the dinghy nestling vertically against it. There are severe limitations to setting sails, but he is a good engineer and his motor never fails, which is just as well as the extra windage is formidable!

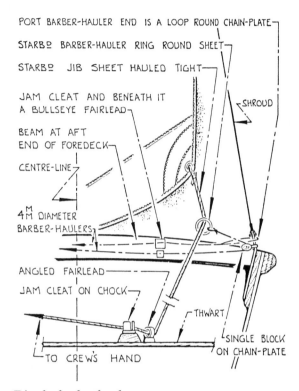

PORT BARBER-HAULER END IS A LOOP ROUND CHAIN-PLATE

STARB⁰ BARBER-HAULER RING ROUND SHEET

STARB⁰ JIB SHEET HAULED TIGHT

JAM CLEAT AND BENEATH IT A BULLSEYE FAIRLEAD

BEAM AT AFT END OF FOREDECK

CENTRE-LINE

4ᴹ DIAMETER BARBER-HAULERS

ANGLED FAIRLEAD

JAM CLEAT ON CHOCK

TO CREW'S HAND

SHROUD

THWART

SINGLE BLOCK ON CHAIN-PLATE

Dinghy barber hauler

This is the view looking forward on the Kilda 12-foot racing dinghy which costs just £300 to build. The barber hauler on the starboard side starts at a plastic ring round the headsail sheet and goes outboard to a little block fixed to the chain-plate then inboard to a bull'seye fairlead on the beam at the aft end of the fore-deck; next it goes to a small jam cleat on the port side, on the same beam, and it terminates in a loop tied loosely round the port chain-plate so that the end does not get lost in the bilge.

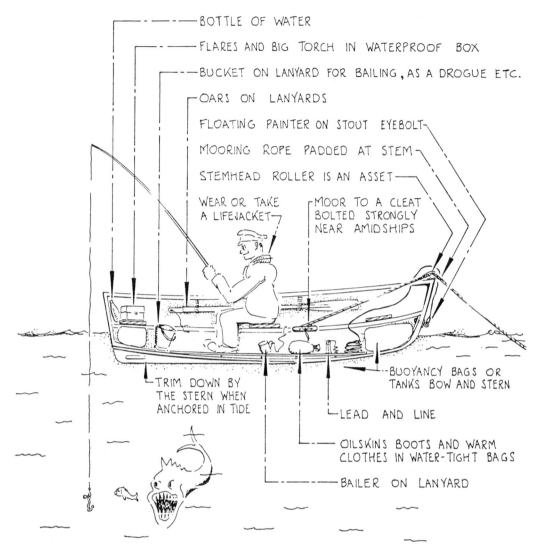

BOTTLE OF WATER

FLARES AND BIG TORCH IN WATERPROOF BOX

BUCKET ON LANYARD FOR BAILING, AS A DROGUE ETC.

OARS ON LANYARDS

FLOATING PAINTER ON STOUT EYEBOLT

MOORING ROPE PADDED AT STEM

STEMHEAD ROLLER IS AN ASSET

WEAR OR TAKE A LIFEJACKET

MOOR TO A CLEAT BOLTED STRONGLY NEAR AMIDSHIPS

TRIM DOWN BY THE STERN WHEN ANCHORED IN TIDE

BUOYANCY BAGS OR TANKS BOW AND STERN

LEAD AND LINE

OILSKINS BOOTS AND WARM CLOTHES IN WATER-TIGHT BAGS

BAILER ON LANYARD

A day's fishing

Accidents afloat are rare, but a substantial proportion of them occur in small open boats. Racing dinghies tend to be supervised by rescue boats, and they are home by dark. Anglers and crews coming ashore from cruisers tend to be unwatched, so if they have trouble they have to cope by themselves.

The rules to follow can be summed up:

Make sure the boat and crew float even when the boat is flooded.

Make sure everything is tied into the boat.

Make sure vulnerable equipment stays dry by putting it in watertight containers.

Have more than one means of calling for help.

This sketch also shows how a mooring rope should be secured so that the crew can haul it in without going right forward and depressing the bow of the boat so that water floods in. While riding at moorings in a strong tide a boat which is down by the bow may sheer about, possibly in a dangerous way, which is why it is important to trim down by the stern.

The lead line is useful to gauge whether the boat is dragging her anchor. If the bucket is to be used as a drogue to check drift it must be one of those tough ones made for farmers. The domestic kind are too flimsy for use afloat.

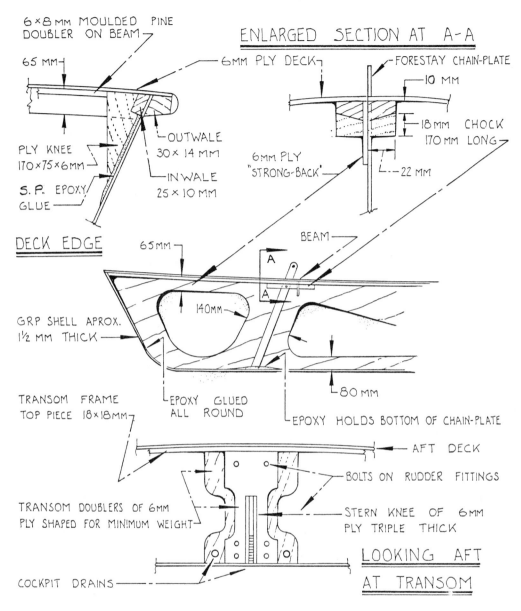

6×8 MM MOULDED PINE
DOUBLER ON BEAM

65 MM

6MM PLY DECK

PLY KNEE
170×75×6 MM

OUTWALE
30×14 MM

INWALE
25×10 MM

S. P. EPOXY
GLUE

ENLARGED SECTION AT A-A

FORESTAY CHAIN-PLATE

10 MM

18 MM CHOCK
170 MM LONG

6MM PLY
"STRONG-BACK"

22 MM

DECK EDGE

65mm

BEAM

A

A

GRP SHELL APROX.
1½ MM THICK

140mm

80 MM

TRANSOM FRAME
TOP PIECE 18×18MM

EPOXY GLUED
ALL ROUND

EPOXY HOLDS BOTTOM OF CHAIN-PLATE

AFT DECK

BOLTS ON RUDDER FITTINGS

STERN KNEE OF 6MM
PLY TRIPLE THICK

TRANSOM DOUBLERS OF 6MM
PLY SHAPED FOR MINIMUM WEIGHT

COCKPIT DRAINS

LOOKING AFT
AT TRANSOM

Contender construction

This drawing shows details of the Contender class dinghy, built by David Spy, but the ideas can be used on other boats. The sketch top left indicates a good way of joining a light ply deck to a glassfibre hull, with strong beam endings.

The centre drawing shows the way that the bow is strengthened to prevent the whole hull flexing in rough conditions. It also shows how the severe stresses on the forestay are contained. Top right the enlarged detail explains how the deck is kept watertight at the forestay.

An attractive feature is the way the main under-deck stringer is tapered to reduce its weight, and the 170 mm long chock nestles on the tapered under surface.

All fast light boats tend to have problems in the area of the pintles so it is worth studying the way this dinghy has tapered-out doublers in way of the rudder fastenings. Inessential wood is cut away, and corners are well rounded. Also (not shown) the ply edges are all rounded as much as possible. This helps the varnish adhere well, and saves a little more weight.

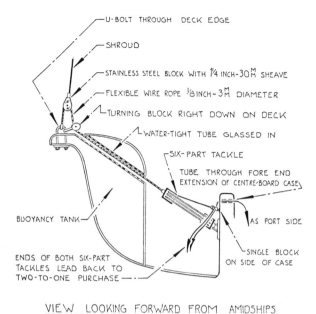

U-BOLT THROUGH DECK EDGE

SHROUD

STAINLESS STEEL BLOCK WITH 1¼ INCH-30ᴹ SHEAVE

FLEXIBLE WIRE ROPE ⅛ INCH-3ᴹ DIAMETER

TURNING BLOCK RIGHT DOWN ON DECK

WATER-TIGHT TUBE GLASSED IN

SIX-PART TACKLE

TUBE THROUGH FORE END EXTENSION OF CENTRE-BOARD CASE

AS PORT SIDE

BUOYANCY TANK

SINGLE BLOCK ON SIDE OF CASE

ENDS OF BOTH SIX-PART TACKLES LEAD BACK TO TWO-TO-ONE PURCHASE

VIEW LOOKING FORWARD FROM AMIDSHIPS

Simple sure shroud tensioner

When running dead down-wind, the crew of a dinghy want to slacken off the shroud tension so that the boom swings as far forward as possible and hence presents the largest possible sail area to the breeze. The arrangement shown here is the one standardised by Milanes and White (formerly Rondar) on their 505s.

Perhaps the most difficult part of the arrangement to fabricate is the tube which passes through the buoyancy tank, because it must be entirely watertight. A more primitive arrangement would consist of a wire leading inboard over the top of the buoyancy tank with chafing strips of half-round stainless steel or brass to protect the tank.

The power at the crew's hand is 24 to one, as the six-part tackle is doubled up at the base of the shroud and also on the hauling part of the six-part tackle (though the latter is not shown in this sketch). The tube through the forward extension of the centre-board has belled out ends to ease the rope's passage, and there is bound to be a little loss to friction here when tightening the shrouds.

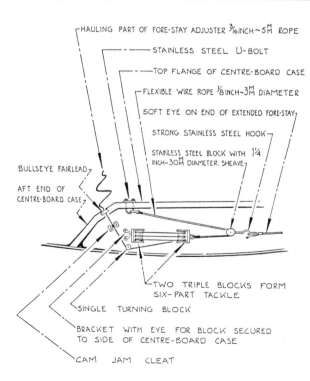

HAULING PART OF FORE-STAY ADJUSTER ³⁄₁₆ INCH~5ᴹ ROPE

STAINLESS STEEL U-BOLT

TOP FLANGE OF CENTRE-BOARD CASE

FLEXIBLE WIRE ROPE ⅛ INCH~3ᴹ DIAMETER

SOFT EYE ON END OF EXTENDED FORE-STAY

STRONG STAINLESS STEEL HOOK

STAINLESS STEEL BLOCK WITH 1¼ INCH-30ᴹ DIAMETER SHEAVE

BULLSEYE FAIRLEAD

AFT END OF CENTRE-BOARD CASE

TWO TRIPLE BLOCKS FORM SIX-PART TACKLE

SINGLE TURNING BLOCK

BRACKET WITH EYE FOR BLOCK SECURED TO SIDE OF CENTRE-BOARD CASE

CAM JAM CLEAT

Forestay tensioner

This is a view looking to port on a standard 505 built by Milanes and White. It shows that the very powerful forestay tensioning arrangements are effective yet simple. They could be adapted with little change for a wide variety of craft, but the anchoring points must be as strong as the loads on them are high.

Some owners will prefer a snap shackle instead of the open hook which engages on the soft eye splice at the end of the forestay. One advantage of this layout is that the forestay precise length is not important. With this arrangement and adjustable shrouds the rake of the whole rig can be adjusted quickly when sailing.

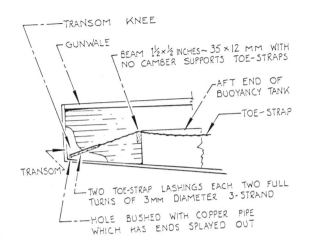

TRANSOM KNEE

GUNWALE

BEAM 1½×½ INCHES~ 35 × 12 MM WITH NO CAMBER SUPPORTS TOE-STRAPS

AFT END OF BUOYANCY TANK

TOE-STRAP

TRANSOM

TWO TOE-STRAP LASHINGS EACH TWO FULL TURNS OF 3MM DIAMETER 3-STRAND

HOLE BUSHED WITH COPPER PIPE WHICH HAS ENDS SPLAYED OUT

Toe-strap securing

The aft ends of the toe-straps must be secured in such a way that there is not the slightest chance of breakages, even with heavy crew throwing themselves outboard energetically. The arrangement shown here has the advantages that it is cheap, easily adjusted and renewed, and the securing lashings are onto a reliable and rugged part of the boat's structure.

The beam across the aft ends of the buoyancy tanks strengthens the boat enormously and is particularly valuable if the transom is light or much cut away.

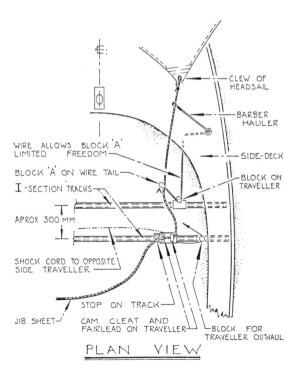

CLEW OF HEADSAIL

BARBER HAULER

WIRE ALLOWS BLOCK 'A' LIMITED FREEDOM

BLOCK 'A' ON WIRE TAIL

I-SECTION TRACKS

SIDE-DECK

BLOCK ON TRAVELLER

APROX 300 MM

SHOCK CORD TO OPPOSITE SIDE TRAVELLER

STOP ON TRACK

JIB SHEET

CAM CLEAT AND FAIRLEAD ON TRAVELLER

BLOCK FOR TRAVELLER OUTHAUL

PLAN VIEW

Racing dinghy headsail arrangement

Though this lay-out was fitted on an Albacore it is suitable for a great variety of boats. It enables the crew to locate the headsail clew wherever they want in a vertical, fore-and-aft and athwartships position.

The I-section tracks across the boat contribute to the strength of the hull and are ideal for sliding carriages because they allow easy movement.

The location of the jib-sheets jam cleat on the lee side suits heavy weather when the crew will be to windward and light conditions when they may be to leeward.

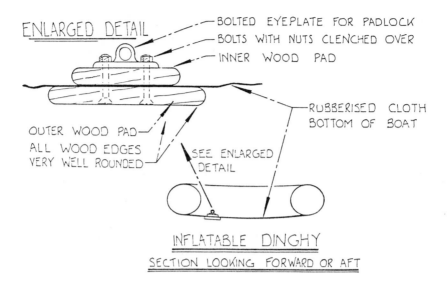

ENLARGED DETAIL

- BOLTED EYEPLATE FOR PADLOCK
- BOLTS WITH NUTS CLENCHED OVER
- INNER WOOD PAD

OUTER WOOD PAD
ALL WOOD EDGES
VERY WELL ROUNDED

SEE ENLARGED DETAIL

RUBBERISED CLOTH
BOTTOM OF BOAT

INFLATABLE DINGHY
SECTION LOOKING FORWARD OR AFT

Burglar-beating

Inflatables are too easy to steal, but this device will deter any thinking thief. An eyeplate is fixed to the inside of the bottom of the boat, with bolts that are clenched over so that they cannot be taken out without slow tedious filing to remove the burred-over heads. A strong padlock and chain secure the dinghy to a railing or electricty pylon or the yacht club commodore's Rolls Royce if he is not using it.

The thief can cut away the bottom of the boat to take it away, but he will have a very leaky vessel and one which he cannot sell to anyone but a very blind yachtsman.

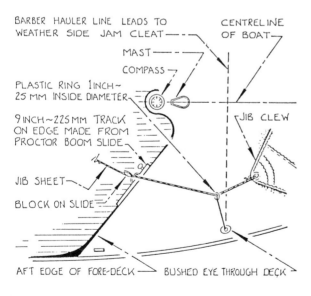

BARBER HAULER LINE LEADS TO
WEATHER SIDE JAM CLEAT

CENTRELINE
OF BOAT

MAST

COMPASS

PLASTIC RING 1INCH~
25 MM INSIDE DIAMETER

9INCH~225MM TRACK
ON EDGE MADE FROM
PROCTOR BOOM SLIDE

JIB CLEW

JIB SHEET

BLOCK ON SLIDE

AFT EDGE OF FORE-DECK

BUSHED EYE THROUGH DECK

Jib sheet control of racing dinghy. (Plan view of port side)

The layout shown here was seen on a 14 foot dinghy, but it can be used on a lot of racing boats. Each barber hauler runs under the foredeck, round a single turning block on the windward side, and aft to a jam cleat near the crew's position.

Eyes like the one which takes the barber hauler through the deck should have smooth metal bushes otherwise they wear too quickly. The lead block on the slide will be a ratchet one on all but the smallest size of dinghy to reduce the load on the crew's hands in strong winds.

Racing dinghy toestraps

If a toestrap fails, the crew fall overboard and the dinghy capsizes. Most failures occur at the fastenings so it is intelligent to minimise the loading on the screws or bolts. This is easily done by wrapping the toestraps round a thwart, as shown here in section. Some people prefer to sew the toestrap back on itself, but two screws are still needed to prevent the strap sliding along the thwart.

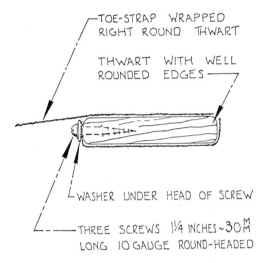

TOE-STRAP WRAPPED RIGHT ROUND THWART

THWART WITH WELL ROUNDED EDGES

WASHER UNDER HEAD OF SCREW

THREE SCREWS 1¼ INCHES ~ 30 M LONG 10 GAUGE ROUND-HEADED

Fixing toestraps to the transom

Because the transom is strong it is an ideal place to fix the aft end of toestraps. However screws should not be used here, and even bolts need more than ordinary washers to prevent the toestraps from tearing away.

Plate washers, which may be made of marine grade aluminium drilled with lightening holes for minimum weight, are the thing for a situation like this. They must have well rounded edges otherwise the toestrap material will quickly chafe through.

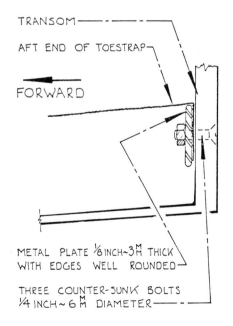

TRANSOM

AFT END OF TOESTRAP

FORWARD

METAL PLATE ⅛ INCH ~ 3 M THICK WITH EDGES WELL ROUNDED

THREE COUNTER-SUNK BOLTS ¼ INCH ~ 6 M DIAMETER

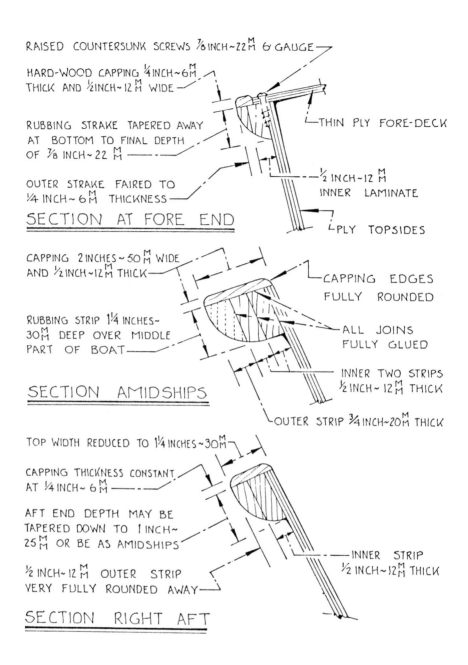

RAISED COUNTERSUNK SCREWS ⅞ INCH ~ 22 M & GAUGE

HARD-WOOD CAPPING ¼ INCH ~ 6 M THICK AND ½ INCH ~ 12 M WIDE

THIN PLY FORE-DECK

RUBBING STRAKE TAPERED AWAY AT BOTTOM TO FINAL DEPTH OF ⅞ INCH ~ 22 M

½ INCH ~ 12 M INNER LAMINATE

OUTER STRAKE FAIRED TO ¼ INCH ~ 6 M THICKNESS

PLY TOPSIDES

SECTION AT FORE END

CAPPING 2 INCHES ~ 50 M WIDE AND ½ INCH ~ 12 M THICK

CAPPING EDGES FULLY ROUNDED

RUBBING STRIP 1¼ INCHES ~ 30 M DEEP OVER MIDDLE PART OF BOAT

ALL JOINS FULLY GLUED

INNER TWO STRIPS ½ INCH ~ 12 M THICK

SECTION AMIDSHIPS

OUTER STRIP ¾ INCH ~ 20 M THICK

TOP WIDTH REDUCED TO 1¼ INCHES ~ 30 M

CAPPING THICKNESS CONSTANT AT ¼ INCH ~ 6 M

AFT END DEPTH MAY BE TAPERED DOWN TO 1 INCH ~ 25 M OR BE AS AMIDSHIPS

INNER STRIP ½ INCH ~ 12 M THICK

½ INCH ~ 12 M OUTER STRIP VERY FULLY ROUNDED AWAY

SECTION RIGHT AFT

12 foot racing dinghy gunwale

These sections show the gunwale of the Kilda dinghy. She cost only £300 complete, but that does not prevent the construction from being strong and elegant.

Each laminate is just thin enough to wrap round the curve of the hull; the thicker outer strip only extends over the mid-ships part of the boat where additional strength is needed and where the extra width makes sitting out more comfortable.

The capping piece is of hard wood to reduce wear and to match up with the mahogany ply of the planking. It protects the ply top edge and is well rounded, like the rest of the gunwale.

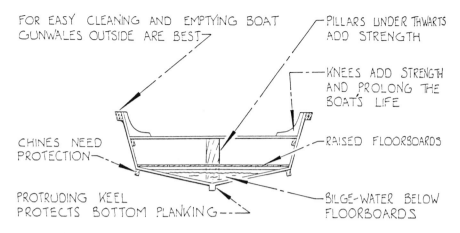

FOR EASY CLEANING AND EMPTYING BOAT GUNWALES OUTSIDE ARE BEST

PILLARS UNDER THWARTS ADD STRENGTH

KNEES ADD STRENGTH AND PROLONG THE BOAT'S LIFE

CHINES NEED PROTECTION

RAISED FLOORBOARDS

PROTRUDING KEEL PROTECTS BOTTOM PLANKING

BILGE-WATER BELOW FLOORBOARDS

Good features in a yacht's tender

Whether buying or building a solid dinghy as a yacht's tender, these are the features which make for comfort and convenience. The mid-section is veed, not flat athwartships, partly for easier rowing and outboarding, partly for strength, and partly to keep the bilge-water under the floorboards.

Most boats get hauled up beaches and slip-ways often, and some protection on the bottom is needed to keep wear to an acceptable level. It is best to have bottom rubbers which are renewable easily, and many builders bolt strips of hardwood fore and aft, with ample bedding at each fastening to prevent leaks. By using bolts the strips are easily renewed when worn out.

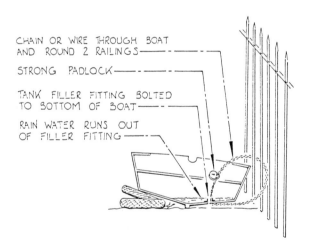

CHAIN OR WIRE THROUGH BOAT AND ROUND 2 RAILINGS

STRONG PADLOCK

TANK FILLER FITTING BOLTED TO BOTTOM OF BOAT

RAIN WATER RUNS OUT OF FILLER FITTING

Thief-proofing

To stop thieves from taking a dinghy fit a drain plug in the bottom. When coming ashore leave the dinghy close to a strong fence or other unmovable structure. Thread a length of chain or old rigging wire with an eye at each end through the drain plug and round the fence. A massive padlock discourages thieves who are by their nature lazy people, easily put off by anything that looks hard to beat. Take the plug home, with the oars and rowlocks, then even if the thief does cut through the chain he will not be able to use the dinghy. The drain unit can be a tank filler fitting, available from any chandler.

This idea can be used on a racing dinghy with the chain through a self-bailer or transom drain.

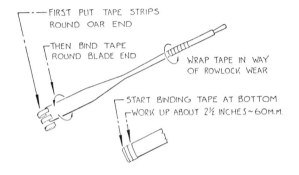

FIRST PUT TAPE STRIPS ROUND OAR END

THEN BIND TAPE ROUND BLADE END

WRAP TAPE IN WAY OF ROWLOCK WEAR

START BINDING TAPE AT BOTTOM
WORK UP ABOUT 2½ INCHES~60M.M.

For better oar worse

The majority of oars these days are used on rubber dinghies. These inflatables often have rowlocks which will not accept oars which are leathered or which have that modern equivalent of leathering, the oar sheath. As a result oars are wearing out faster than boats, an absurd state of affairs since oars used to last almost indefinitely.

One answer is to protect the end and the wearing part of the loom with lengths of glassfibre tape bonded with resin. One inch (25 mm) wide tape works well, though if it is not available 1½ oz chopped strand mat with a finishing cloth over can be used. To avoid chafing a glued-on rubber rowlock the resin should be applied thickly to give a smooth final finish.

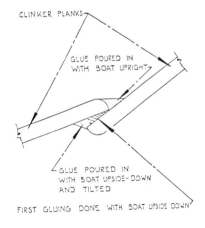

CLINKER PLANKS

GLUE POURED IN WITH BOAT UPRIGHT

GLUE POURED IN WITH BOAT UPSIDE-DOWN AND TILTED

FIRST GLUING DONE WITH BOAT UPSIDE DOWN

Modern clinker planking

Using epoxy glue it is now quite easy to build a clinker dinghy. No metal fastenings are needed, but each plank join should be reinforced with three runs of glue.

The boat will first be assembled by gluing up each plank edge join, and when all the planks are on the boat is turned upside down and more epoxy glue run into the outsides of each join. It will probably be necessary to tilt the dinghy and thicken the glue a little to ensure the resin fills the gap between the planks. Finally the dinghy is set the right way up and the same procedure followed inside. Filling the 'lands' makes cleaning and varnishing or painting easier, and makes each plank edge join massively strong.

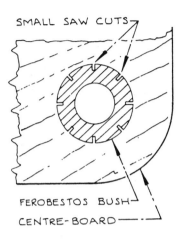

SMALL SAW CUTS

FEROBESTOS BUSH

CENTRE-BOARD

Centreboard bushing

It is bad practice to allow the pivot pin of a centreboard to bear directly on wood or metal without bushing the hole. A metal plate will wear the pin and a wood board will become sloppy through the hole being enlarged. It is not unusual to find bushes simply pressed home and in general this is often adequate, but the bush may rotate in its hole or drop out and get lost when the board is removed, so there is a good case for gluing in the bush.

However, the glue is unlikely to hold efficiently on a self-lubricating bearing pressed into a tight hole. For this reason it is a good plan to make a series of tiny saw cuts round the outside of the bearing to give a key to the glue.

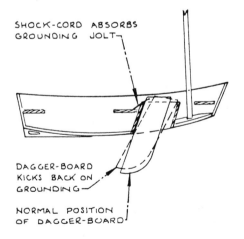

SHOCK-CORD ABSORBS
GROUNDING JOLT

DAGGER-BOARD
KICKS BACK ON
GROUNDING

NORMAL POSITION
OF DAGGER-BOARD

Dagger board safety device

When adding sails to a knockabout dinghy there is a temptation to fit a pivoting centreboard. The argument goes like this: if we run aground the board may get a bit chipped but it will swing up and there will not be much damage.

However, the long slot needed for a good centreboard chops so much strength out of the hull which may not have been designed originally for such radical surgery. As knockabout dinghies need a deep plate, the problem cannot be solved by fitting a short centreboard.

A reasonable compromise is a dagger board with a slightly over-long case and a slot about half the length of that required for a pivoting centreboard. The board is held down and aft by shock cord, which can be adjusted for tension by trial and error. If the boat grounds the board pivots a few degrees and deceleration is not too violent. In this way damage is minimised.

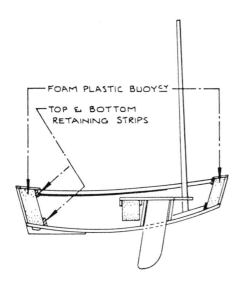

FOAM PLASTIC BUOYCY

TOP & BOTTOM
RETAINING STRIPS

Economical buoyancy

A simple form of buoyancy can be made from slabs of
expanded polystyrene. This material is available from
many timber merchants and home decorator's shops
which supply insulation, decorative and other types of
boarding. It is sold in sheets 8 ft by 4 ft, in various
thicknesses – generally up to 3 inches thick. It is also
available in thicker slabs, but few retailers hold these in
stock. However, it is easy enough to use several pieces to
build up the required thickness. Buoyancy from
polystyrene is not necessarily cheaper than buoyancy
bags, as far as initial outlay is concerned, but it does
not develop punctures, so it is probably cheaper in the
long run.

Its main weakness is a tendency to chip at the corners,
but if the retaining battens are placed at the edges they
will provide protection.

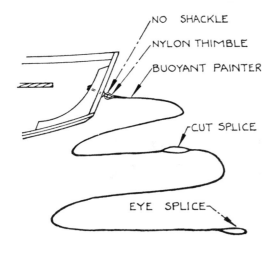

NO SHACKLE

NYLON THIMBLE

BUOYANT PAINTER

CUT SPLICE

EYE SPLICE

A modern painter

There are two modern ropes which float and are therefore
most suitable for dinghy painters. They are Courlene and
Ulstron. The former is very tough and hard-wearing
under the most adverse conditions as well as being very
springy. It lasts for ages even when scuffed by gravel and
mud on hards or chafed on quay walls. In many respects
it is ideal, but its very special qualities also make it hard
to knot and inclined ιo come undone. For this reason it is
best to splice an eye in the end to fit exactly over the
parent yacht's cleats. A second splice about halfway
down is useful when it is necessary to secure the dinghy
on a short scope.

The advantages of a floating painter are not only the
unlikelihood of the rope becoming wound round the
propeller, but the line is easy to fish out of the water.

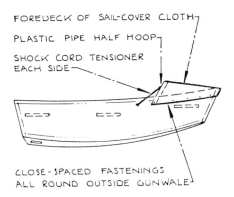

FOREDECK OF SAIL-COVER CLOTH
PLASTIC PIPE HALF HOOP
SHOCK CORD TENSIONER EACH SIDE

CLOSE-SPACED FASTENINGS ALL ROUND OUTSIDE GUNWALE

Safer dinghies

Yachtsmen most often have accidents when going to and from their yachts, while in the tender. This is small wonder when the size and shape of some yachts' dinghies are examined. Making a dinghy more seaworthy is a relatively simple job. Naturally plenty of buoyancy material is the first requirement. Just as valuable is any arrangement which stops water coming aboard. A simple turtle deck can be made which will throw off any errant wave, yet add little to the weight or windage of the dinghy, but it will be in the way if someone wants to sit on the bow thwart. However that may discourage overloading, which in itself is a major cause of accidents.

A variety of materials can be used for this turtle deck, but it is advisable to avoid any which will rot if left permanently wet. Also the best materials are those which can withstand rough usage, such as Terylene, canvas and heavy plastic tubing.

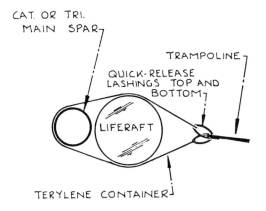

CAT. OR TRI. MAIN SPAR
TRAMPOLINE
QUICK-RELEASE LASHINGS TOP AND BOTTOM
LIFERAFT
TERYLENE CONTAINER

Cruising cat safety

There is the ever-present risk that a cruising cat (or tri) will turn over, if she is one of the unballasted type. If this occurs the liferaft is likely to be needed and any raft stowed snugly inside one of the hulls is going to be quite inaccessible.

It is therefore essential to devise stowages which make it possible, in fact downright easy, to get the liferaft launched regardless of which way up the multihulled craft is floating.

A simple solution is to have part of the trampoline in the form of an envelope which can be opened from on top or 'underneath'. The envelope must be rot-proof material and laced up over hooks or similarly fastened so that release is obvious and quick.

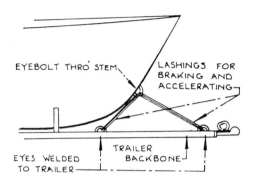

Stemhead eyebolt

When trailing it is imperative that the boat is securely lashed down. It is fairly easy to keep the hull in place with straps taken from a strongback athwartships on the gunwales down to the main frame of the trailer. When we look at the lashings and chocks and other securing members, however, we find there is little or nothing to stop the boat sliding forward when the brakes are slammed on in an emergency.

A really stout eyebolt fitted to the stem just above the forefoot is particularly useful on any boat which spends a considerable proportion of its life on a road trailer.

It can take lashings extending forward and aft to eyes on the trailer. There is often a suitable point to take the forward lashing but a second point further aft to take the other lashing will usually have to be fitted. It may be a welded eye, or a bolted eyeplate or U-bolt.

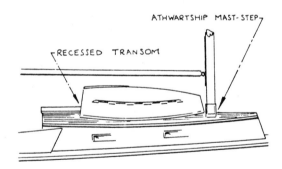

Dinghy space

Getting a dinghy to fit on to a cabin top is one of those multiple compromise plans. The dinghy should be as large as possible, but a large tender overlaps the hatch, restricts access and reduces forward visibility. If the dinghy is too small it is useless for going ashore, being insufficiently seaworthy. It is also too small to get a kedge off, too small to carry a week-end's gear and too small to carry an outboard. Factors of top weight, windage and boom clearance must also be taken into consideration.

When the mast is stepped on the cabin top the mast step often forces the bow of the dinghy aft. This is because the step is usually fairly long fore and aft. However it is sometimes possible to make the step extend arthwartships with quite a small fore and aft dimension which allows the stem of the dinghy to nestle right up to the mast.

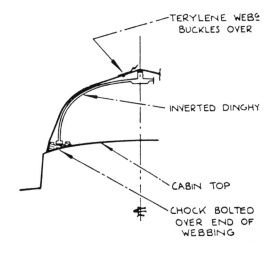

Dinghy on deck

Even experienced yachtsmen have difficulty in lashing a dinghy down really tight. The suitable knots, like a Carter's Hitch, are not popularly known, and other knots are too prone to leave the lashings slightly slack.

By using Terylene webbing with buckles even beginners will be able to get the dinghy tightly strapped down. At least two sets of webbing are needed, and it is usual to cross them.

Fixing down the ends of the webbing straps must be done carefully, since anything so slovenly as a couple of screws will soon let go. A good scheme is to slip the webbing straps under the dinghy chocks before the latter are bolted down. The bolts must pass through the webbing, and drilling through the webbing calls for care. The best technique is to melt the holes out using a bolt heated over a cooker flame.

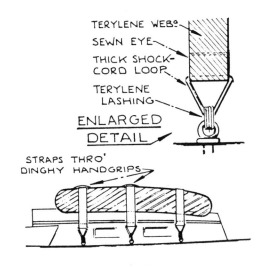

Secure dinghy straps

A rubber dinghy which has been inflated is quite difficult to fix down. It is hard to secure due to the resilience of the hull and also it varies in size according to the temperature. When the sun beats down the air inside gets hot and expands, especially if the rubber is dark and absorbs a lot of heat. At night the dinghy cools and its lashings are likely to slacken.

The use of combined shock cord and Terylene webbing makes an inflatable's lashings easier to secure and safer. For offshore work there should be more than the usual crossed pair and for ocean cruising one would advocate four or even more. Flat Terylene webbing is to be preferred to rope which will chafe at one particular point. It is true that firms like Avon can do a remarkable job renewing large panels of their inflatables but one does not want to have to make repairs before the season is over.

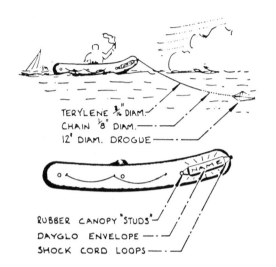

TERYLENE ⅜" DIAM.
CHAIN ⅛" DIAM.
12' DIAM. DROGUE

RUBBER CANOPY "STUDS"
DAYGLO ENVELOPE
SHOCK CORD LOOPS

Drogue for inflatables

Inflatable rubber dinghies present problems when it comes to attaching accessories and painting names. Painting is not easy, so it is worth while making up a name panel and tying it to the bow. If the name is sewn on a piece of brightly coloured material such as Dayglo plastic the dinghy will be easy to pick out in a crowd.

Inflatables drift down-wind very fast. If an oar is lost the situation can quickly get out of hand. The boat will drift faster than the oar and this type of boat is impossible to paddle with one oar in a strong wind.

If the name panel is made in the form of an envelope, a drogue can be stowed inside complete with a short length of light chain (to make the drogue sink).

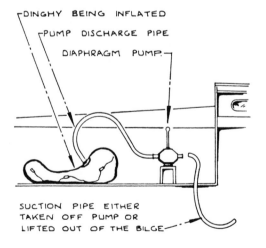

DINGHY BEING INFLATED
PUMP DISCHARGE PIPE
DIAPHRAGM PUMP

SUCTION PIPE EITHER TAKEN OFF PUMP OR LIFTED OUT OF THE BILGE

When the bellows are lost

Inflatable dinghies can be blown up with a diaphragm bilge pump. If the bellows have been left at home, dropped overboard or broken there is no need to be marooned aboard.

The first job is to make sure there is no water left in the pump or its piping. If the pump inspection cover is removed this will drain the casing; the piping should be held at a slope to get all the dregs out. The suction can either be detached from the pump casing, or it may be easier to lift the bottom end up to cabin level, taking care it cannot drop back into the bilge. If any water gets into the dinghy it will be hard to remove!

The pump is worked in the ordinary way with the discharge pipe end held over each valve in turn until the dinghy is fully inflated.

Inexpensive inflatables

On a small sailing or motor-cruiser, under 22 ft overall, the dinghy can be a massive problem. Towing the dinghy, even with ample horse-power in a calm sea, is a miserable business. There is the constant worry that the tender will break adrift or fill or turn over, or do all three in succession.

Anyone who tries to tow a sensible size of conventional dinghy behind a small sailing cruiser soon finds that useful progress is tedious work except down wind and tide.

Naturally the next consideration is an inflatable dinghy. Costs rear their ugly head. A conventional inflatable dinghy can cost 15% of the parent yacht or even more. The student or newly married couple, pinching to buy a mini-cruiser, do not have much cash to spare for a dinghy. They could make a wood one for about the cost of

the materials, but this is often too bulky and heavy to carry aboard. On the other hand a little inflatable can be carried in the fore peak or deflated and lashed on deck of a cruiser only 17 ft long. These blow-up boats tend to have a short life but they are so cheap that it is good economics to write them off every three years. There is virtually no maintenance whereas a wood boat can easily cost 8% of its new value to maintain each year.

One trouble about these little inflatables is that they are hard to row in a strong tide or wind. A combination of adverse tide and fresh wind makes them impossible. For this reason their use is limited to going ashore in reasonably protected moorings. Also the very small versions are no more than toys. An overall length of 7 ft is the bottom limit and even 8 ft is rather small for most moorings.

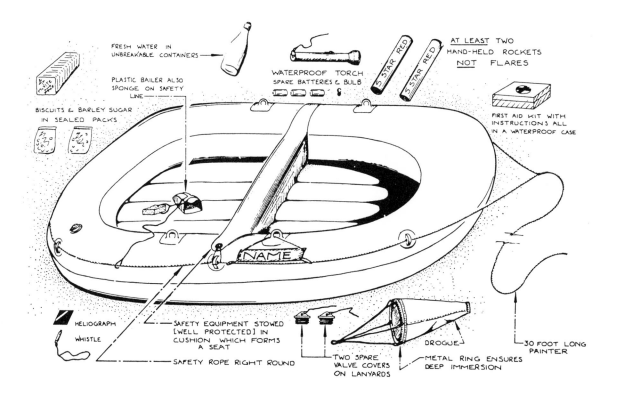

Naturally this cheap inflatable can never be a substitute for a proper liferaft. But then on a small cruiser there is not room for a full-blooded inflatable raft. Its weight, especially with a glassfibre casing, is unacceptable on many boats under 25 ft overall. The cost can be as much as 20% of the total cost of a secondhand four-berth cruiser. This is often too much for a hard-up owner, who may seldom go on a serious cruise anyway.

Safety is partly a matter of seamanship, and this in turn is largely a matter of preparation. It is not enough to equip a dinghy with emergency equipment. Practice with the gear is also essential. This is how I came to discover just how ineffective the average hand-held flare is. No! I didn't sit offshore of a Coastguard station lighting hand-flares and timing the arrival of my rescuers. I took ashore at the end of the season the flares and rockets. On November 5th, having assembled a crowd of children, we had a firework display. The hand-flares proved less reliable than 5-Star rockets, burned less brightly and were hard to start. In contrast the 5-Star rockets seem to have a longer shelf-life, go much higher so are likely to be seen even over high waves, and each star moves in a trajectory so that it is more likely to draw attention to itself than a relatively motionless hand-flare – even one whirled overhead.

On some cruisers the dinghy can be carried fully inflated. Particularly on motor-cruisers where weight and windage aloft are less pressing, the dinghy might be stowed fully blown-up on wheelhouse top, cabin top or foredeck. Anywhere in fact where it is out of the way and does not impede vision. On a sailing cruiser the stowage situation is likely to be more acute. However it may be possible to fit the dinghy snugly by deflating one half and folding that part over. The fold should be carefully made because a crease along one line subject to any pressure on the fold will wear the material and cause leaks. A half-inflated dinghy gives a better chance of survival than a life-ring and if the pump is available and can be worked the result will be much better than a water-logged solid dinghy.

Some of the small inflatables are sold with inadequate painters and grab-lines. Depending on such factors as the local rise-and-fall height of tide, the painter should be around 25 or 45 ft. If it is of ⅜ inch (8 mm) diameter Ulstron it will float and so is unlikely to get wound round propellers.

An expensive inflatable dinghy needs some modifications to make it suitable for general cruising. The cheaper types need even more attention. And because an inflatable is sometimes called upon to act as a lifeboat, it is sensible to equip it for the job. Even if an inflatable liferaft is carried the dinghy may have to save life. There are more accidents, far more, between the shore and the parent yacht than there are on full-sized yachts.

In some places frequented by yachts the tide is so strong that it is easy for a strong oarsman to be swept out to sea, especially in an inflatable which is relatively hard to row. A beginner or a man getting on in years can find himself in trouble in rivers and estuaries even during a neap ebb. Such places as Burnham, Fleetwood, parts of Poole can be awkward if not downright dangerous. It is not too bad if one can flash a torch or burn a 5-Star rocket and get help. To drift helpless within sight of friends and potential rescuers is enough to make one die of frustration before something more serious occurs.

Incidentally the 5-Star rockets, which cost a bit more than hand-flares, seem to retain their red colour, which not all flares do. A white-looking flare will just be mistaken for a steamer-scarer, and not bring help.

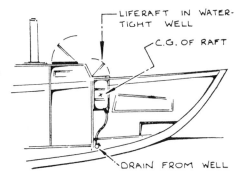

LIFERAFT IN WATER-TIGHT WELL

C.G. OF RAFT

DRAIN FROM WELL

Liferaft locker

All safety equipment should be stowed so that it is readily available in an emergency. In the case of a liferaft this means stowage on deck, usually on the foredeck or aft deck because these are the only convenient locations. When building a new yacht or modernising an old one this deep deck locker arrangement can be used. The weight is relatively low and the raft does not clutter up the deck; there is no risk of a heavy sea washing the raft overboard. A rope handle should be attached to the liferaft container and led to an eye on the underside of the hatch. A drain should be fitted so that the locker can be drained.

Anchors, Chain and Warps

Anchoring is something of an art, in that it is far from an exact science. Whereas some can achieve neat success even when alone aboard, in a cramped harbour, in spite of a raging gale, others fail miserably and drag. They drag their two anchors even when the fates and geography are in their favour. It is usually because they have insufficient scope.

Scope and weight, these two are the arch-angels which look after yachtsmen. The boat which never seems in trouble when anchored probably has been designed by someone who follows a simple rule: double everything; put aboard at least two anchors, and for distant cruising have four. Make the anchors, chain and warps twice as long and as strong as calculation and common usage suggests.*

This may sound excessive, but go aboard any yacht which has sailed over the far far horizon and come back unscathed. In the old days she would have had baggy-wrinkle and ratlines. Nowadays she looks like a great number of other yachts, till her ground tackle is examined.

One trouble about this double-everything rule is that special gear may be needed to handle the resulting weight. This results in more heavy equipment, including winches, maybe a cat davit, or a long tackle and bearing-out spar, perhaps special flat bow-fenders. There is scope here for the ingenious designer, because this is a relatively neglected field.

---

* Tables of sizes of anchors and gear are given in the author's publication *Boat Data Book*.

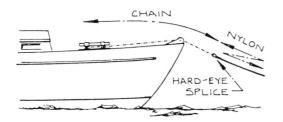

Safe anchoring

The increasing popularity of nylon and Terylene for anchoring calls for new techniques. It is usual to insert a length of chain between the anchor and the warp to take the ground chafe and also to give a nearly horizontal pull on the anchor.

At the top of the warp various ideas have been used to absorb the chafe at the stemhead. A piece of canvas bandaged round the rope is scarcely adequate for even one night. Some owners use a length of plastic tube over the rope. But plastic chafes and bends sharply at the nip over the roller.

When the chips are down it is hard to beat metal on metal. This means either wire or chain. In practice wire is lightest but awkward to handle and liable to fatigue failure, especially if the same part always bears on the roller. This brings us back to chain, which has few disadvantages.

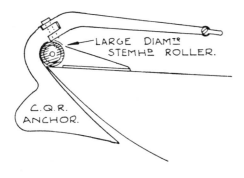

Ready-for-use anchors

Say what you like, the motor-yacht owner has one great advantage over his sailing friends. On a power yacht you can have a hawse-pipe, so that when you want to anchor you release the chain and the anchor roars out, all within seconds.

This is seldom possible on sailing yachts. However, a near substitute is to have a big stemhead roller, with a CQR anchor hauled up onto it. The chain will be easier to pull over the large diameter roller, but that is just a secondary asset.

The idea of the large roller is that it will act as a comfortable stowage for the anchor. With the chain tightened firmly and with flanges up either side of the roller, that anchor is there to stay, even if the yacht capsizes. To anchor, it is only necessary to release the chain and tip the aft end of the stock up a little. Gravity and the big roller do the rest.

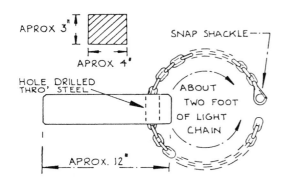

APROX 3"

APROX 4'

HOLE DRILLED
THRO' STEEL

SNAP SHACKLE

ABOUT
TWO FOOT
OF LIGHT
CHAIN

APROX. 12"

Anchor weight

It is well appreciated that anchors can be made to hold in bad weather by hanging a weight on the chain about half way between the yacht and the anchor. This weight has two functions. It makes the lead of the chain from the anchor more nearly horizontal, so that the anchor is less likely to pull out. Secondly the weight damps down the snatch as the boat throws her bows up when a wave passes under her. It is this jerk upwards that often dislodges an anchor.

It used to be traditional to use a pig of ballast as the weight. These normally weigh about 56 lb. For many people they are too heavy to handle on a small yacht in rough weather.

To get over this, it is suggested that a steel bar be used. It has a hole drilled in one end through which passes a light chain. The chain is shackled round the anchor chain outboard, with the weight *still on deck*. A line is tied to the bar which is then lifted outboard and slid down the anchor chain.

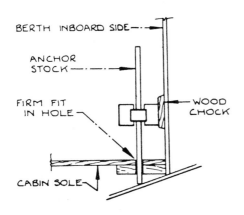

BERTH INBOARD SIDE

ANCHOR
STOCK

FIRM FIT
IN HOLE

WOOD
CHOCK

CABIN SOLE

Secure anchor

If an anchor is stowed on the fore cabin sole its weight is low and forward, and so in the best place to improve performance. A good stowing arrangement is shown here. A hole in the sole exactly fits the stock so that to stow the anchor, it is just dropped on edge into its home. It is wedged by a wood pad which also prevents the anchor from damaging the berth side. The anchor is ready for instant use, since there are not even any lashings round it, yet it takes up no important space.

It is worth copying this arrangement for the second anchor (or the third) where the main anchor is stowed ready for use on deck. Naturally the deck stowage arrangement will not be used by anyone who is all out for racing speed. Boats which go far offshore do need a safety lashing on each anchor stowed below.

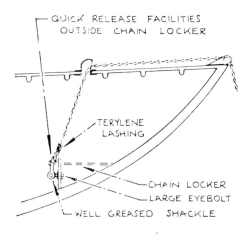

The chain end

All the cruising books describe how the inner end of the anchor chain should be well lashed so that it can be let go in an emergency. But this is only half the story. The lashing must be of Terylene, nylon, or of Courlene, otherwise it will rot. It must be accessible, so that it can be cut or untied even when the bulk of the chain is in the locker. Above all, it should not be a simple lashing between the last link and the eyebolt, since this would fail when there was a sudden heavy jolting load on the chain. The chain should be passed through a big shackle and lashed back on itself. By keeping the shackle well greased the crew have the choice in an emergency of cutting the lashing or undoing the shackle.

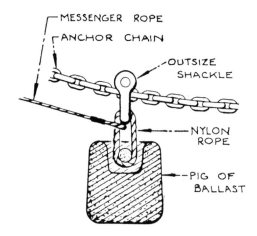

Home-made angel

To improve the holding power of an anchor there is a well-established technique involving the use of a pig of ballast. This weight is lowered down the chain until it hangs about half way between the sea-bed and the yacht. In this position it prevents the chain pulling taut easily and also lowers the angle at which the chain leads away from the anchor.

It is possible to buy special large shackles called angels for securing the weight to the chain. However a large shackle, such as is sometimes found in a dusty corner of an old-style ships' chandler, works well, and provides weight itself. This type of shackle cannot normally be hooked into a ballast pig, so a link is needed. A loop of nylon or similar rope can be used, but natural fibres like hemp or manilla are less satisfactory as they chafe too easily.

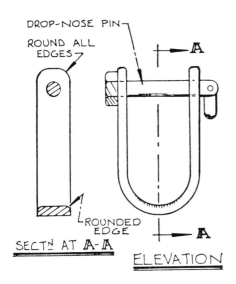

DROP-NOSE PIN

ROUND ALL
EDGES

ROUNDED
EDGE

SECT<u>N</u> AT A-A

ELEVATION

Angel shackle

Because a yacht's ground tackle is her best insurance, it should be given every aid to efficient operation. For instance anchor flukes should be kept sharp. Once the anchor is down, a weight on the chain helps it to hold.

To get the weight down on the chain, this simple shackle is worth making. It can be fabricated from 1 inch by ¼ inch steel for yachts up to 25 feet and from 1½ inch by ⅜ inch steel for yachts up to about 35 feet.

For craft around the 45 foot size it would be best to use something like 2 inch or 2½ inch by ½ inch or even ⅝ inch. The pin should have a diameter of about one third of the major size of the shackle. So for sizes under 25 feet a ⅜ inch diameter pin would be about right.

The shackle should be galvanised after completion. The pin is easy enough for an amateur to make out of bronze.

The Belfast anchor

The Belfast anchor, illustrated on page 196, will suit racing yachts because it comes apart and so can be stowed below the sole, which is the best place for weighty gear. On a cruising yacht there must be two anchors in case one is lost, or the boat has to be moored in severe weather. Normally one anchor is carried on the foredeck but it can be quite a problem to find space for the other. Wherever it is put, it knocks shins, chafes sail bags and damages all sorts of less flinty equipment. Under the sole it will do very little damage but it must be a Belfast type – others are almost always too wide to fit.

On a big yacht, even with a strong crew, it can be quite a job getting the anchor up from below onto the foredeck. The Belfast can be lugged up in pieces and assembled at the bow, then lifted over the side by the cat davit or a foresail halyard, or spinnaker boom and its topping loft. For assembly on a pitching foredeck nuts and bolts could with advantage be replaced by quick-action fasteners which must of course be non-corrosive.

Another attraction of this anchor is that it can be amateur made. Not everyone has a welding set, but the cutting, drilling and filing are all easy enough. This means it is possible to fabricate an anchor to suit a particular boat instead of taking the best of a poor selection. Naturally all sorts of refinements can be introduced, to make the anchor easier to assemble, though in practice these will make the anchor more complex. This will put up its price if professionally fabricated.

This plan gives proportions which are based on what past experience recommends. Anyone making a larger or smaller anchor should maintain the proportions, but for use in very soft mud the palm area can be increased. If the anchor is *only* used in soft mud then the arms can be set at a wider angle to the shank.

Sometimes an owner has to leave his boat on her own anchor while he goes home for a few days. This is always a worry because the tide may swing the yacht round several times, till the anchor chain is thoroughly wound round the upstanding arm. With the Belfast pattern this risk is eliminated by taking off one arm. A shackle is put through one of the then unused bolt holes and the anchor is lowered in a horizontal position by rope down to the sea-bed, so as to make sure the remaining arm digs in. To make quite certain, the yacht's engine should be run astern to check that the anchor is holding.

For this sort of situation the shank can be filled with lead or iron to give it extra weight.

Another advantage relates to the sharpness of the palms. These should cut easily into the sea-bed. Normally it is difficult to sharpen an anchor's flukes, and once done the whole anchor needs regalvanising. With this pattern the arms are removed for sharpening on a grindstone. Notice how the tips are pointed outwards, that is to say, the grinding off is on the inner face of the palm. Once the re-grinding is complete only the arms need regalvanising.

This anchor got its name because its original design and early development were sponsored by the Belfast Ropework Co.

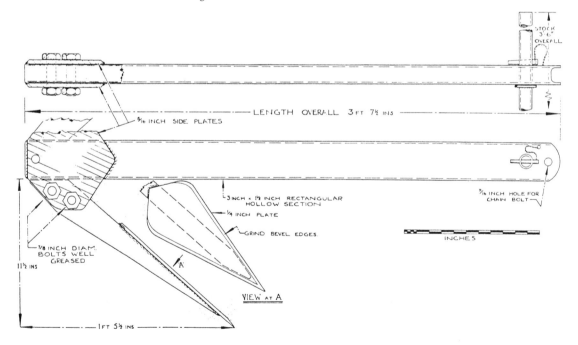

Fitting Out and Laying Up

In some yacht yards each new boat, as building commences, is allocated a special notebook. This contains all her vital statistics and information. On one page will be a list of rigging sizes, on another a schedule of blocks, on another the type and bore of the seacocks and so on. I remember visiting one yard and finding an air of subdued conspiracy mixed with mirth. The resident designer had lost this all-important notebook and as he was young and too bumptious no-one would help him find it. The poor fellow was in a great state, because it is vastly inconvenient to have so much important information mislaid. Much of it, but by no means all, is on the plans. However it takes a lot of time and trouble to extract the details which will be scattered through several plans.

When fitting out a similar notebook is at least a help, and often essential if all the details are to be remembered. If the book is kept aboard all summer then a jotted note of each defect as it occurs will save hours in the winter. It is probably best to divide the book into sections relating to rigging, engine, electrics and so on. Each job will have its own page, as space is needed to list parts and material needed to make each repair.

Another help is a few big photos of the boat on moorings and under way. These will show up all sorts of details from rust streaks to sail puckers, from bent stanchions to the need to realign the boot-top.

Both the photos and the notebook should be kept from year to year and used as references. Another asset is a text book because this acts as a reminder. It is so easy to forget to look at the skin fitting bolts annually, yet they are just as vulnerable and important as keel bolts.

Fitting out is easiest in the autumn when other people are slacking off. Yards are not pressurised, chandlers have time to discuss the best make and type of fitting, sail-makers are looking for work.

Fitting out afloat takes twice as long as ashore, and when actually at sea, even very simple jobs are difficult or impossible.

Once the information is available, good tools are the next essential. Every boat bigger than a dinghy needs such basic things as a hacksaw and spare blades, the best available hand drill and a range of drills from $\frac{1}{16}$ up to $\frac{1}{2}$ inch (1 to 12 mm), a set of chromed spanners, big and small screwdriver, a set of new files, adjustable Stillsons, and so on. Some larger and expensive tools, like a super-long set of Stillsons and an electric orbital sander, might be shared between owners, because they are not needed often.

One good technique is to explain to one's family how undesirable socks and ties are at Christmas. Point out that even *yacht club* ties are nothing like so acceptable as a new ratchet brace when the old one has rusted up, or a key-hole saw, a spare set of drills because they *break* so often, or one of those handy saws which seem designed for small cruisers because they cut wood or metal, and have adjustable handles to cope with awkward corners.

Once the tool locker is properly stocked then the cunning owner leaves carefully marked chandlers' catalogues lying about the house. Fitting out is so much easier if there is a ready supply of spare shackles of all sizes, a full range of spare blocks, plenty of thin line for lashings and whippings and seizings.

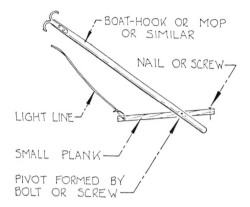

BOAT-HOOK OR MOP
OR SIMILAR

NAIL OR SCREW

LIGHT LINE

SMALL PLANK

PIVOT FORMED BY
BOLT OR SCREW

Bilge salvage

In a boat with a deep bilge, if a tool is dropped it can be
impossible to reach down to retrieve the lost item. This
simple recovery tool can be made up from gear on board.
It can also be used to get things up from the sea-bed
where the water is too dirty for bathing, as it tends to be
in commercial harbours. Yet another use is recovering a
halyard tail which has gone aloft. When a boat is laid up
is the ideal time to recover all those tools and treasures
which have dropped into deep inaccessible corners of the
bilge.

Ocean cruisers

Those that are purpose-built for the job are, on the
whole, better suited to their task than conversions.
If a conversion it has to be, however, see that cockpit
coamings are adequately deep and strong, change
lightweight portlights for a sturdier pattern. See that
the tiller is very strong. If a really prolonged passage is
contemplated, see that a new suit of sails is ordered and
choose a sailmaker who is used to producing a rugged
sail. New sails should be used for a fortnight or so and
then sent back to the sailmaker to have any necessary
chafing patches sewn on in the right places. Protect the
areas chafed by the lower shrouds and crosstrees as a
matter of course.

All deck hardware should be the best that is available,
though the depth of the owner's pocket must be
considered here. The mooring post must be capable of
holding the boat during a hurricane and navigation
lights should be displayed so that they are unlikely to be
hidden by high waves. After long exposure to sea and
weather, corrosion can become a particular enemy. Make
sure that rigging screws are kept in good working order
and wire up their barrels so that they cannot unscrew.

Efficient ventilation for the ends of the yacht and the
main accommodation is particularly important. See that
fresh air can get below even in bad weather. Make
arrangements to keep the hatches open to some degree as
long as possible. If conditions degenerate to a point
where it becomes necessary to batten down completely,
see that the measures make the boat as tight as a
submarine.

To lessen rigging stresses, rigging angles should be
wide. Twin backstays are better than a single wire and
two lower forward shrouds are preferable to just one wire
taken from the mast to the centreline.

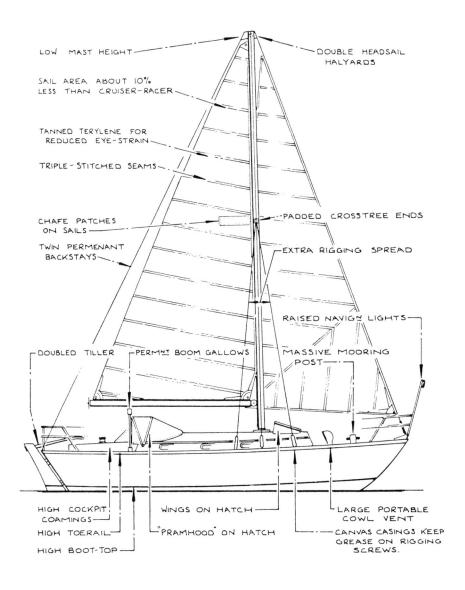

LOW MAST HEIGHT

DOUBLE HEADSAIL HALYARDS

SAIL AREA ABOUT 10% LESS THAN CRUISER-RACER

TANNED TERYLENE FOR REDUCED EYE-STRAIN

TRIPLE-STITCHED SEAMS

CHAFE PATCHES ON SAILS

PADDED CROSSTREE ENDS

TWIN PERMENANT BACKSTAYS

EXTRA RIGGING SPREAD

RAISED NAVIGN LIGHTS

DOUBLED TILLER

PERMNT BOOM GALLOWS

MASSIVE MOORING POST

HIGH COCKPIT COAMINGS

WINGS ON HATCH

LARGE PORTABLE COWL VENT

HIGH TOERAIL

"PRAMHOOD" ON HATCH

CANVAS CASINGS KEEP GREASE ON RIGGING SCREWS.

HIGH BOOT-TOP

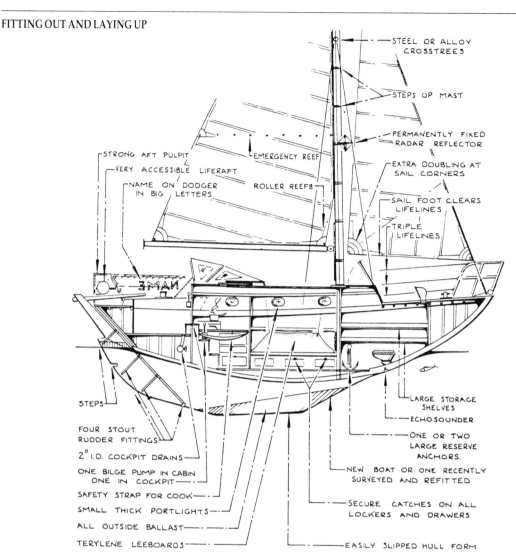

STEEL OR ALLOY CROSSTREES

STEPS UP MAST

PERMANENTLY FIXED RADAR REFLECTOR

EXTRA DOUBLING AT SAIL CORNERS

SAIL FOOT CLEARS LIFELINES

TRIPLE LIFELINES

STRONG AFT PULPIT

VERY ACCESSIBLE LIFERAFT

EMERGENCY REEF

NAME ON DODGER IN BIG LETTERS

ROLLER REEFS

LARGE STORAGE SHELVES

ECHO SOUNDER

ONE OR TWO LARGE RESERVE ANCHORS.

NEW BOAT OR ONE RECENTLY SURVEYED AND REFITTED

SECURE CATCHES ON ALL LOCKERS AND DRAWERS

EASILY SLIPPED HULL FORM

STEPS

FOUR STOUT RUDDER FITTINGS

2" I.D. COCKPIT DRAINS

ONE BILGE PUMP IN CABIN ONE IN COCKPIT

SAFETY STRAP FOR COOK

SMALL THICK PORTLIGHTS

ALL OUTSIDE BALLAST

TERYLENE LEEBOARDS

More and more skippers are taking their yachts further afield, and a number of crews have taken unmodified stock cruisers for long trips even though the boats, originally, may have been designed for short period cruising or cruiser racing. A yacht which is intended for ocean cruising must be easy to handle and maintain. Because such a yacht is likely to find herself in remote corners of the globe where spare parts and overhaul facilities may be hard to come by, it is important that the boat is fitted out so that she is as self-sufficient as possible and equipped with gear that is particularly reliable. The yacht should be fitted with substantial lifelines all round to prevent a man from falling overboard. If, in spite of this, a member of the crew is unfortunate enough to fall over the side, then it can be an advantage to have footholds in the trailing edge of the rudder to aid recovery. The true offshore yacht requires a secondary pump in case the main pump fails. There are reef points in the mainsail just in case the roller gear fails, and fit metal crosstrees because even the strongest ones in wood have some tendency to split. Two anchors are too few except in the smallest ocean cruiser and the inflatable liferaft should be stowed aboard in such a way that it can be launched in a rush.

With synthetic materials there is less tendency to chafe, but precautions are still necessary to help protect sails and rigging. Crew comfort is most important: make sure that bunks are fitted with deep leeboards and that there are high fiddles on all shelves. The cook and navigator must be able to work efficiently while the yacht is in a seaway. See that all locker fronts are provided with catches which will hold everything shut while the yacht is being flung about at sea.

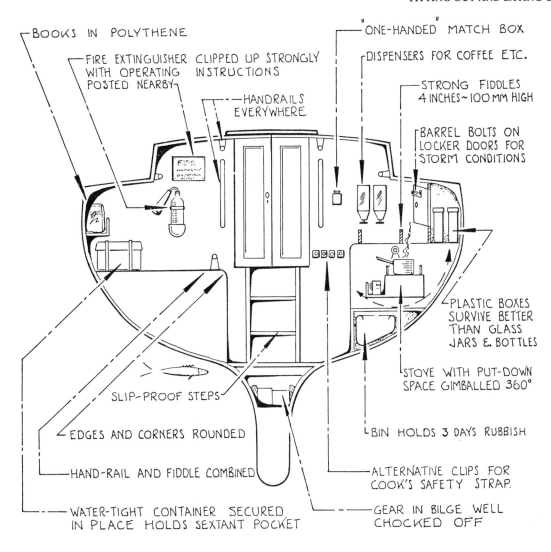

BOOKS IN POLYTHENE

FIRE EXTINGUISHER CLIPPED UP STRONGLY
WITH OPERATING INSTRUCTIONS
POSTED NEARBY

HANDRAILS
EVERYWHERE

"ONE-HANDED" MATCH BOX

DISPENSERS FOR COFFEE ETC.

STRONG FIDDLES
4 INCHES ~ 100 MM HIGH

BARREL BOLTS ON
LOCKER DOORS FOR
STORM CONDITIONS

PLASTIC BOXES
SURVIVE BETTER
THAN GLASS
JARS & BOTTLES

STOVE WITH PUT-DOWN
SPACE GIMBALLED 360°

SLIP-PROOF STEPS

EDGES AND CORNERS ROUNDED

HAND-RAIL AND FIDDLE COMBINED

WATER-TIGHT CONTAINER SECURED
IN PLACE HOLDS SEXTANT POCKET

BIN HOLDS 3 DAYS RUBBISH

ALTERNATIVE CLIPS FOR
COOK'S SAFETY STRAP.

GEAR IN BILGE WELL
CHOCKED OFF

Deep sea details

Comfort and safety offshore depend on ideas like the
ones shown here. That 'one-handed' matchbox, secured
to the bulkhead just aft of the cooker, is such a boon when
the boat is heavily heeled and jumping about. So are the
dispensers which make it easy to meter out the correct
amount of coffee, powdered soup or sugar into each mug.

Under the galley the gash bin has turned-over top
edges to prevent rubbish escaping even in rough
conditions. If the boat gets a knock-down the stove will
swing over without hitting the hull or galley lining.

All doors and drawers need reliable fixings to keep
them shut regardless of what antics the boat gets up to,
and barrel bolts are ideal for this job. They are widely
available, cheap, easy to keep lubricated and easy to open
and close.

Items like fire extinguishers which are sold complete
with supporting brackets often need extra clips or
straps to hold them in place. The common type of bracket
is possibly satisfactory in a caravan, but inadequate
afloat.

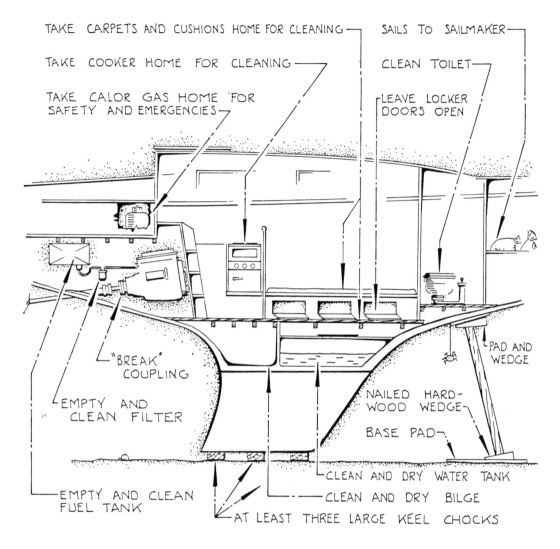

TAKE CARPETS AND CUSHIONS HOME FOR CLEANING

TAKE COOKER HOME FOR CLEANING

TAKE CALOR GAS HOME FOR SAFETY AND EMERGENCIES

SAILS TO SAILMAKER

CLEAN TOILET

LEAVE LOCKER DOORS OPEN

"BREAK" COUPLING

EMPTY AND CLEAN FILTER

EMPTY AND CLEAN FUEL TANK

PAD AND WEDGE

NAILED HARD-WOOD WEDGE

BASE PAD

CLEAN AND DRY WATER TANK

CLEAN AND DRY BILGE

AT LEAST THREE LARGE KEEL CHOCKS

Laying up reminder

It is easy to feel that a modern glassfibre boat needs no attention. But a glance at this drawing shows just some of the jobs which should be done each time a yacht is put away for the off-season.

Taking the calor gas home is partly to make the boat safe, partly because many insurance companies and boat yards insist that such inflammable equipment must not be left aboard during a lay-up; but also it can be useful if there is an emergency at home such as a power failure.

Most gear can be cleaned more thoroughly and more conveniently if taken home where there is ample space, plenty of hot water and hopefully all the conveniences of a workshop. Gear which has to be taken to specialists, such as life-rafts and sails, should always be delivered as soon as the yacht is ashore and not a week before she goes back afloat. If all owners did this the price of sails would come down for everyone.

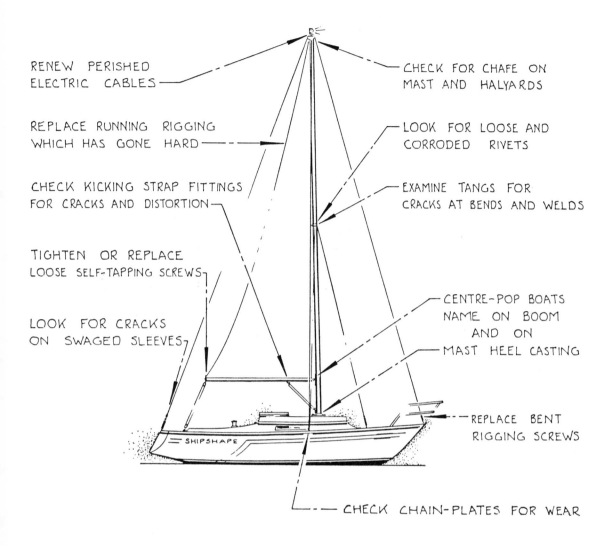

RENEW PERISHED
ELECTRIC CABLES

REPLACE RUNNING RIGGING
WHICH HAS GONE HARD

CHECK KICKING STRAP FITTINGS
FOR CRACKS AND DISTORTION

TIGHTEN OR REPLACE
LOOSE SELF-TAPPING SCREWS

LOOK FOR CRACKS
ON SWAGED SLEEVES

CHECK FOR CHAFE ON
MAST AND HALYARDS

LOOK FOR LOOSE AND
CORRODED RIVETS

EXAMINE TANGS FOR
CRACKS AT BENDS AND WELDS

CENTRE-POP BOATS
NAME ON BOOM
AND ON
MAST HEEL CASTING

REPLACE BENT
RIGGING SCREWS

CHECK CHAIN-PLATES FOR WEAR

SHIPSHAPE

After the last weekend's sail

Before coming ashore, after the last sail of the season, it is best to go over a boat with a critical eye and make a list of work needed during the months when the yacht is laid up.

The name of the boat should be marked in pencil on the mast and boom; the name is made permanent by punching with a 'centre-pop'. This indents the aluminium with a row of holes along the pencil lines which form each letter of the name.

Someone should go aloft, because it is possible to miss a defect when examining a mast laid out in a gloomy spar shed, or when it is set on some high-up rack on the side of the laying-up shed. Masts should not be left standing on boats which are ashore, not least because it greatly increases the chance of the boat being blown over by a gale.

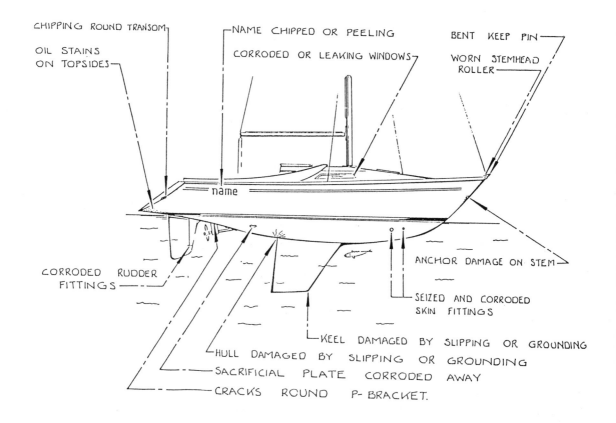

CHIPPING ROUND TRANSOM

OIL STAINS
ON TOPSIDES

NAME CHIPPED OR PEELING

CORRODED OR LEAKING WINDOWS

BENT KEEL PIN

WORN STEMHEAD
ROLLER

name

CORRODED RUDDER
FITTINGS

ANCHOR DAMAGE ON STEM

SEIZED AND CORRODED
SKIN FITTINGS

KEEL DAMAGED BY SLIPPING OR GROUNDING

HULL DAMAGED BY SLIPPING OR GROUNDING

SACRIFICIAL PLATE CORRODED AWAY

CRACKS ROUND P-BRACKET.

End of season damage

There are certain things to look for when laying a boat up, or buying one. Modern boats are built as lightly as possible to make them fast . . . and, let's be honest, to make them as cheap as possible. One result of this light construction is that quite a small 'incident' results in damage because there are no great factors of safety built in to most craft.

In the course of a season's cruising or racing it is inevitable that a boat will nudge a quay, scrape against another boat when coming into a marina, bump on the bottom when trying to take a short cut, and suffer minor damage when roaring into a crowded mooring in a rising gale.

If these little troubles are not mended each winter the boat will soon look sad, start to lose value, and in time become unseaworthy. Yet each trouble, if caught early, should only cost a small sum to put right, and most of the defects shown here are curable by the average competent amateur.

How long is my topping lift?

Anyone who drops into a yacht chandlery to buy a new topping lift is likely to get a surprise – how much rope should be bought?

The ideal procedure is to take along the worn-out rope and measure the new one against it. But so often that chafe in the topping lift (or any other item of running rigging) is only noticed just when everyone is packing up after a weekend afloat. Either there is not time to unreeve the rope, or it is needed to support the boom during the week.

Very few people know the lengths of any of the pieces of rigging on their boat. As a result some sort of guide is badly needed. This guide has to be based on a dimension which is well known, so the obvious selection is the yacht's overall length. To be sure, not many owners know the precise length of their own boat but in this case an error of 2% or 3% does not matter.

The guide on page 206 naturally errs on the safe side. It tends to give rope lengths which are longer than actually needed. It could hardly be otherwise. A rope which is 6 inches too short is a disaster whereas one which is 6 or even 16 ft too long is the right length plus a little to spare. That short extra length is cut off to make a dinghy lashing, or a reefing pennant or a personal lifeline or a bosun's chair or even a tow-rope for the car.

Because one moderately long offcut is more use than several short ones the following procedure should be followed when buying several pieces of rope: make up a list of all items of the same type and diameter. This might include:

76 ft of 1¼ inch circumference 3-strand jib halyard plus 76 ft of 1¼ inch circumference 3-strand main halyard plus 60 ft of 1¼ inch circumference 3-strand topping lift Total 212 ft

Get the chandlers to cut off a single length 212 ft long.

Take this to the boat and reeve it off, item by item. Each end is cut at exactly the right point. If each item has been given as, say, 5 ft too long by the guide, then we end up with a single useful piece of rope 15 ft long. But if the chandler had been told to cut off two pieces 76 ft and one at 60 ft there would have been three offcuts each 5 ft long after reeving off.

The guide is designed for the average modern sailing yacht between 18 ft and 48 ft. It is not much help to the owner of a barquentine, or a traditional Tancook Island schooner. (Yes! They do exist! I had a Bermudan sloop-rigged version once, and *she* would have fitted the guide because she had a modern rig.)

An increasing number of pure cruisers have halyards made entirely of pre-stretched 3-strand Terylene. Provided that no chafe occurs these halyards will last a very long time. They are pleasant to handle and there is no rope-to-wire join which can involve a complex splice. On racing yachts the all-Terylene halyard, even though it is pre-stretched, is found unsuitable because the sail's luff cannot be hauled up sufficiently taut and kept that way. This explains the difference between the racing and cruising criteria in the guide.

Because this guide is based on an average yacht due allowance must be made for divergences from the norm. For instance boats used inland on sheltered waters tend to have big sail areas and hence high masts and long booms. In America there is a tendency to set more sail than in Europe – largely because the eastern US seaboard is a weather shore. This again means higher masts.

The substance of all this is that the guide must be used as such, and not as an exact indicator. It was designed for use in conjunction with the Belfast Ropework Company table which gives the *diameter* and *type* of rope to be used. This table is on page 207.

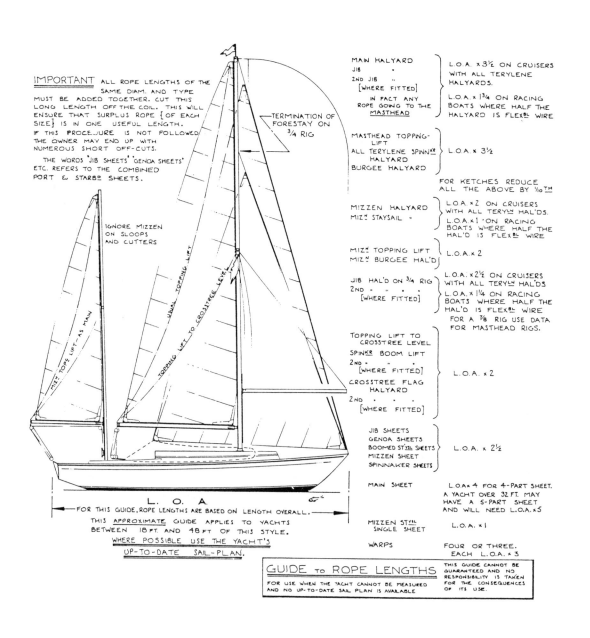

IMPORTANT ALL ROPE LENGTHS OF THE SAME DIAM. AND TYPE MUST BE ADDED TOGETHER. CUT THIS LONG LENGTH OFF THE COIL. THIS WILL ENSURE THAT SURPLUS ROPE {OF EACH SIZE} IS IN ONE USEFUL LENGTH. IF THIS PROCEDURE IS NOT FOLLOWED THE OWNER MAY END UP WITH NUMEROUS SHORT OFF-CUTS.

THE WORDS "JIB SHEETS" "GENOA SHEETS" ETC. REFERS TO THE COMBINED PORT & STARBD. SHEETS.

TERMINATION OF FORESTAY ON ¾ RIG

IGNORE MIZZEN ON SLOOPS AND CUTTERS

MIZN ROPE LIFT—AS MAIN

JIB & TOPPING LIFT

TOPPING LIFT TO CROSSTREE LEVEL

MAIN HALYARD JIB " 2ND JIB " [WHERE FITTED] IN FACT ANY ROPE GOING TO THE MASTHEAD	L.O.A. × 3½ ON CRUISERS WITH ALL TERYLENE HALYARDS. L.O.A. × 1¾ ON RACING BOATS WHERE HALF THE HALYARD IS FLEXBL WIRE
MASTHEAD TOPPING-LIFT ALL TERYLENE SPINNKR HALYARD BURGEE HALYARD	L.O.A. × 3½
	FOR KETCHES REDUCE ALL THE ABOVE BY 1/10TH
MIZZEN HALYARD MIZN STAYSAIL "	L.O.A. × 2 ON CRUISERS WITH ALL TERYLN HAL'DS. L.O.A. × 1·ON RACING BOATS WHERE HALF THE HAL'D IS FLEXBL WIRE
MIZN TOPPING LIFT MIZN BURGEE HAL'D	L.O.A. × 2
JIB HAL'D ON ¾ RIG 2ND " " " " [WHERE FITTED]	L.O.A. × 2½ ON CRUISERS WITH ALL TERYLN HAL'DS L.O.A. × 1¼ ON RACING BOATS WHERE HALF THE HAL'D IS FLEXBL WIRE FOR A ⅞ RIG USE DATA FOR MASTHEAD RIGS.
TOPPING LIFT TO CROSSTREE LEVEL SPINKR BOOM LIFT 2ND " " " [WHERE FITTED] CROSSTREE FLAG HALYARD 2ND " " " [WHERE FITTED]	L.O.A. × 2
JIB SHEETS GENOA SHEETS BOOMED STSL SHEETS MIZZEN SHEET SPINNAKER SHEETS	L.O.A. × 2½
MAIN SHEET	L.O.A. × 4 FOR 4-PART SHEET. A YACHT OVER 32 FT. MAY HAVE A 5-PART SHEET AND WILL NEED L.O.A. × 5
MIZZEN STSL SINGLE SHEET	L.O.A. × 1
WARPS	FOUR OR THREE. EACH L.O.A. × 3

L.O.A.

FOR THIS GUIDE, ROPE LENGTHS ARE BASED ON LENGTH OVERALL. THIS APPROXIMATE GUIDE APPLIES TO YACHTS BETWEEN 18 FT. AND 48 FT OF THIS STYLE. WHERE POSSIBLE USE THE YACHT'S UP-TO-DATE SAIL-PLAN.

GUIDE to ROPE LENGTHS
FOR USE WHEN THE YACHT CANNOT BE MEASURED AND NO UP-TO-DATE SAIL PLAN IS AVAILABLE

THIS GUIDE CANNOT BE GUARANTEED AND NO RESPONSIBILITY IS TAKEN FOR THE CONSEQUENCES OF ITS USE.

MINIMUM recommended sizes

All ropes are listed in circumferences

Yacht's length overall	Up to 18 ft	18–24 ft	24–30 ft	30–36 ft	36–44 ft	44–54 ft	54–66 ft	66–80 ft
Thames tonnage	Dinghies and dayboats	2–4 tons	4–8 tons	8–12 tons	12–18 tons	18–30 tons	30–55 tons	55–90 tons
Main halyard and masthead jib halyard	¾" 3 strand	⅞" 3 strand	1¼" 3 strand	1½" 3 strand	1½" 3 strand	1½" 3 strand	1¾" 3 strand	2" 3 strand
Mizzen halyard and staysail halyard	¾" 3 strand	⅞" 3 strand	⅞" 3 strand	1¼" 3 strand	1½" 3 strand	1½" 3 strand	1½" 3 strand	1¾" 3 strand
Main topping lift	½" plaited	¾" plaited	¾" plaited	1" plaited	1¼" plaited	1¼" plaited	1½" plaited	2" plaited
Mizzen topping lift	½" plaited	½" plaited	½" plaited	¾" plaited	1" plaited	1" plaited	1¼" plaited	1½" plaited
Burgee halyard	¼" plaited	⅜" plaited	⅜" plaited	⅜" plaited	⅜" plaited	½" plaited	½" plaited	⅝" plaited
Main and headsail sheets	1¼" plaited	1¼" plaited	1½" plaited	1½" plaited	2" plaited	2" plaited	2" plaited	2" plaited
Spinnaker and mizzen sheets	¾" plaited	1" plaited	1¼" plaited	1½" plaited	1½" plaited	1½" plaited	2" plaited	2" plaited
Light weather spinnaker sheets	½" plaited	¾" plaited	¾" plaited	1" plaited	1" plaited	1" plaited	1¼" plaited	1½" plaited
Anchor rope (Protect at bow fairlead against chafe)	100 ft of 1" plaited plus 12 ft of ¼" chain	140 ft of 1½" plaited plus 18 ft of ⁵⁄₁₆" chain	180 ft of 1¾" 3 strand plus 18 ft of ⅜" chain	240 ft of 2" 3 strand plus 24 ft of ⁷⁄₁₆" chain	300 ft of 2" 3 strand plus 24 ft of ⁷⁄₁₆" chain			
Mooring warps 3 strand or plaited	2, 3 or 4 required each 30 ft of 1"	3 or 4 required each 45 ft of 1¼"	4 required each 60 ft of 1½"	4 required each 75 ft of 1¾"	4 required each 90 ft of 2"	4 required each 100 ft of 2"		

Recommended sheave sizes for ropes

Rope size	¼" & ⅜"	½"	¾"	⅞"	1"	1¼"	1½"	1¾"	2"
Recommended sheave diameter	1"	1½"	1¾"	2"	2¼"	2½"	2¾"	3¼"	3½"
Minimum sheave diameter	Metal eye or ⅝" dia sheave	1"	1"	1⅛"	1¼"	1¾"	2¼"	2⅝"	2⅞"

CONVERSION SCALE

Inches	Millimetres
$\frac{1}{16}$	1.59
$\frac{1}{8}$	3.18
$\frac{1}{4}$	6.35
$\frac{3}{8}$	9.53
$\frac{1}{2}$	12.70
$\frac{5}{8}$	15.88
$\frac{3}{4}$	19.05
$\frac{7}{8}$	22.23
1	25.40
2	50.80
3	76.2
6	152.4
9	228.6
12	305

To convert	Into	Multiplier	Reciprocal
Inches	Millimetres	25.4	0.0394
$\frac{1}{8}$ths of inches	Millimetres	3.175	0.315
$\frac{1}{16}$ths of inches	Millimetres	1.587	0.630
Inches	Metres	0.025	39.37
Feet	Metres	0.305	3.281